# web2py Application Development Cookbook

Over 110 recipes to master this full-stack Python web framework

Mariano Reingart

Bruno Cezar Rocha

Jonathan Lundell

Pablo Martín Mulone

Michele Comitini

Richard Gordon

Massimo Di Pierro

[PACKT] PUBLISHING

open source
community experience distilled

BIRMINGHAM - MUMBAI

# web2py Application Development Cookbook

Copyright © 2012 Packt Publishing

All rights reserved. No part of this book may be reproduced, stored in a retrieval system, or transmitted in any form or by any means, without the prior written permission of the publisher, except in the case of brief quotations embedded in critical articles or reviews.

Every effort has been made in the preparation of this book to ensure the accuracy of the information presented. However, the information contained in this book is sold without warranty, either express or implied. Neither the authors, nor Packt Publishing, and its dealers and distributors will be held liable for any damages caused or alleged to be caused directly or indirectly by this book.

Packt Publishing has endeavored to provide trademark information about all of the companies and products mentioned in this book by the appropriate use of capitals. However, Packt Publishing cannot guarantee the accuracy of this information.

First published: March 2012

Production Reference: 1070312

Published by Packt Publishing Ltd.
Livery Place
35 Livery Street
Birmingham B32PB, UK..

ISBN 978-1-84951-546-7

www.packtpub.com

Cover Image by Asher Wishkerman (wishkerman@hotmail.com)

# Credits

**Authors and Reviewers**
Mariano Reingart
Bruno Cezar Rocha
Jonathan Lundell
Pablo Martín Mulone
Michele Comitini
Richard Gordon
Massimo Di Pierro

**Reviewer**
Alan Etkin

**Acquisition Editor**
Usha Iyer

**Lead Technical Editor**
Hyacintha D'souza

**Technical Editor**
Lubna Shaikh

**Project Coordinator**
Michelle Quadros

**Proofreader**
Aaron Nash

**Indexer**
Monica Ajmera

**Graphics**
Manu Joseph

**Production Coordinator**
Prachali Bhiwandkar

**Cover Work**
Prachali Bhiwandkar

# About the Authors and Reviewers

**Mariano Reingart** lives in Buenos Aires (Argentina), and is a specialist in database administration, and development of software applications and libraries (web services, PDF, replication, and so on), with more than 10 years of experience. Currently, he is the PostgreSQL regional contact for Argentina and a web2py contributor, with more than 14 open source projects, including interface for Free Electronic Invoice web services (PyAfipWs) and Pythonic Replication for PostgreSQL (PyReplica).

Mariano has a bachelor's degree in Computer Systems Analysis from the University of Morón, and currently works on his own funded startup formed by an open group of independent professionals, which is dedicated to software development, training, and technical support, focusing on open source tools (GNU/Linux, Python, PostgreSQL and web2py).

Mariano has worked for local Python companies in large business applications (ERP, SCM, and CRM) and mission critical systems (election counting, electronic voting, and 911 emergency events support). He has contributed to the book *web2py Enterprise Web Framework 3rd Edition*, and for several Spanish translation efforts of the PostgreSQL official documentation. You can find his resume at: `http://reingart.blogspot.com/p/resume.html`.

**Bruno Cezar Rocha** is a web developer and entrepreneur. He is the co-founder and lead developer at http://www.blouweb.com, a micro-company dedicated to web2py/Python web development and training. He is the lead teacher in Curso de Python (http://www.CursoDePython.com.br), an initiative to offer online courses of Python and web2py to Brazilian companies and educational institutes.

He is the Vice President of the Python Brazilian Association, which is the organizer of PyCon Brazil, and other Python-related events in his country.

He is an entrepeneur focused on SaaS products powered by web2py at http://www.ansy.me/en, which is a pioneer in web-based systems for veterinarians and pet shops, and creator of http://www.movu.ca, a social network engine and CMS powered by web2py.

You can find his resume at: http://www.rochacbruno.com.br

**Jonathan Lundell** leveraged a background in the philosophy of Ludwig Wittgenstein, into an exciting career in computer systems design. These days, he uses web2py to provide cloud services to his iOS apps, written for Lobitos Creek. He's getting used to Objective-C, but can't help wishing that Steve Jobs had been a Python fan.

**Pablo Martín Mulone** is a full-time web developer and software designer. He co-runs his own company located in Argentina, which is dedicated to bring IT solution to libraries, archives, and government in matter of documentary preservation. He has an extensive experience in FLOSS projects and associated tools. He is the creator of instant2press and CMS/ blog that is developed in web2py framework. His company created the patrimoniosf.gov.ar heritage database, which was built for the state government of Santa Fe.

**Michele Comitini** is a programmer, a consultant, and an entrepreneur, with 20 years of experience in the field of open source software development. Michele has worked with many of the top Information and Communication Technology (ICT) companies in Italy. His skills include the ability to program in many languages and some of the most popular web frameworks. Michele was a Linux early adopter, and he has developed a deep knowledge of the Linux/Unix operating systems as well as its use in embedded systems.

Michele is the owner and CEO of GliscoS.R.L., a consulting and development firm that is specialized in mission critical or highly customized software. His customers are mostly companies in the ICT and in the financial sectors.

**Richard Gordon** has 30 years of experience in agile web development and industrial design-automation software. He has a Master's degree in Electrical Engineering from Stanford University and a Science Baccalaureate with honors from Brown University. His career spans microprocessor design at AT&T Bell laboratories, electronic-design-automation, software development at Mentor Graphics and Tera Systems, which he founded. He is the founder and lead YAK at YAKiToMe! Co., the Internet's first text-to-speech SaaS portal.

**Massimo Di Pierro** is an associate professor at the School of Computing of DePaul University in Chicago, where he directs the Master's program in Computational Finance. He also teaches courses on various topics, including web frameworks, network programming, computer security, scientific computing, and parallel programming.

Massimo has a PhD in High Energy Theoretical Physics from the University of Southampton (UK), and he has previously worked as an associate researcher for Fermi National Accelerator Laboratory.

Massimo is the author of a book on web2py, and more than 50 publications in the fields of Physics and Computational Finance, and he has contributed to many open source projects. He started the web2py project in 2007, and is currently the lead developer.

> We wish to thank all the web2py contributors and web2py users, but, in particular, we want to thank those users who have contributed examples on http://www.web2pyslices.com/, as some of them have been used as a basis for the recipes in this book. They are:
>
> Nathan Freeze, Hans Christian von Stockhausen, BenignoCalvo, Chih-Hsiang Hsu, Renato Caliari, Rob Powell, David Harrison, Richard Penman, Teru Homma, Brian M., Jon Vlachoyiannis, KubaKucharski, Anton Georg Mückl, Falko Krause, Mike Ellis, Karl Bochert, Alexandre Andrade, Mark Carrier, Timothy Farrell, Martin Sagastume, Carlos Costa, Fred Gansevles, John Heenan, Ionel Anton, Alex Pearson, Dmitry Sherbina, Evan Gray, Nico de Groot, Igor Gassko, John Tynan, Karol Grobski, Dieter Asman, Mark Pettit, Marco Laspe, Yarin Kessler, PietroBertera, Jeffrey Berube, huimies, Janis Vizulis, Jose Jachuf, Chris Steel, Patrick Breitenbach, Patrick Breitenbach, Ariel Gonzalez, ArunRajeevan, Victhor, Zimba, BogdanHlevca, Nico de Groot, Pierre Thibault, Ai Lau, Gilson Filho, Matt Gorecki, UolterUolter, and Jim Karsten.
>
> Also, particular thanks go to Anthony Bastardi and Patrick Breintenbach for their continuous help and support to the web2py community, Alan Etkin and Timothy Dietrich for their help in proofreading the book, Muqeet Khan for help with the IIS recipes, and Thadeus Burgess for his help with the recipes on database queues and template blocks.

# About the Reviewer

**Alan Etkin** has been gradually migrating from I.T. support to the application development field, and his preferred programming language is Python. He is a devoted user of web2py, and participates as a developer in various web2py-powered projects. He also has contributed with fixes and features to the framework. If you want to reach Alan, type `spametki` in your search engine.

# www.PacktPub.com

## Support files, eBooks, discount offers and more

You might want to visit `www.PacktPub.com` for support files and downloads related to your book.

Did you know that Packt offers eBook versions of every book published, with PDF and ePub files available? You can upgrade to the eBook version at `www.PacktPub.com` and as a print book customer, you are entitled to a discount on the eBook copy. Get in touch with us at `service@packtpub.com` for more details.

At `www.PacktPub.com`, you can also read a collection of free technical articles, sign up for a range of free newsletters and receive exclusive discounts and offers on Packt books and eBooks.

**PACKTLiB®**

`http://PacktLib.PacktPub.com`

Do you need instant solutions to your IT questions? PacktLib is Packt's online digital book library. Here, you can access, read and search across Packt's entire library of books.

## Why Subscribe?

- Fully searchable across every book published by Packt
- Copy and paste, print and bookmark content
- On demand and accessible via web browser

## Free Access for Packt account holders

If you have an account with Packt at `www.PacktPub.com`, you can use this to access PacktLib today and view nine entirely free books. Simply use your login credentials for immediate access.

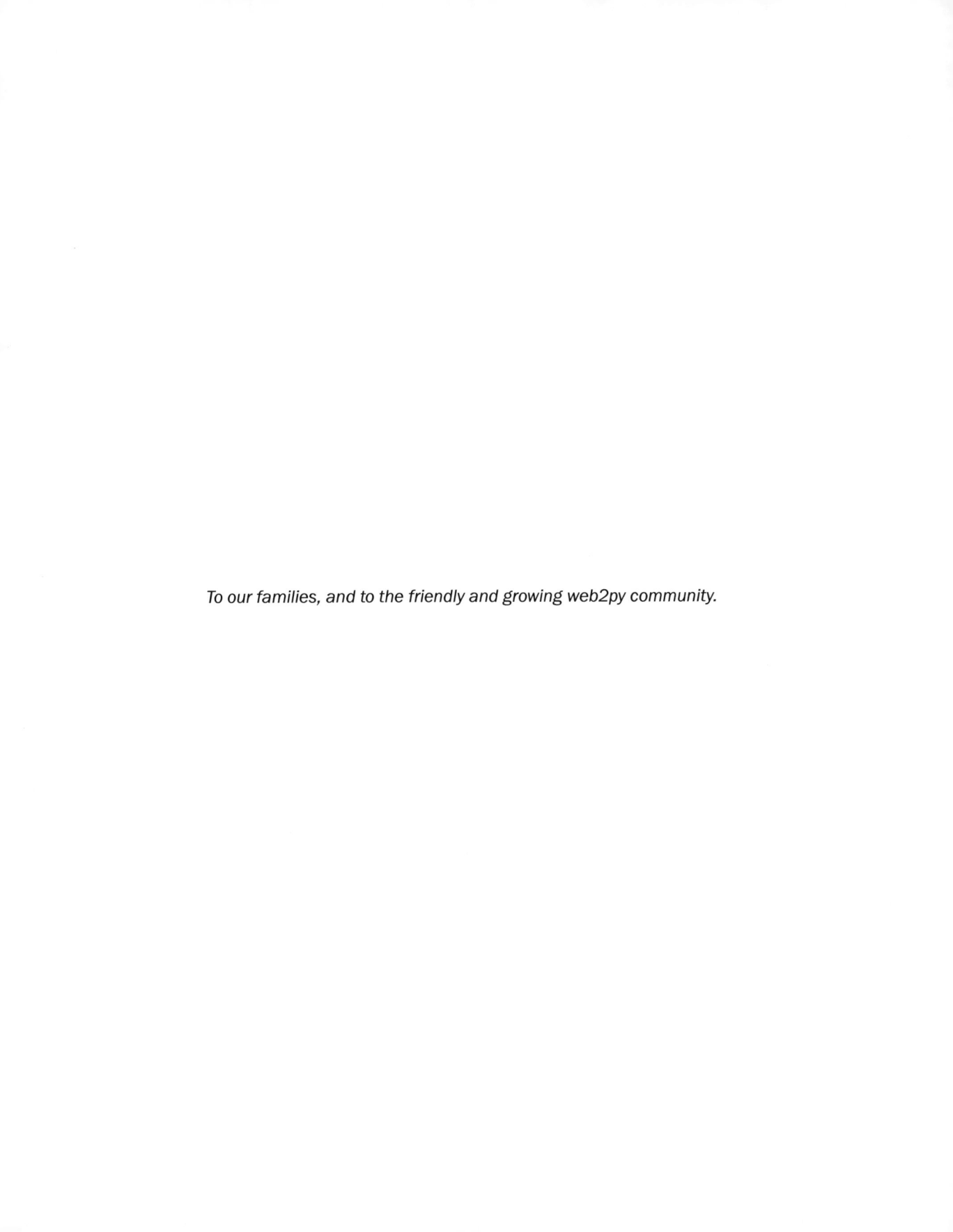

*To our families, and to the friendly and growing web2py community.*

# Table of Contents

**Preface** — 1

**Chapter 1: Deploying web2py** — 7
- Introduction — 7
- Installing web2py on Windows (from source code) — 8
- Installing web2py in Ubuntu — 10
- Setting up a production deployment on Ubuntu — 12
- Running web2py with Apache, mod_proxy, and mod_rewrite — 16
- Running web2py with Lighttpd — 23
- Running web2py with Cherokee — 26
- Running web2py with Nginx and uWSGI — 31
- Running web2py on shared hosts using CGI — 34
- Running web2py on shared hosts with mod_proxy — 35
- Running web2py from a user-defined folder — 36
- Installing web2py as a service in Ubuntu — 39
- Running web2py with IIS as a proxy — 39
- Running web2py with ISAPI — 45

**Chapter 2: Building Your First Application** — 49
- Introduction — 50
- Improving the scaffolding application — 50
- Building a simple contacts application — 53
- Building a Reddit clone — 61
- Building a Facebook clone — 68
- Using crud.archive — 76
- Converting an existing static site into a web2py application — 78
- Creating semi-static pages (flatpages) — 79
- Adding your custom logo — 84

| | |
|---|---|
| Creating menus and submenus | 87 |
| Customizing menus with icons | 88 |
| Creating a navigation bar | 89 |
| Using cookies to set the language | 92 |
| Designing modular applications | 94 |
| Speeding up downloads | 96 |

## Chapter 3: Database Abstraction Layer — 99

| | |
|---|---|
| Introduction | 99 |
| Creating a new model | 100 |
| Creating a model from a CSV file | 102 |
| Batch upload of your data | 104 |
| Moving your data from one database to another | 106 |
| Creating a model from existing MySQL and PostgreSQL databases | 107 |
| Efficiently searching by tag | 110 |
| Accessing your database from multiple applications | 112 |
| Hierarchical category tree | 114 |
| Creating records on demand | 116 |
| OR, LIKE, BELONGS, and more on Google App Engine | 117 |
| Replacing slow virtual fields with DB views | 121 |

## Chapter 4: Advanced Forms — 125

| | |
|---|---|
| Introduction | 126 |
| Adding confirmation on form submit | 127 |
| Searching data dynamically | 128 |
| Embedding multiple forms in one page | 130 |
| Detecting and blocking concurrent updates | 133 |
| Creating a form wizard | 134 |
| De-normalizing data temporarily | 136 |
| Removing form labels | 138 |
| Using fileuploader.js | 139 |
| Uploading files using a LOADed component | 142 |
| Making image thumbnails from uploaded images | 144 |
| Monitoring upload progress | 146 |
| Auto tooltips in forms | 148 |
| Color picker widget | 150 |
| Shortening text fields | 151 |
| Creating multi-table forms | 153 |
| Creating a multi-table form with references | 154 |
| Creating a multi-table update form | 156 |
| Star rating widget | 158 |

## Chapter 5: Adding Ajax Effects — 161
- Introduction — 161
- Using jquery.multiselect.js — 162
- Creating a select_or_add widget — 163
- Using an autocompletion plugin — 169
- Creating a drop-down date selector — 171
- Improving the built-in ajax function — 173
- Using a slider to represent a number — 174
- Using jqGrid and web2py — 175
- Improving data tables with WebGrid — 180
- Ajaxing your search functions — 183
- Creating sparklines — 187

## Chapter 6: Using Third-party Libraries — 191
- Introduction — 191
- Customizing logging — 191
- Aggregating feeds — 195
- Displaying Tweets — 197
- Plotting with matplotlib — 200
- Extending PluginWiki with an RSS widget — 203

## Chapter 7: Web Services — 207
- Introduction — 207
- Consuming a web2py JSON service with jQuery — 208
- Consuming a JSON-RPC service — 210
- JSON-RPC from JavaScript — 211
- Making amf3 RPC calls from Flex using pyamf — 220
- PayPal integration in Web2py — 222
- PayPal web payments standard — 235
- Getting Flickr photos — 243
- Sending e-mails with Boto through Amazon Web Services (AWS) — 245
- Making GIS amps using mapscript — 246
- Google groups and Google code feeds reader — 248
- Creating SOAP web services — 248

## Chapter 8: Authentication and Authorization — 253
- Introduction — 253
- Customizing Auth — 254
- Using CAPTCHA on login failure — 255
- Using pyGravatar to get avatars for user profile pages — 256
- Multi-user and teacher modes — 262
- Authenticating with Facebook using OAuth 2.0 — 263

*Table of Contents*

## Chapter 9: Routing Recipes — 267
- Introduction — 267
- Making cleaner URLs with routes.py — 268
- Creating a simple router — 270
- Adding a URL prefix — 272
- Associating applications with domains — 272
- Omitting the application name — 273
- Removing application name and controllers from URLs — 274
- Replacing underscores with hyphens in URLs — 275
- Mapping favicons.ico and robots.txt — 275
- Using URLs to specify the language — 276

## Chapter 10: Reporting Recipes — 279
- Introduction — 279
- Creating PDF reports — 279
- Creating PDF listings — 282
- Creating pdf labels, badges, and invoices — 284

## Chapter 11: Other Tips and Tricks — 295
- Introduction — 295
- Using PDB and the embedded web2py debugger — 296
- Debugging with Eclipse and PyDev — 302
- Updating web2py using a shell script — 304
- Creating a simple page statistics plugin — 307
- Rounding corners without images or JavaScript — 308
- Setting a cache.disk quota — 310
- Checking if web2py is running using cron — 311
- Building a Mercurial plugin — 312
- Building a pingback plugin — 315
- Changing views for mobile browsers — 323
- Background processing with a database queue — 324
- How to effectively use template blocks — 327
- Making standalone applications with web2py and wxPython — 330

## Index — 335

# Preface

we2py is a framework for rapid development of secure database-driven Internet applications. It is written in and is programmable in Python. It comprises libraries, applications, and reusable examples.

Created in 2007, web2py has grown, evolved, and improved tremendously, thanks to the work of many developers who have been using the framework. We thank them all.

web2py has evolved rapidly in the last two years, so much so that it has been difficult to keep the official documentation current. Although web2py is always backwards-compatible, new APIs have been created, providing new ways to solve old problems.

A large body of knowledge has accumulated in third-party websites, such as wikis, blogs, and mailing lists. Two resources, in particular, have been very valuable to web2py users: the web2py Google Group and the http://www.web2pyslices.com/website. Yet the quality of the information provided there varies, as some of the recipes have become outdated.

This book started from the need to collect that information, clean it up, update it, and separate the important and recurrent problems that users try to solve from other issues, which do not represent the general interest.

The most recurrent problems encountered by users include deploying web2py in a production-ready configuration, building complex applications using reusable components, generating PDF reports, customizing forms and authentication, using third-party libraries (jQuery plugins in particular), and interfacing with third-party web services.

Collecting this information and organizing it in this book has taken us more than a year. More people than the listed authors have knowingly and unknowingly contributed. Some of the code used here is, in fact, based on code already published online, although that code has been refactored, tested, and documented better here.

*Preface*

The code in this book is released under the BSD license, unless otherwise specified, and is available online on a dedicated GitHub repository listed below. Python code should follow a style convention called PEP 8. We have followed that convention for the code posted online, but we have compressed the listings in the printed book in order to follow the Packt style guide, and reduce the need for wrapping long lines.

We trust this book will be a valuable resource for both new web2py developers and experienced ones. Our goal is still to make the web a more open and accessible place. We contribute by providing web2py and its documentation to enable anyone to build new infrastructure and services with agility and efficiency.

## What this book covers

*Chapter 1, Deploying web2py*. In this chapter, we discuss how to configure various web servers to work with web2py. This is a necessary setup for a production environment. We consider the most popular servers, such as Apache, Cherokee, Lighttpd, Nginx, CGI, and IIS. The corresponding recipes provide examples of usage of the different adapters, such as `mod_wsgi`, `FastCGI`, `uWSGI`, and `ISAPI`. Therefore, they can easily be extended to many other web servers. Using a production web server guarantees speedier serving of static files, better concurrency, and enhanced logging capabilities.

*Chapter 2, Building Your First Application*. We guide the reader through the process of creating a few non-trivial applications, including a `Contacts` application, a `Reddit` clone, and a `Facebook` clone. Each of these applications provides user authentication, multiple tables connected by relations, and Ajax functionality. In the second part of the chapter, we discuss further customization of generic web2py applications, such as building a plugin to serve flat pages, adding a logo to the header, customizing the menu, and allowing users to select their preferred language. The main focus of this chapter is on modularity and reusability.

*Chapter 3, Database Abstraction Layer*. The DAL is arguably the most important component of web2py. In this chapter, we discuss various ways to import models and data from existing sources (`csv` files, `mysql`, and `postgresql` databases), and how to create new models. We deal with recurrent situations, such as tagging data and efficiently searching the database using tags. We implement a tree representation using the pre-order tree traversal method. We demonstrate how to work around some of the limitations of the Google App Engine platform.

*Chapter 4, Advanced Forms*. One of the strengths of web2py is its ability to automatically generate forms from the data representation. Yet, inevitably, the most demanding users feel the need to customize these forms. In this chapter, we provide examples of typical customizations, such as adding buttons, adding an upload progress bar, adding tooltips, and adding thumbnails for uploaded images. We also show how to create wizard forms and add multiple forms on one page.

*Chapter 5, Adding Ajax Effects*. This chapter is an extension of the previous one. Here we further enhance forms and tables, using various jQuery plugins to make them more interactive using Ajax.

*Chapter 6, Using Third-party Libraries*. web2py can use any Python third-party library. In this chapter we give some examples by using libraries that ship with web2py (`feedparser`, `rss`) as well as libraries that do not (`matplotlib`). We also provide a recipe that allows customized logging at the application-level, and an application that can retrieve and display Twitter feeds.

*Chapter 7, Web Services*. Computers can talk to each other through protocols, such as JSON, JSONRPC, XMLRPC, and SOAP. In this chapter, we provide recipes that allow web2py to both create services based on these protocols and consume services provided by others. In particular, we provide example of integration with Flex, Paypal, Flickr, and GIS.

*Chapter 8, Authentication and Authorization*. web2py has a built-in Auth module that deals with authentication and authorization. In this chapter, we show various ways to customize it, including adding CAPTCHA to registration and login forms, adding Globally Recognized Avatars (gravatars) for representing users, and integrating with services using OAuth 2.0 (for example Facebook). We also show how to utilize the `teacher/students` mode.

*Chapter 9, Routing Recipes*. This chapter includes recipes for exposing web2py actions using shorten, cleaner, and legacy URLs. For example, adding a prefix to, or omitting the application name from the URLs. We also show advanced uses of the web2py router mechanism to handle special characters in the URL, use the URL to specify a preferred language, and map special files, such as `favicons.ico` and `robots.txt`.

*Chapter 10, Reporting Recipes*. There are many ways to create reports in web2py using standard Python libraries, such as `reportlab` or `latex`. Yet for the convenience of the users web2py ships with `pyfpdf`, a library created by *Mariano Reingart* to convert HTML directly to PDF. This chapter presents recipes to create PDF reports, listings, labels, badges, and invoices using the web2py template system and the `pyfpdf` library.

*Chapter 11, Other Tips and Tricks*. Here we look at those recipes that did not fit into any other chapter, and yet were considered important by typical web2py users. An example is how to use web2py with Eclipse, a very popular Java IDE that works with Python. Other examples include how to develop applications that are mobile-friendly, and how to develop standalone applications that use a wxPython GUI.

# What you need for this book

The only software required is web2py, which is common to all recipes. web2py comes in source version, and binary versions for Mac and Windows. It can be downloaded from `http://web2py.com`.

We do recommend running web2py from source, and in this case, users should also install the most recent Python 2.7 interpreted, which can be downloaded from `http://python.org`.

When a recipe has additional requirements, it is stated explicitly in the recipe (for example some require Windows, some require IIS, and some require additional Python modules or jQuery plugins).

## Who this book is for

This book is aimed at Python developers with a basic knowledge of web2py, who want to master this framework.

## Conventions

In this book, you will find a number of styles of text that distinguish between different kinds of information. Here are some examples of these styles, and an explanation of their meaning.

Code words in text are shown as follows: "Running web2py with `Lighttpd`."

A block of code is set as follows:

```
from gluon.storage import Storage
settings = Storage()

settings.production = False

if settings.production:
    settings.db_uri = 'sqlite://production.sqlite'
    settings.migrate = False
else:
    settings.db_uri = 'sqlite://development.sqlite'
    settings.migrate = True
```

When we wish to draw your attention to a particular part of a code block, the relevant lines or items are set in bold:

```
{{extend 'layout.html'}}
<h2>Companies</h2>
<table>
  {{for company in companies:}}
<tr>
  <td>
    {{=A(company.name, _href=URL('contacts', args=company.id))}}
  </td>
  <td>
    {{=A('edit', _href=URL('company_edit', args=company.id))}}
  </td>
</tr>
  {{pass}}
<tr>
<td>{{=A('add company', _href=URL('company_create'))}}</td>
</tr>
</table>
```

Any command-line input or output is written as follows:

```
python web2py.py -i 127.0.0.1 -p 8000 -a mypassword --nogui
```

New terms and important words are shown in bold. Words that you see on the screen, in menus or dialog boxes for example, appear in the text like this: "Once the site is created, double-click the **URLRewrite** as shown in the following screenshot:".

> Warnings or important notes appear in a box like this.

> Tips and tricks appear like this.

# Reader feedback

Feedback from our readers is always welcome. Let us know what you think about this book—what you liked or may have disliked. Reader feedback is important for us to develop titles that you really get the most out of.

To send us general feedback, simply send an e-mail to `feedback@packtpub.com`, and mention the book title via the subject of your message.

If there is a book that you need and would like to see us publish, please send us a note in the **SUGGEST A TITLE** form on `www.packtpub.com` or e-mail `suggest@packtpub.com`.

If there is a topic that you have expertise in and you are interested in either writing or contributing to a book, see our author guide on `www.packtpub.com/authors`.

# Customer support

Now that you are the proud owner of a Packt book, we have a number of things to help you to get the most from your purchase.

## Downloading the example code

You can download the example code files for all Packt books you have purchased from your account at `http://www.PacktPub.com`. If you purchased this book elsewhere, you can visit `http://www.PacktPub.com/support`, and register to have the files e-mailed directly to you. The code files are also uploaded at the following repository: `https://github.com/mdipierro/web2py-recipes-source`.

All the code is released under the BSD license (`http://www.opensource.org/licenses/bsd-license.php`) unless otherwise stated in the source file.

## Errata

Although we have taken every care to ensure the accuracy of our content, mistakes do happen. If you find a mistake in one of our books—maybe a mistake in the text or the code—we would be grateful if you would report this to us. By doing so, you can save other readers from frustration and help us improve subsequent versions of this book. If you find any errata, please report them by visiting http://www.packtpub.com/support, selecting your book, clicking on the **errata submission form** link, and entering the details of your errata. Once your errata are verified, your submission will be accepted and the errata will be uploaded on our website, or added to any list of existing errata, under the Errata section of that title. Any existing errata can be viewed by selecting your title from http://www.packtpub.com/support.

## Piracy

Piracy of copyright material on the Internet is an ongoing problem across all media. At Packt, we take the protection of our copyright and licenses very seriously. If you come across any illegal copies of our works, in any form, on the Internet, please provide us with the location address or website name immediately so that we can pursue a remedy.

Please contact us at copyright@packtpub.com with a link to the suspected pirated material.

We appreciate your help in protecting our authors, and our ability to bring you valuable content.

## Questions

You can contact us at questions@packtpub.com if you are having a problem with any aspect of the book, and we will do our best to address it.

# 1
# Deploying web2py

In this chapter, we will cover the following recipes:

- Installing web2py on Windows (from source code)
- Installing web2py on Ubuntu
- Setting up a production deployment on Ubuntu
- Running web2py with Apache, `mod_proxy`, and `mod_rewrite`
- Running web2py with `Lighttpd`
- Running web2py with Cherokee
- Running web2py with Nginx and uWSGI
- Running web2py on shared hosts using CGI
- Running web2py on shared hosts with `mod_proxy`
- Running web2py from a user-defined folder
- Installing web2py as a service in Ubuntu
- Running web2py with IIS as proxy
- Running web2py with ISAPI

## Introduction

In this chapter, we discuss how to download, set up, and install web2py in different systems and with different web servers.

*Deploying web2py*

> All of them require that you download the latest web2py source from the website: `http://web2py.com`, unzip it under `/home/www-data/web2py` on Unix and Linux systems, and on `c:/web2py` on Windows systems. In various places, we will assume that the public IP address of the host machine is `192.168.1.1`; replace this with your own IP address or host name. We will also assume web2py starts on port `8000`, but there is nothing special about this number; change it if you need to.

# Installing web2py on Windows (from source code)

Although there is a binary distribution for Windows environments (packaging executables and standard libraries), web2py is open source, and can be used with a normal Python installation.

This method allows working with the latest releases of web2py, and customizing the python modules to be used.

## Getting ready

First of all, you must install **Python**. Download your preferred 2.x version (not 3.x) from: `http://www.python.org/download/releases/`.

Although newer versions include more enhancements and bug fixes, previous versions have more stability and third-party library coverage. Python 2.5.4 has a good balance within features and proven stability history, with good binary libraries support. Python 2.7.2 is the latest production release for this platform at the time of this writing, so we will use it for the examples.

After downloading your preferred Windows Python installer (that is **python-2.7.2.msi**), double-click to install it. The default values are fine for most cases, so press **Next** until it finishes the installation.

You will need **Python Win32 extensions** to use the web2py taskbar or Windows service. You can install **pywin32** from: `http://starship.python.net/~skippy/win32/Downloads.html`.

Prior to using web2py, you may also need some dependencies to connect to databases. SQLite and MySQL drivers are included in web2py. If you plan to use another RDBMS, you will need to install its driver.

For **PostgreSQL**, you can install the **psycopg2** binary package (for Python 2.7, you should use `psycopg2-2.3.1.win32-py2.7-pg9.0.1-release.exe`): `http://www.stickpeople.com/projects/python/win-psycopg/` (notice that web2py requires **psycopg2** and not **psycopg**).

For MS SQLServer or DB2, you need **pyodbc**: `http://code.google.com/p/pyodbc/downloads/list`.

## How to do it...

At this point, you can use web2py with your preferred database.

1. Download the source package from web2py official website: `http://www.web2py.com/examples/static/web2py_src.zip`, and unzip it.

   As web2py doesn't requires installation, you can unzip it in any folder. Using `c:\web2py` is convenient, to keep pathnames short.

2. To start it, double-click `web2py.py`. You can also start it from the console:

   `cd c:\web2py`

   `c:\python27\python.exe web2py.py`

3. Here you can add command-line parameters (`-a` to set an admin password, `-p` to specify an alternate port, and so on). You can see all the startup options with:

   `C:\web2py>c:\python27\python.exe web2py.py --help`

## How it works...

web2py is written in Python, a portable, interpreted and dynamic language that doesn't require compilation or complicated installation to run. It uses a virtual machine (such as Java and .Net), and it can transparently byte-compile your source code on the fly when you run your scripts.

For novice users' convenience, there is web2py Windows binary distribution available at the official site, which is precompiled to a bytecode, packaged in a zip file with all the required libraries (`dll/pyd`), and is present with an executable entry-point file (`web2py.exe`), but there is no noticeable difference running web2py from source.

## There's more...

Running web2py from the source package in Windows has many advantages, a few of which are listed as follows:

- You can more easily use third-party libraries, such as Python Imaging (look at Python package index, where you can install more than ten thousand modules!).
- You can import web2py functionality (for example, the **Database Abstraction Layer** (**DAL**)) from other Python programs.
- You can keep web2py updated with the latest changes, help to test it, and submit patches.
- You can browse the web2py source code, tweak it for your custom need, and so on.

*Deploying web2py*

# Installing web2py in Ubuntu

This recipe covers how to install web2py in a development environment using the Ubuntu desktop. Installation in a production system will be covered in the next recipe.

We assume that you know how to use a console and install applications using the console. We will use the latest Ubuntu desktop, at this writing: Ubuntu Desktop 10.10.

## Getting ready

We are going to install web2py in your home directory, so fire up the console.

## How to do it...

1. Download web2py.

    ```
    cd /home
    mkdir www-dev
    cd www-dev
    wget http://www.web2py.com/examples/static/web2py_src.zip
    (get web2py)
    ```

2. When the download is complete, unzip it:

    ```
    unzip -x web2py_src.zip
    ```

3. Optionally install the `tk` library for Python, if you want the GUI.

    ```
    sudo apt-get install python-tk
    ```

> **Downloading the example code**
>
> You can download the example code files for all Packt books you have purchased from your account at `http://www.PacktPub.com`. If you purchased this book elsewhere, you can visit `http://www.PacktPub.com/support`, and register to have the files e-mailed directly to you. The code files are also uploaded at the following repository: `https://github.com/mdipierro/web2py-recipes-source`.
>
> All the code is released under the BSD license (`http://www.opensource.org/licenses/bsd-license.php`) unless otherwise stated in the source file.

4. To start web2py, access the web2py directory and run web2py.

    ```
    cd web2py
    python web2py.py
    ```

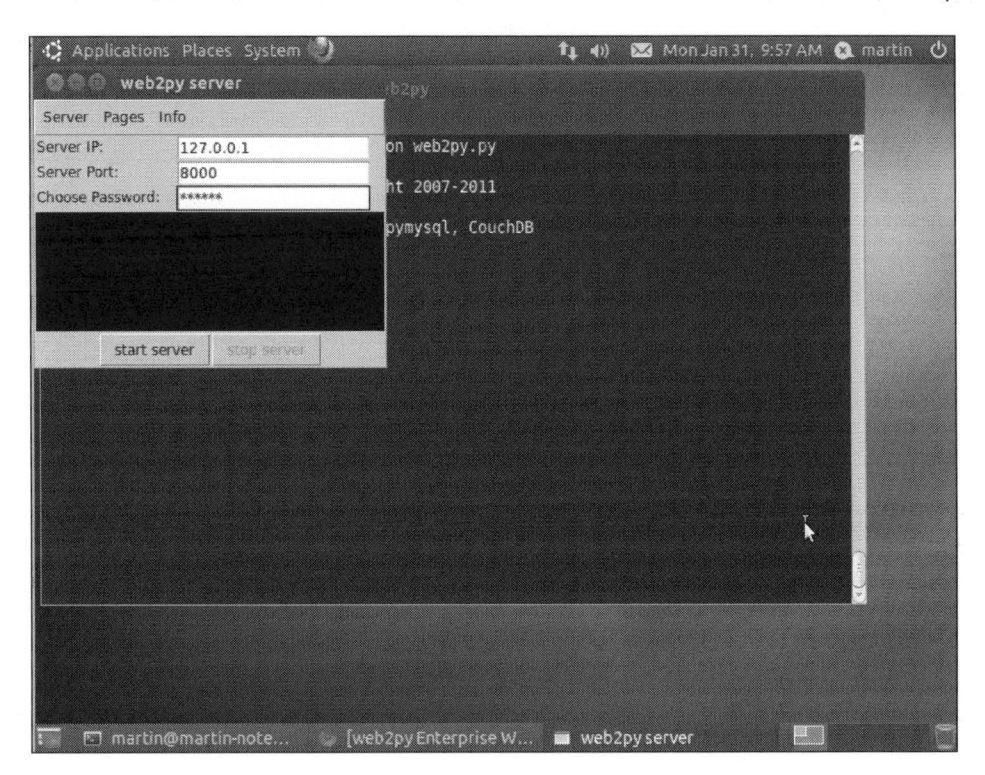

After installation, each time you run it, web2py will ask you to choose a password. This password is your administrative password. If the password is left blank, the administrative interface will be disabled.

5. Enter `127.0.0.1:8000/` in your browser to check if everything is working OK.

> The administrative interface: `http://127.0.0.1:8000/admin/default/index` is only accessible through `localhost`, and always requires a password. It can also be accessed through an SSH tunnel.

## There's more...

You can use some other options. For example, you can specify the port with the option `-p port` and IP address with the option `-i 127.0.0.1`. It's useful to specify the password, so you don't have to enter it every time you start web2py; use option `-a password`. If you want help on other options, run web2py with the `-h` or `-help` option.

For example:

```
python web2py.py -i 127.0.0.1 -p 8000 -a mypassword --nogui
```

## Setting up a production deployment on Ubuntu

This recipe describes how to install web2py in a production environment using the Ubuntu server. This is the recommended method to deploy web2py in production.

### Getting ready

We assume that you know how to use a console and install applications using a repository and commands. We will use the latest Ubuntu server at the time of writing: Ubuntu Server 10.04 LTS.

In this recipe we will learn how to:

- Install all modules needed to run web2py on Ubuntu
- Install web2py in `/home/www-data/`
- Create a self-signed SSL certificate
- Set up web2py with `mod_wsgi`
- Overwrite `/etc/apache2/sites-available/default`
- Restart Apache

```
Ubuntu 10.04.1 LTS ubuntu tty1

ubuntu login: martin
Password:
Last login: Mon Jan 31 12:10:05 ART 2011 on tty1
Linux ubuntu 2.6.32-24-generic #39-Ubuntu SMP Wed Jul 28 06:07:29 UTC 2010 i686
GNU/Linux
Ubuntu 10.04.1 LTS

Welcome to Ubuntu!
 * Documentation:  https://help.ubuntu.com/

  System information as of Mon Jan 31 14:27:59 ART 2011

  System load:   1.93              Processes:            83
  Usage of /:    9.3% of 7.23GB    Users logged in:      0
  Memory usage:  4%                IP address for lo:    127.0.0.1
  Swap usage:    0%                IP address for eth0:  192.168.1.102

  Graph this data and manage this system at https://landscape.canonical.com/

64 packages can be updated.
32 updates are security updates.

martin@ubuntu:~$
```

First, we need to be sure that the system is up-to-date. Upgrade the system with these commands:

```
sudo apt-get update
sudo apt-get upgrade
```

## How to do it...

1. Let's start by installing `postgreSQL`:

    ```
    sudo apt-get install postgresql
    ```
    *[handwritten: mysql-server]*

2. We need to unzip and open `ssh-server`, if it's not installed already.

    ```
    sudo apt-get install unzip
    sudo apt-get install openssh-server
    ```

3. Install Apache 2 and `mod-wsgi`:

    ```
    sudo apt-get install apache2
    sudo apt-get install libapache2-mod-wsgi
    ```

4. Optionally, if you plan to manipulate images, we can install the **Python Imaging Library** (**PIL**):

    ```
    sudo apt-get install python-imaging
    ```

5. Now we need to install web2py. We'll create `www-data` in `/home`, and extract the web2py source there.

    ```
    cd /home
    sudo mkdir www-data
    cd www-data
    ```

6. Get the web2py source from the web2py site:

    ```
    sudo wget http://web2py.com/examples/static/web2py_src.zip
    sudo unzip web2py_src.zip
    sudo chown -R www-data:www-data web2py
    ```

7. Enable the Apache SSL and EXPIRES modules:

    ```
    sudo a2enmod expires
    sudo a2enmod ssl
    ```

8. Create a self-signed certificate:

    You should obtain your SSL certificates from a trusted **Certificate Authority**, such as `verisign.com`, but for testing purposes you can generate your own self-signed certificates. You can read more about it at: `https://help.ubuntu.com/10.04/serverguide/C/certificates-and-security.html`.

Deploying web2py

9. Create the SSL folder, and put the SSL certificates inside it:

    ```
    sudo openssl req -new -x509 -nodes -sha1 -days 365 -key \
    /etc/apache2/ssl/self_signed.key > \
    /etc/apache2/ssl/self_signed.cert
    sudo openssl x509 -noout -fingerprint -text < \
    /etc/apache2/ssl/self_signed.cert > \
    /etc/apache2/ssl/self_signed.info
    ```

10. If you have problem with permissions, use `sudo -i`.
11. Edit the default Apache configuration with your editor.

    ```
    sudo nano /etc/apache2/sites-available/default
    ```

12. Add the following code to the configuration:

    ```
    NameVirtualHost *:80
    NameVirtualHost *:443


    <VirtualHost *:80>
      WSGIDaemonProcess web2py user=www-data group=www-data
      WSGIProcessGroup web2py
      WSGIScriptAlias / /home/www-data/web2py/wsgihandler.py

      <Directory /home/www-data/web2py>
        AllowOverride None
        Order Allow,Deny
        Deny from all
        <Files wsgihandler.py>
          Allow from all
        </Files>
      </Directory>

      AliasMatch ^/([^/]+)/static/(.*) \
         /home/www-data/web2py/applications/$1/static/$2
      <Directory /home/www-data/web2py/applications/*/static/>
        Options -Indexes
        Order Allow,Deny
    ```

14

```
      Allow from all
    </Directory>

    <Location /admin>
      Deny from all
    </Location>

    <LocationMatch ^/([^/]+)/appadmin>
      Deny from all
    </LocationMatch>

    CustomLog /var/log/apache2/access.log common
    ErrorLog /var/log/apache2/error.log
</VirtualHost>

<VirtualHost *:443>
    SSLEngine on
    SSLCertificateFile /etc/apache2/ssl/self_signed.cert
    SSLCertificateKeyFile /etc/apache2/ssl/self_signed.key

    WSGIProcessGroup web2py

    WSGIScriptAlias / /home/www-data/web2py/wsgihandler.py

    <Directory /home/www-data/web2py>
      AllowOverride None
      Order Allow,Deny
      Deny from all
      <Files wsgihandler.py>
        Allow from all
      </Files>
    </Directory>

    AliasMatch ^/([^/]+)/static/(.*) \
      /home/www-data/web2py/applications/$1/static/$2
```

```
        <Directory /home/www-data/web2py/applications/*/static/>
          Options -Indexes
          ExpiresActive On
          ExpiresDefault "access plus 1 hour"
          Order Allow,Deny
          Allow from all
        </Directory>

        CustomLog /var/log/apache2/access.log common
        ErrorLog /var/log/apache2/error.log
        </VirtualHost>
```

13. Restart the Apache server:

    ```
    sudo /etc/init.d/apache2 restart
      cd /home/www-data/web2py
      sudo -u www-data python -c "from gluon.widget import console; \
    console();"

      sudo -u www-data python -c "from gluon.main \
    import save_password; \
    save_password(raw_input('admin password: '),443)"
    ```

14. Enter `http://192.168.1.1/` in your browser to check if everything is working OK, replacing `192.168.1.1` with your public IP address.

## There's more...

Everything that we did can be done automatically using a script provided by web2py:

```
wget http://web2py.googlecode.com/hg/scripts/setup-web2py-\
  ubuntu.sh

chmod +x setup-web2py-ubuntu.sh

sudo ./setup-web2py-ubuntu.sh
```

# Running web2py with Apache, mod_proxy, and mod_rewrite

**Apache httpd** is the most popular HTTP server, and having Apache httpd on a large installation is a must, just like panettone on Christmas day in Italy. Like the panettone, Apache comes in many flavors and with different fillings. You have to find the one you like.

In this recipe, we configure Apache with `mod_proxy`, and refine it through `mod_rewrite` rules. This is a simple, but robust solution. It can be used to increase web2py scalability, throughput, security, and flexibility. These rules should satisfy both the connoisseur and the beginner.

This recipe will show you how to make a web2py installation on a host appear as part of a website, even when hosted somewhere else. We will also show how Apache can be used to improve the performance of your web2py application, without touching web2py.

## Getting ready

You should have the following:

- web2py installed and running on `localhost` with the built-in Rocket webserver (port 8000)
- Apache HTTP server (`httpd`) version 2.2.x or later
- `mod_proxy` and `mod_rewrite` (included in the standard Apache distribution)

On Ubuntu or other Debian-based servers, you can install Apache with:

**apt-get install apache**

On CentOS or other Fedora-based Linux distributions, you can install Apache with:

**yum install httpd**

For most other systems you can download Apache from the website `http://httpd.apache.org/`, and install it yourself with the provided instructions.

## How to do it...

Now that we have Apache HTTP server (from now on we will refer to it simply as Apache) and web2py both running locally, we must configure it.

Apache is configured by placing directives in plain text configuration files. The main configuration file is usually called `httpd.conf`. The default location of this file is set at compile time, but may be overridden with the `-f` command line flag. `httpd.conf` may include other configuration files. Additional directives may be placed in any of these configuration files.

*Deploying web2py*

The configuration files may be located in /etc/apache2, in /etc/apache, or in /etc/httpd, depending on the details of the OS and the Apache version.

1. Before editing any of the files, make sure that the required modules are enabled from the command-line shell (bash), type:

   **a2enmod proxy**

   **a2enmod rewrite**

   With mod_proxy and mod_rewrite enabled, we are now ready to set up a simple rewrite rule to proxy forward HTTP requests received by Apache to any other HTTP server we wish. Apache supports multiple VirtualHosts, that is, it has the ability to handle different virtual host names and ports within a single Apache instance. The default VirtualHost configuration is in a file called /etc/<apache>/sites-available/default, where <apache> is apache, apache2, or httpd.

2. In this file each VirtualHost is defined by creating an entry as follows:

   ```
   <VirtualHost *:80>
       ...
   </VirtualHost>
   ```

   You can read the in-depth VirtualHost documentation at http://httpd.apache.org/docs/2.2/vhosts/.

3. To use RewriteRules, we need to activate the **Rewrite Engine** inside the VirtualHost:

   ```
   <VirtualHost *:80>
       RewriteEngine on
       ...
   </VirtualHost>
   ```

4. Then we can configure the rewrite rule:

   ```
   <VirtualHost *:80>
       RewriteEngine on
       # make sure we handle the case with no / at the end of URL
       RewriteRule ^/web2py$ /web2py/ [R,L]

       # when matching a path starting with /web2py/ do use a reverse
       # proxy
       RewriteRule ^/web2py/(.*) http://localhost:8000/$1 [P,L]
       ...
   </VirtualHost>
   ```

The second rule tells Apache to do a reverse proxy connection to `http://localhost:8000`, passing all the path components of the URL called by the user, except for the first, web2py. The syntax used for rules is based on regular expressions (`regex`), where the first expression is compared to the incoming URL (the one requested by the user).

If there is a match, the second expression is used to build a new URL. The flags inside `[and]` determine how the resulting URL is to be handled. The previous example matches any incoming request on the default `VirtualHost` with a path that begins with `/web2py`, and generates a new URL prepending `http://localhost:8000/` to the remainder of the matched path; the part of the incoming URL that matches the expression `.*` replaces `$1` in the second expression.

The flag `P` tells Apache to use its proxy to retrieve the content pointed by the URL, before passing it back to the requesting browser.

Suppose that the Apache Server responds at the domain `www.example.com`; then if the user's browser requests `http://www.example.com/web2py/welcome`, it will receive a response with the contents from the scaffolding application of web2py. Thats is, it would be as if the browser had requested `http://localhost:8000/welcome`.

5. There is a catch: web2py could send an HTTP redirect, for instance to point the user's browser to the default page. The problem is that the redirect is relative to web2py's application layout, the one that the Apache proxy is trying to hide, so the redirect is probably going to point the browser to the wrong location. To avoid this, we must configure Apache to intercept redirects and correct them.

```
<VirtualHost *:80>

   ...

   #make sure that HTTP redirects generated by web2py are reverted
     / -> /web2py/
   ProxyPassReverse /web2py/ http://localhost:8000/
   ProxyPassReverse /web2py/ /


   # transform cookies also
   ProxyPassReverseCookieDomain localhost localhost
   ProxyPassReverseCookiePath / /web2py/

   ...
</VirtualHost>
```

*Deploying web2py*

6. There is yet another issue. Many URLs generated by web2py are also relative to the web2py context. These include the URLs of images or CSS style sheets. We have to instruct web2py how to write the correct URL, and of course, since it is web2py, it is simple and we do not have to modify any code in our application code. We need to define a file `routes.py` in the root of web2py's installation, as follows:

    ```
    routes_out=((r'^/(?P<any>.*)', r'/web2py/\g<any>'),)
    ```

7. Apache can, at this point, transform the received content before sending it back to the client. We have the opportunity to improve website speed in several ways. For example, we can compress all content before sending it back to the browser, if the browser accepts compressed content.

    ```
    # Enable content compression on the fly,
    # speeding up the net transfer on the reverse proxy.
    <Location /web2py/>
      # Insert filter
      SetOutputFilter DEFLATE
      # Netscape 4.x has some problems...
      BrowserMatch ^Mozilla/4 gzip-only-text/html
      # Netscape 4.06-4.08 have some more problems
      BrowserMatch ^Mozilla/4\.0[678] no-gzip
      # MSIE masquerades as Netscape, but it is fine
      BrowserMatch \bMSIE !no-gzip !gzip-only-text/html
      # Don't compress images
      SetEnvIfNoCase Request_URI \
            \.(?:gif|jpe?g|png)$ no-gzip dont-vary
      # Make sure proxies don't deliver the wrong content
      Header append Vary User-Agent env=!dont-vary
    </Location>
    ```

It is possible in the same way, just by configuring Apache, to do other interesting tasks, such as SSL encryption, load balancing, acceleration by content caching, and many other things. You can find information for those and many other setups at `http://httpd.apache.org`.

Here is the complete configuration for the default VirtualHost as used in the following recipe:

```
<VirtualHost *:80>
  ServerName localhost
  # ServerAdmin: Your address, where problems with the server
  # should
```

```
# be e-mailed.  This address appears on some server-generated
# pages,
# such as error documents.   e.g. admin@your-domain.com
ServerAdmin root@localhost

# DocumentRoot: The directory out of which you will serve your
# documents. By default, all requests are taken from this
# directory,
# but symbolic links and aliases may be used to point to other
# locations.
# If you change this to something that isn't under /var/www then
# suexec will no longer work.
DocumentRoot "/var/www/localhost/htdocs"

# This should be changed to whatever you set DocumentRoot to.
<Directory "/var/www/localhost/htdocs">
    # Possible values for the Options directive are "None", "All",
    # or any combination of:
    #   Indexes Includes FollowSymLinks
    #   SymLinksifOwnerMatch ExecCGI MultiViews
    #
    # Note that "MultiViews" must be named *explicitly* ---
    # "Options All"
    # doesn't give it to you.
    #
    # The Options directive is both complicated and important.
    # Please
    # see http://httpd.apache.org/docs/2.2/mod/core.html#options
    # for more information.
    Options Indexes FollowSymLinks
    # AllowOverride controls what directives may be placed in
    # .htaccess
    # It can be "All", "None", or any combination of the keywords:
    #   Options FileInfo AuthConfig Limit
    AllowOverride All

    # Controls who can get stuff from this server.
```

```
    Order allow,deny
    Allow from all
</Directory>

### WEB2PY EXAMPLE PROXY REWRITE RULES
RewriteEngine on
# make sure we handle when there is no / at the end of URL
RewriteRule ^/web2py$ /web2py/ [R,L]

# when matching a path starting with /web2py/ do a reverse proxy
RewriteRule ^/web2py/(.*) http://localhost:8000/$1 [P,L]

# make sure that HTTP redirects generated by web2py are reverted
# / -> /web2py/
ProxyPassReverse /web2py/ http://localhost:8000/
ProxyPassReverse /web2py/ /

# transform cookies also
ProxyPassReverseCookieDomain localhost localhost
ProxyPassReverseCookiePath / /web2py/

# Enable content compression on the fly speeding up the net
# transfer on the reverse proxy.
<Location /web2py/>
  # Insert filter
  SetOutputFilter DEFLATE
  # Netscape 4.x has some problems...
  BrowserMatch ^Mozilla/4 gzip-only-text/html
  # Netscape 4.06-4.08 have some more problems
  BrowserMatch ^Mozilla/4\.0[678] no-gzip
  # MSIE masquerades as Netscape, but it is fine
  BrowserMatch \bMSIE !no-gzip !gzip-only-text/html
  # Don't compress images
  SetEnvIfNoCase Request_URI \
      \.(?:gif|jpe?g|png)$ no-gzip dont-vary
```

```
# Make sure proxies don't deliver the wrong content
Header append Vary User-Agent env=!dont-vary
   </Location>
</VirtualHost>
```

You must restart Apache for any change to take effect. You can use the following command for the same:

```
apachectl restart
```

# Running web2py with Lighttpd

**Lighttpd** is a secure, fast, compliant, and a very flexible web-server that has been optimized for high-performance environments. It has a very low memory footprint as compared to other web servers, and takes care of the cpu-load. Its advanced feature-set (FastCGI, CGI, Auth, Output-Compression, URL-Rewriting, and many more) make Lighttpd the perfect web server software for every server that suffers load problems.

This recipe was derived from official web2py book, but while the book uses FastCGI `mod_fcgi` to expose web2py functionality behind a Ligthttpd web server, here, we use SCGI instead. The SCGI protocol that we use here is similar in intent to FastCGI, but simpler and faster. It is described at the following website:

http://python.ca/scgi

**SCGI** is a binary protocol for inter-process communication over IP. SCGI is tailored for the specific task of web server to CGI application communication. The CGI standard defines how a web server can delegate to an external application the dynamic generation of an HTTP response.

The problem with CGI is that, for every incoming request a new process has to be created. Process creation can take longer than response generation in some contexts. This is true in most interpreted language environments, where the time to load a new instance of the interpreter can be longer than the execution of the program itself.

**FastCGI** addresses this problem by using long-running processes to answer to more than one request without exiting. This is beneficial, in particular, for interpreted programs, because the interpreter does not need to be restarted each time. SCGI was developed after FastCGI experience to reduce the complexity required to convert a CGI to a FastCGI application, allowing better performance. SCGI is a standard module of Lighttpd, and is available for Apache as well.

*Deploying web2py*

## Getting ready

You should have:

- web2py installed and running on localhost (port `8000`)
- Lighttpd (download and install from `http://www.lighttpd.net`)
- SCGI (download and install from `http://python.ca/scgi`)
- Python Paste (download and install from `http://pythonpaste.org/`), or WSGITools (`http://subdivi.de/helmut/wsgitools`)

If you have `setuptools`, you can install SCGI, paste, and wsgitools, as follows:

`easy_install scgi`

`easy_install paste`

`easy_install wsgitools`

You will also need a script to start an SCGI server, configured for web2py that may or may not come with web2py, depending on the version, so we have supplied one to this recipe.

## How to do it...

Now, you have to write the script to start the SCGI server that will be listening to Lighttpd requests. Don't worry, even if it is very short and easy, we provide one ready to copy here:

```python
#!/usr/bin/env python
# -*- coding: utf-8 -*-

LOGGING = False
SOFTCRON = False

import sys
import os

path = os.path.dirname(os.path.abspath(__file__))
os.chdir(path)
sys.path = [path]+[p for p in sys.path if not p==path]

import gluon.main

if LOGGING:
```

```
  application = gluon.main.appfactory(
    wsgiapp=gluon.main.wsgibase,
    logfilename='httpserver.log',
  profilerfilename=None)
else:
  application = gluon.main.wsgibase

if SOFTCRON:
  from gluon.settings import global_settings
  global_settings.web2py_crontype = 'soft'

try:
  import paste.util.scgiserver as scgi
  scgi.serve_application(application, '', 4000).run()
except ImportError:
  from wsgitools.scgi.forkpool import SCGIServer
  SCGIServer(application, port=4000).run()
```

1. Copy the previous script, and put it in the root of your web2py installation with the name `scgihandler.py`. Start the SCGI server, and leave it running in the background:

   ```
   $ nohup python ./scgihandler.py &
   ```

   Now we are ready to configure `lighttpd`.

   We provide a simple `lighttpd.conf` configuration file here, as an example. Of course, real-world configurations can be much more complex, but the important parts will not differ much.

2. Append the following lines to your `lighttpd.conf`:

   ```
   server.modules += ( "mod_scgi" )
   server.document-root="/var/www/web2py/"
   # for >= linux-2.6
   server.event-handler = "linux-sysepoll"

   url.rewrite-once = (
     "^(/.+?/static/.+)$" => "/applications$1",
     "(^|/.*)$" => "/handler_web2py.scgi$1",
   )
   scgi.server = ( "/handler_web2py.scgi" =>
   ```

```
            ("handler_web2py" =>
              ( "host" => "127.0.0.1",
              "port" => "4000",
              "check-local" => "disable", # important!
              )
            )
          )
```

3. This configuration does the following:
   - Loads the SCGI module into Lighttpd
   - Configures the server document root to the root of web2py installation
   - Rewrites the URL, using `mod_rewrite`, so that incoming requests to static files are served directly by Lighttpd, while all the rest are rewritten to a **fake** URL beginning with `/handler_web2py.scgi`
   - **Creates an SCGI server stanza**: For every request beginning with `/handler_web2py.scgi` the request is routed to the SCGI server running on `127.0.0.1` at port `4000`, skipping the check for the existence of a corresponding local file on the filesystem

4. Now, check that your configuration is ok:

   `$ lighttpd -t -f lighttpd.conf`

5. Then start the server for testing:

   `$ lighttpd -D -f lighttpd.conf`

6. You can start/stop/restart the server with the following command:

   `$ /etc/init.d/lighttpd start|stop|restart`

You will see your web2py application go to the speed of Light(ttpd).

# Running web2py with Cherokee

This recipe explains how to run web2py behind a Cherokee web server using **uWSGI**.

**Cherokee** is a webserver written in C, similar in intent to Lighttpd: fast, compact, and modular. Cherokee comes with an administrative interface that allows one to manage its configuration, which is difficult to read and modify otherwise. uWSGI is described in its website as a fast (pure C), self-healing, developer/sysadmin-friendly application container server. Cherokee has an included module to talk to uWSGI servers.

## How to do it...

1. Install the package or download, compile, and install the required components. Create the following file in the installation root of web2py, and call it `uwsgi.xml`:

   ```
   <uwsgi>
       <pythonpath>/home/web2py</pythonpath>
       <module>wsgihandler</module>
       <socket>127.0.0.1:37719</socket>
       <master/>
       <processes>8</processes>
       <memory-report/>
   </uwsgi>
   ```

   This configuration spawns eight processes to manage multiple requests from the HTTP server. Change it as needed, and configure `<pythonpath>` to the installation root of web2py.

2. As the user that owns the web2py installation, start the uWSGI server:

   ```
   $ uWSGI -d uwsgi.xml
   ```

3. Now launch the Cherokee administrative interface to create a new configuration:

   ```
   $ cherokee-admin
   ```

4. Connect to the admin interface with the browser at the following link: `http://localhost:9090/`.

5. Go to the **Sources** section - **(A)**, then click on the **+** button - **(B)**.

*Deploying web2py*

6. Select **Remote Host** on **(C)**, then fill the text field at **(D)** with the IP address, and port to match the configuration in the previous `uswgi.xml` file.

   Having configured the uWGI source, it is now possible to configure a Virtual Host, and redirect requests through it. In this recipe, we choose the **default** Virtual Host that is used when no other Virtual Host has a better match for the incoming request.

7. Click on button (C) to go to **Rule Management**.

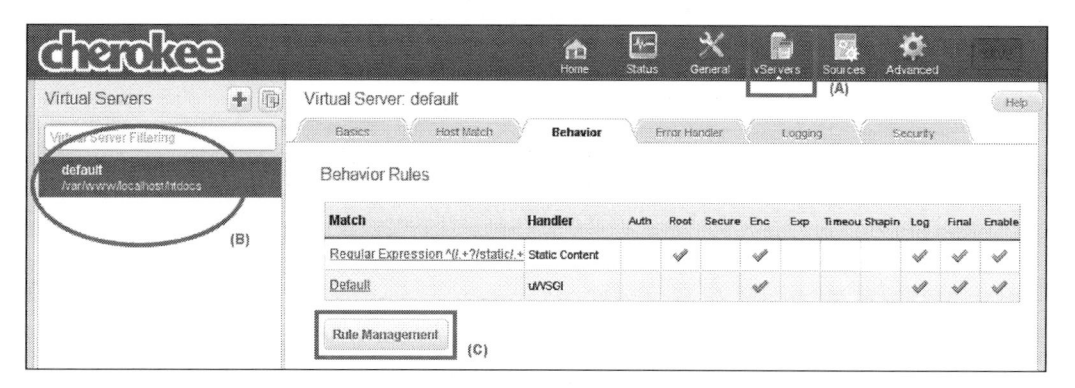

8. Delete all rules listed on the left. Only the **default** rule will remain.

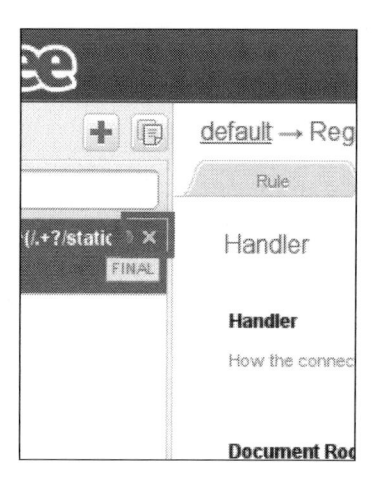

9. Configure the **default** rule with a uWSGI **Handler**. Leave the other values unchanged.

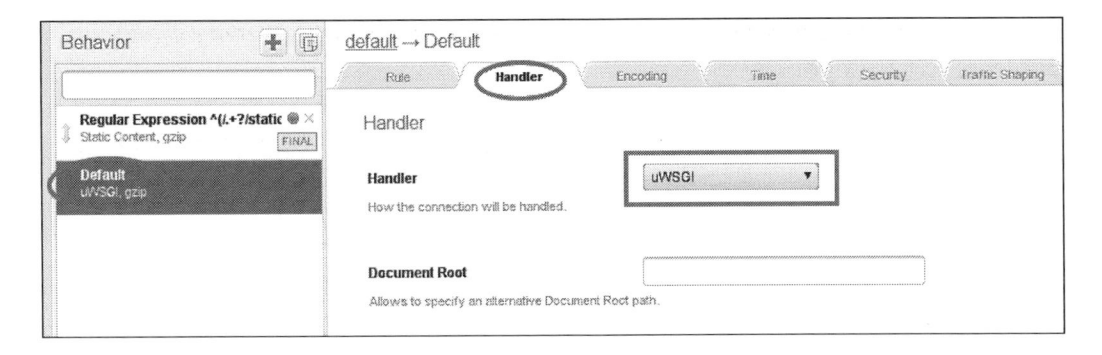

10. If you want Cherokee to serve static files directly from web2py folders, you can add a **Regular Expression** rule. Click button **(A)**, and select **Regular Expression** from the drop-down menu at **(B)**. Be aware that this configuration works only if the web2py directory is on the same file system, and is accessible to Cherokee.

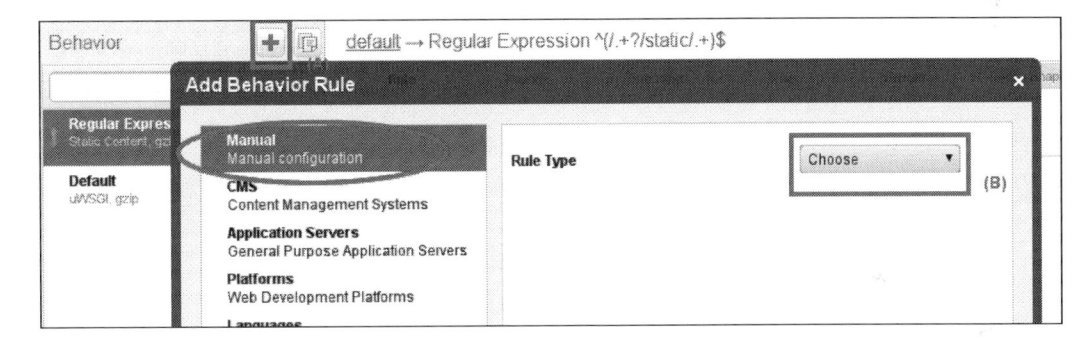

11. Configure the **Regular Expressions**:

12. Now you can configure the Static Handler pointing to the applications subdirectory of your web2py installation:

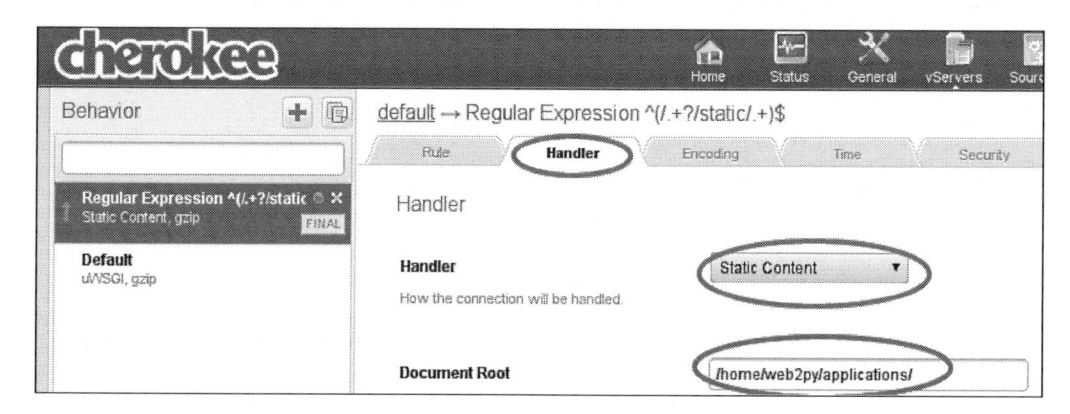

Remember to save the configuration, and reload or restart Cherokee from the administrative interface; then you are ready to start the uWSGI server.

13. Change to the correct user ID that was used to install web2py; be aware that using root is not recommended.

14. Go into the root directory of web2py installation, where you saved the configuration file `uwsgi.xml`.

15. Run uWSGI with the `-d <logfile>` option, so that it runs in the background:

```
$ su - <web2py user>
$ cd <web2py root>
$ uwsgi -x uwsgi.xml -d /tmp/uwsgi.log
```

Enjoy the speed!

## Getting ready

You should have the following:

- web2py (installed but not running)
- uWSGI (download and install from `http://projects.unbit.it/uwsgi/wiki`)
- Cherokee (download and install from `http://www.cherokee-project.com/`)

# Running web2py with Nginx and uWSGI

This recipe explains how to run web2py with the Nginx web server using uWSGI.

**Nginx** is a free, open-source, high-performance HTTP server, and reverse proxy, written by **Igor Sysoev**.

Nginx, unlike traditional servers, does not rely on threads to handle requests, rather, it implements an asynchronous architecture. This implies that Nginx uses a predictable amount of memory, even under heavy load, resulting in higher stability and low resource consumption. Nginx now hosts more than seven percent of all domains worldwide.

It should be stressed that even if Nginx is asynchronous, web2py is not. Therefore, web2py will use more resources, the more concurrent requests it handles concurrently. uWSGI is described on its website as a fast (pure C), self-healing, developer/sysadmin-friendly application container server. We will configure Nginx to serve dynamic web2py pages through uWSGI, and serve static pages directly, taking advantage of its low footprint capabilities.

## Getting ready

You should have the following:

- web2py (installed but not running)
- uWSGI (download and install from `http://projects.unbit.it/uwsgi/wiki`)
- Nginx (download and install from `http://nginx.net/`)

On Ubuntu 10.04 LTS, you can install uWSGI and Nginx using `apt-get`, as follows:

```
apt-get update
apt-get -y upgrade
apt-get install python-software-properties
add-apt-repository ppa:nginx/stable
add-apt-repository ppa:uwsgi/release
apt-get update
apt-get -y install nginx-full
apt-get -y install uwsgi-python
```

## Deploying web2py

### How to do it...

1. First we need to configure Nginx. Create or edit a file called `/etc/nginx/sites-available/web2py`.
2. In the file, write the following:

```
server {
  listen          80;
  server_name     $hostname;
  location ~* /(\w+)/static/ {
    root /home/www-data/web2py/applications/;
  }
  location / {
    uwsgi_pass    127.0.0.1:9001;
    include       uwsgi_params;
  }
}

server {
  listen          443;
  server_name     $hostname;
  ssl                     on;
  ssl_certificate         /etc/nginx/ssl/web2py.crt;
  ssl_certificate_key     /etc/nginx/ssl/web2py.key;
  location / {
    uwsgi_pass    127.0.0.1:9001;
    include       uwsgi_params;
    uwsgi_param   UWSGI_SCHEME $scheme;
  }
}
```

As you can see, it passes all dynamical requests to `127.0.0.1:9001`. We need to get uWSGI running there.

3. Create the following file in the installation root of web2py, and call it `web2py.xml`:

   ```xml
   <uwsgi>
     <socket>127.0.0.1:9001</socket>
     <pythonpath>/home/www-data/web2py/</pythonpath>
     <app mountpoint="/">
       <script>wsgihandler</script>
     </app>
   </uwsgi>
   ```

   This script assumes that web2py is installed as usual at `/home/www-data/web2py/`.

4. Now disable the default configuration, and enable the new one:

   ```
   rm /etc/nginx/sites-enabled/default
   rm /etc/nginx/sites-available/default
   ln -s /etc/nginx/sites-available/web2py /etc/nginx/sites-enabled/\
   web2py
   ln -s /etc/uwsgi-python/apps-available/web2py.xml /etc/uwsgi-\
   python/apps-enabled/web2py.xml
   ```

5. In order to use HTTPS, you may need to create a self-signed certificate:

   ```
   mkdir /etc/nginx/ssl
   cd /etc/nginx/ssl
   openssl genrsa -out web2py.key 1024
   openssl req -batch -new -key web2py.key -out web2py.csr
   openssl x509 -req -days 1780 -in web2py.csr -signkey web2py.key \
   -out web2py.crt
   ```

6. You will also need to enable web2py admin:

   ```
   cd /var/web2py
   sudo -u www-data python -c "from gluon.main import save_password;\
   save_password('$PW', 443)"
   ```

7. Once you are done, restart both uWSGI and Nginx:

   ```
   /etc/init.d/uwsgi-python restart
   /etc/init.d/nginx restart
   ```

web2py comes with a script that will perform this setup for you automatically:

```
scrips/setup-web2py-nginx-uwsgi-ubuntu.sh
```

*Deploying web2py*

# Running web2py on shared hosts using CGI

This recipe explains how to configure web2py to run on a shared host with login (but not root) access.

With login or FTP access to a shared host, the user isn't able to configure the web server, and must live within the host's configured constraints. This recipe assumes a typical Unix-based or Linux-based shared host running Apache.

Two deployment methods are possible, depending on how the system is configured. If Apache's `mod_proxy` is available, and the host permits long-running processes, running web2py's built-in server as an Apache proxy is straightforward and efficient. If `mod_proxy` is not available, or the host prohibits long-running processes, we're limited to the CGI interface, which is simple to configure and almost universally available, but is also slow, since the Python interpreter must run and load web2py for each request.

We'll start with CGI deployment, the simpler case.

## Getting ready

We'll assume that the root of your website is `/usr/www/users/username`, and that `/usr/www/users/username/cgi-bin` is your CGI binaries directory. If your details differ, obtain the actual values from your provider, and modify these instructions accordingly.

For security reasons, here, we also assume your host supports running CGI scripts as the local user (`cgiwrap`). This procedure may vary from host to host, if it's available at all; check with your provider.

Download the web2py source to your `cgi-bin` directory. For example:

```
cd cgi-bin
wget http://www.web2py.com/examples/static/web2py_src.zip
unzip web2py_src.zip
rm web2py_src.zip
```

Alternatively, unzip the web2py source locally, and upload it to the host through FTP.

## How to do it...

1. In your web root directory, create the file `.htaccess`, if necessary, and add the following lines (changing paths as required):

   ```
   SuexecUserGroup <yourusername> <yourgroup>
   RewriteEngine on
   ```

```
RewriteBase /usr/www/users/username
RewriteRule ^(welcome|examples|admin)(/.*)?$ \
            /cgi-bin/cgiwrap/username/web2py/cgihandler.py
```

2. Change its permissions with the following:

    `chown 644 .htaccess`

3. Now access `http://yourdomain.com/welcome`, or (depending on your provider) `http://hostingdomain.com/username/welcome`.

4. If you get access errors at this point, examine the most recent file in `web2py/applications/welcome/errors/`, using the `tail` command. This format isn't especially friendly, but it can provide useful clues. If the `errors` directory is empty, you may need to double-check that the `errors` directory is writable by the web server.

# Running web2py on shared hosts with mod_proxy

Using `mod_proxy` has two major advantages over CGI deployment discussed in the previous recipe: web2py runs continuously, so performance is considerably better, and it runs as your local user, which improves security. Because from web2py's perspective it appears to be running on localhost, the admin application can run, but if you don't have SSL operation available, you may want to disable admin for security reasons. SSL sctup is discussed in the *Setting up a production deployment on Ubuntu* recipe.

## Getting ready

Here we assume that you have already downloaded and unzipped web2py somewhere in your home folder. We also assume that your web hosting provider has mod_proxy enabled, supports long running processes, allows you to open a port (8000 in the example but you can change if this port is occupied by another user).

## How to do it...

1. In your base web directory, create a file `.htaccess`, if necessary, and add these lines:

```
RewriteEngine on
RewriteBase /usr/www/users/username
RewriteRule ^((welcome|examples|admin)(/.*)?)$ \
            http://127.0.0.1:8000/$1 [P]
```

*Deploying web2py*

2. Download and unzip web2py as described previously for CGI operation, except that web2py need not be installed in your `cgi-bin` directory, or even in your web documents tree. For this recipe, we'll assume that you install it in your login home directory $HOME.

3. Start web2py running on localhost and port `8000` with the following command:

   `nohup python web2py.py -a password -p 8000 -N`

   The `password` is the one time admin password that you choose. The `-N` is optional and it disables web2py cron to save memory. (Notice that this last step cannot be accomplished trhough FTP, so login access is required.)

## Running web2py from a user-defined folder

This recipe explains how to relocate the web2py `applications` folder.

With web2py, each application lives in a folder under the `applications/` folder, which in turn is located in the web2py `base` or `root` folder (the folder that also contains `gluon/`, the web2py core code).

When web2py is deployed using its built-in web server, the `applications/` folder can be relocated to some other location in your file system. When `applications/` is relocated, certain other files are relocated as well, including `logging.conf`, `routes.py`, and `parameters_port.py`. Additionally, a `site-packages` in the same folder as the relocated `applications/`, is inserted into `sys.path` (this `site-packages` directory need not exist).

### How to do it...

When web2py is run from the command line, the folder relocation is specified with the `-f` option, which should specify the parent folder of the relocated `applications/` folder, for example:

`python web2py.py -i 127.0.0.1 -p 8000 -f /path/to/apps`

### There's more...

When web2py is run as a Windows service (`web2py.exe -W`), the relocation can be specified in a file `options.py` in the web2py main folder. Change the default folder: `os.getcwd()` to specify the parent folder of the relocated `applications/` folder. Here is an example of the `options.py` file:

`import socket`

`import os`

```
ip = '0.0.0.0'
port = 80
interfaces=[('0.0.0.0',80),
   ('0.0.0.0',443,'ssl_key.pem','ssl_certificate.pem')]
password = '<recycle>'   # <recycle> means use the previous password
pid_filename = 'httpserver.pid'
log_filename = 'httpserver.log'
profiler_filename = None
#ssl_certificate = 'ssl_cert.pem'   # certificate file
#ssl_private_key = 'ssl_key.pem'   # private key file
#numthreads = 50 # ## deprecated; remove
minthreads = None
maxthreads = None
server_name = socket.gethostname()
request_queue_size = 5
timeout = 30
shutdown_timeout = 5
folder = "/path/to/apps" # <<<<<<<< edit this line
extcron = None
nocron = None
```

Applications relocation is not available when web2py is deployed with an external web server.

## How to do it...

1. First, create a web2py unprivileged user:

   `sudo adduser web2py`

2. For security, disable the web2py user password to prevent remote logins:

   `sudo passwd -l web2py`

3. Download the source package from web2py's official website, uncompress it in a suitable directory (for example /opt/web2py), and set the access permissions appropriately:

   `wget http://www.web2py.com/examples/static/web2py_src.zip`

   `sudo unzip -x web2py_src.zip -d /opt`

   `sudo chown -Rv web2py. /opt/web2py`

*Deploying web2py*

4. Create an `init` script in `/etc/inid.d/web2py` (you can use the one in `web2py/scripts/` as a starting point):

   `sudo cp /opt/web2py/scripts/web2py.ubuntu.sh /etc/init.d/web2py`

5. Edit the `init` script:

   `sudo nano /etc/init.d/web2py`

6. Set the basic configuration parameters:

   `PIDDIR=/opt/$NAME`

   `DAEMON_DIR=/opt/$NAME`

   `APPLOG_FILE=$DAEMON_DIR/web2py.log`

   `DAEMON_ARGS="web2py.py -p 8001 -i 127.0.0.1 -c server.crt -k server.key -a<recycle> --nogui --pid_filename=$PIDFILE -l \ $APPLOG_FILE"`

7. Change `127.0.0.1` and `8001` to your desired IP and port. You can use `0.0.0.0` as a wildcard IP that match all the interfaces.

8. Create a self-signed certificate, if you plan on using admin remotely:

   `sudo openssl genrsa -out /opt/web2py/server.key 1024`

   `sudo openssl req -new -key /opt/web2py/server.key -out /opt/\ web2py/server.csr`

   `sudo openssl x509 -req -days 365 -in /opt/web2py/server.csr \ -signkey /opt/web2py/server.key -out /opt/web2py/server.crt`

9. If you use `print` statements for debugging purposes, or want to record web2py output messages, you can redirect standard output, by adding the following line after the `imports` in `web2py.py`:

   `sys.stdout = sys.stderr = open("/opt/web2py/web2py.err","wa", 0)`

10. Finally, start your web2py service:

    `sudo /etc/init.d/web2py start`

11. To install it permanently (so it starts and stop automatically with the rest of the operating system services), issue the following command:

    `sudo update-rc.d web2py defaults`

If all works correctly, you'll be able to open your web2py admin:

`https://127.0.0.1:8001/welcome/default/index`

## Installing web2py as a service in Ubuntu

For simple sites and intranets, you may need a simple installation method that keeps web2py running. This recipe shows how to start web2py in a simple way without further dependencies (no Apache webserver!).

### There's more...

You can see what is happening using `bash` to debug the `init` script:

```
sudo bash -x /etc/init.d/web2py start
```

Also, you can change `start-stop-daemon` options to be more verbose, and use the web2py user to prevent interference with other Python daemons:

```
start-stop-daemon --start \
 ${DAEMON_USER:+--chuid $DAEMON_USER} --chdir $DAEMON_DIR \
 --background --user $DAEMON_USER --verbose --exec $DAEMON \
 --$DAEMON_ARGS || return 2
```

Remember to set up a password to be able to use the administrative interface. This can be done by executing the following command (change `mypass` to your desired password):

```
sudo -u web2py python /opt/web2py/web2py.py -p 8001 -a mypasswd
```

## Running web2py with IIS as a proxy

IIS is the primary web server for the Windows OS. It can run multiple concurrent domains and several application pools. When you deploy web2py on IIS, you want to set up a new site, and have a separate application pool for its root application. In this way, you have separate logs and ability to start/stop the application pool, independently on the others. Here we explain how.

This is the first of three recipes in which we repeat the process using different configurations. In this first recipe, we set up IIS to act as a proxy for the web2py **Rocket** web server.

This configuration is desirable when IIS default site is already in production with enabled ASP.NET, ASP, or PHP applications, and at the same time, your web2py sites may be under-development and may require frequent restarting (for example, due to changes in `routes.py`).

## Getting ready

In this recipe, we assume that you have IIS version 7 or later, already installed. We do not discuss the steps to install IIS7, since it is a commercial product and they are well documented somewhere else.

You also need to have web2py unzipped in a local folder. Start web2py on port `8081`.

```
python web2py -p 8081 -i 127.0.0.1 -a 'password'
```

Note that when running web2py as a proxy, you should be careful about unintentionally exposing admin without encryption.

Finally, you need to be able to use a IIS Proxy. For this, you will need **Application Request Routing** (**ARR**) **2.5**. ARR can be downloaded and installed from Microsoft Web Platform Installer available here:

```
http://www.microsoft.com/web/downloads/platform.aspx
```

## How to do it...

1. After you download the web platform installer for ARR, open the application and browse to **Products** on the left-hand side of the screen, as shown in the following screenshot:

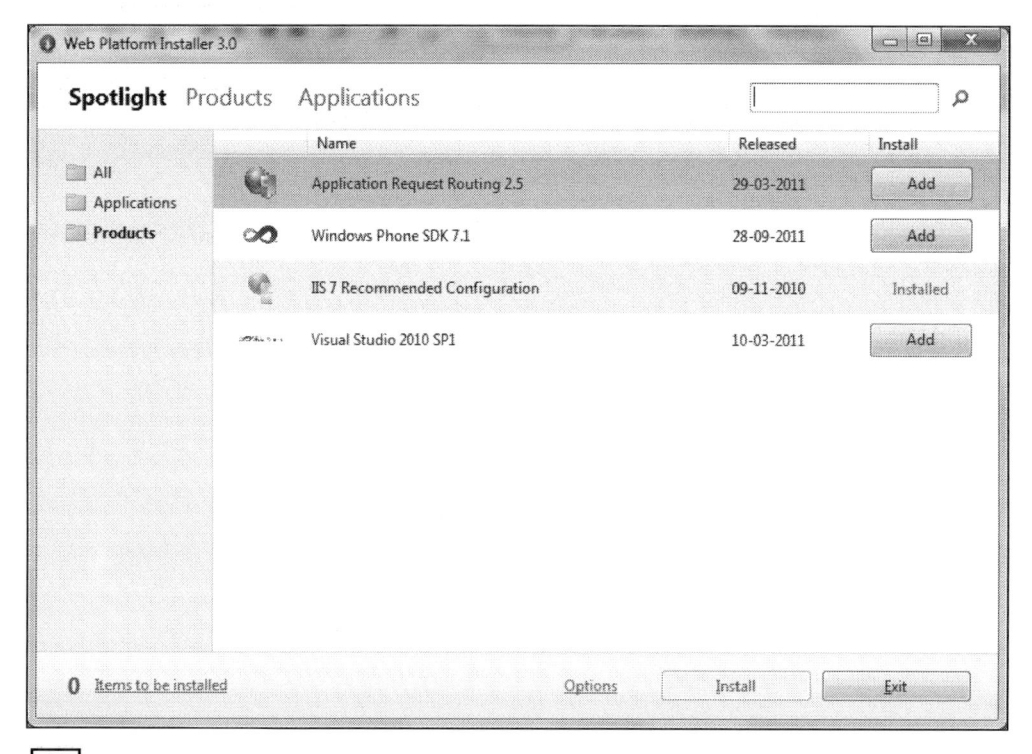

2. Next, click on **Add** - **Application Request Routing 2.5**, and then click on **Install**. This will take you to a new screen, as shown in the following screenshot; click on **I Accept**:

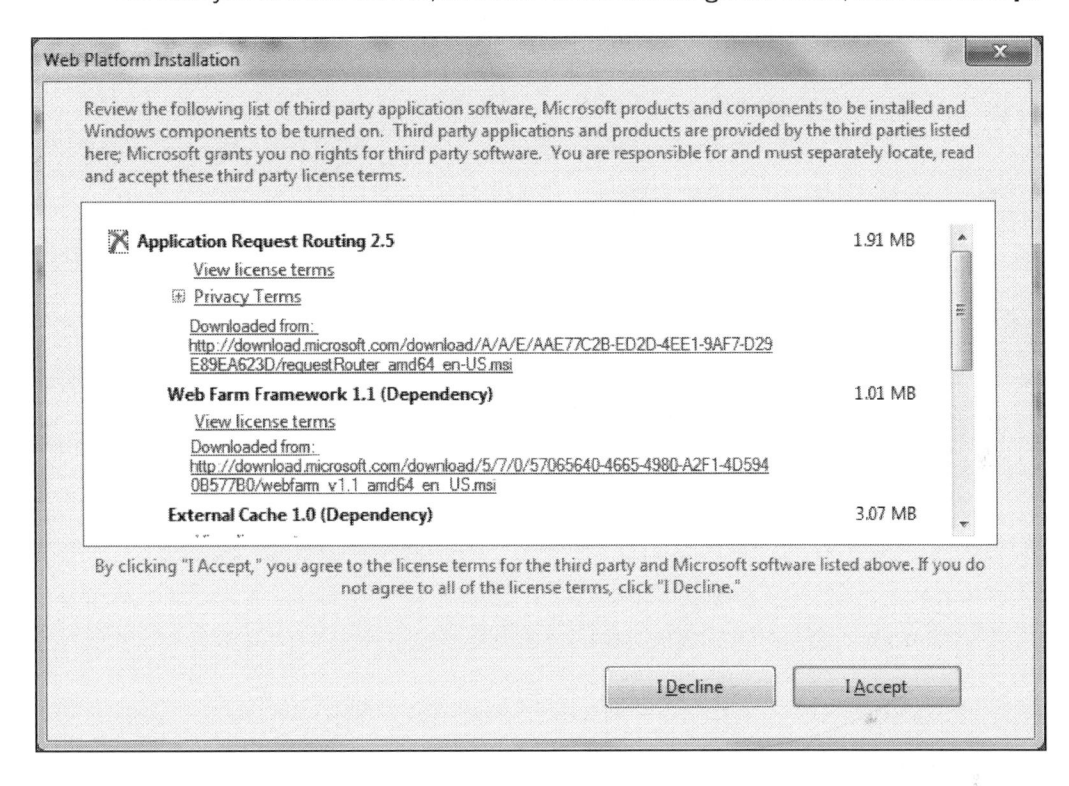

3. Web Platform installer will automatically select and install all the dependencies required for **Application Request Routing 2.5** to work. Click on **Finish**, and this will bring you to the **Download and Installation** screen.

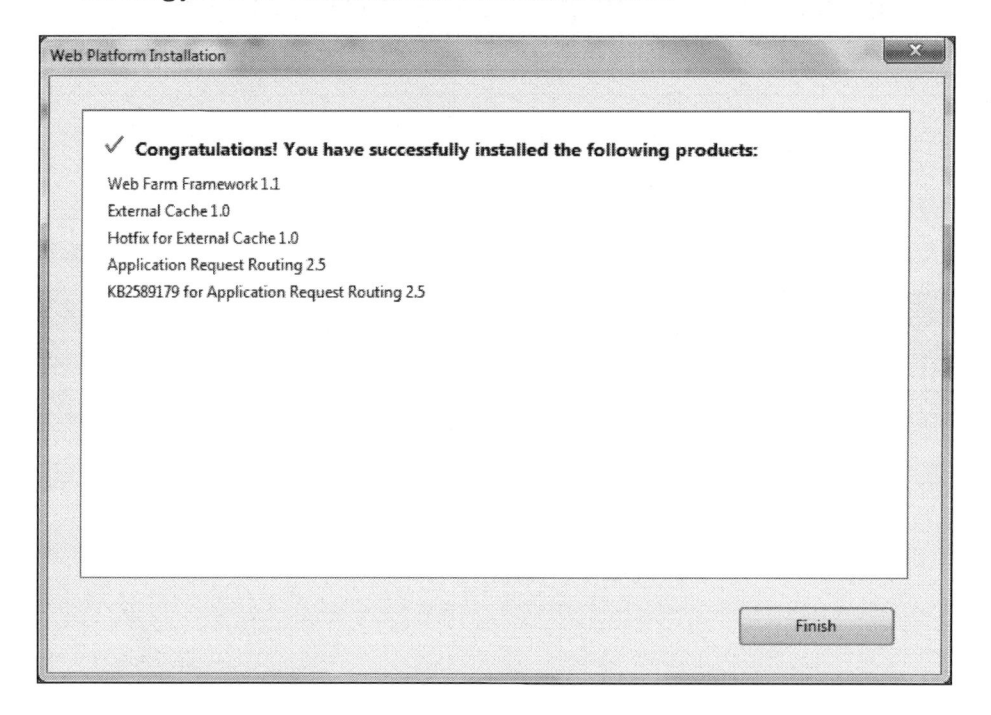

4. Once you receive the successful message, you can close Microsoft web platform application.
5. Now open the IIS Manager, and create a new website as directed.
6. First, right-click on **Sites** on the top-left in the **IIS Manager**, and select **New Website**. This will take you to the following screen. Fill in the details as shown here:

*Chapter 1*

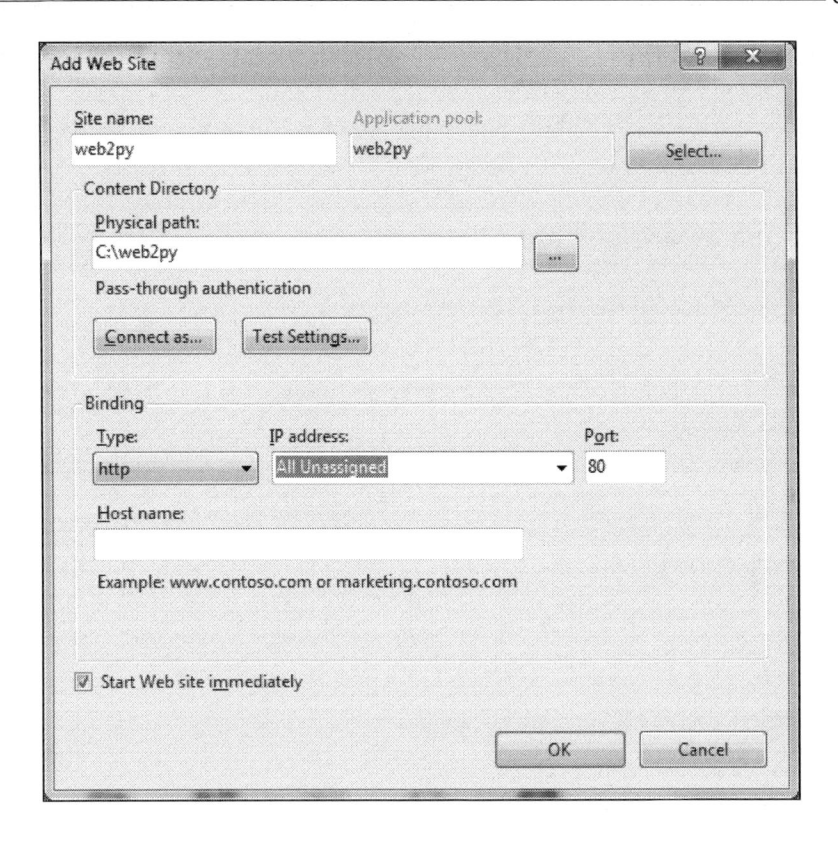

Make sure you select the right IP on which your site will run.

7. Once the site is created, double-click the **URL Rewrite** as shown in the following screenshot:

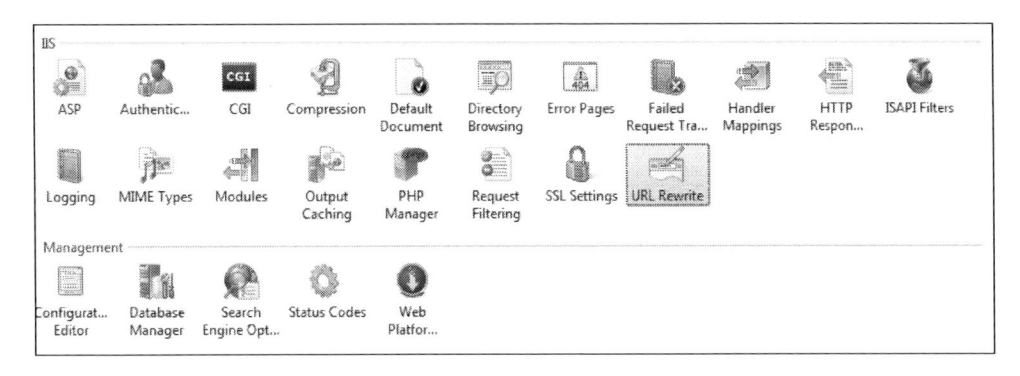

*Deploying web2py*

8. Once in **URL Rewrite** module, click on **Add Rule** on the top-right-hand side, as shown in the next screenshot.
9. Select the **Reverse Proxy** template under **Inbound and Outbound Rules**.
10. Fill out the details as shown here:

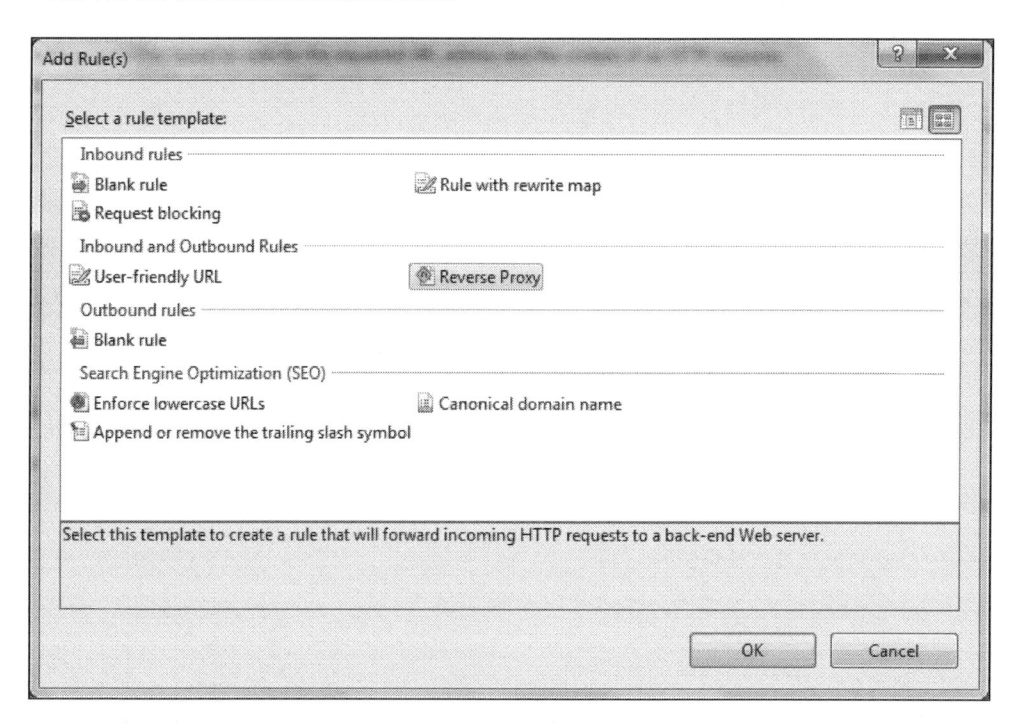

11. Since the **Server IP** field is the most important, it must contain the IP and port where web2py is running: `127.0.0.1:8081`. Also, make sure that **SSL Offloading** is checked. In the outbound rules for the **TO** field, write the domain name assigned to the website. When done, click **OK**.

    At this point, everything on your web2py installation should be working, except for the admin interface. Web2py requires that we use HTTPS when a request for the admin interface is coming for a non-localhost server. In our example, localhost for web2py is `127.0.0.1:8081`, while IIS is currently operational on `127.0.0.1:80`.

12. To enable the admin, you will need a certificate. Create a certificate and add it to your server certificates in IIS 7, then repeat the previous steps to bind `443` to the web2py website we created previously.
13. Now, visit: `https://yourdomain.com/admin/`, and you will be able to browse the web2py admin web interface. Enter the password for your web2py admin interface, and proceed normally.

# Running web2py with ISAPI

Here, we present a production quality configuration, which uses a dedicated application pool run natively in IIS using the ISAPI handler. It is similar to a typical Linux/Apache configuration, but is a Windows native.

## Getting ready

As before you will need IIS installed.

You should have web2py already downloaded and unzipped. If you have it already running on port **8081** (or other port) on localhost, you can leave it there, since it should not interfere with this installation. We will assume web2py is installed into `C:\path\to\web2py`.

You can place it anywhere else you like.

Then you need to download and install `isapi-wsgi`. This is explained below.

## How to do it...

1. First of all, you need to download `isapi-wsgi` from: http://code.google.com/p/isapi-wsgi/.

   It is a mature WSGI adapter for IIS, based on pywin32. Most of this recipe is based on the documentation and the examples about `isapi-wsgi`.

   You can install `isapi-wsgi` using the win32 installer: http://code.google.com/p/isapi-wsgi/downloads/detail?name=isapi_wsgi-0.4.2.win32.exe.

   You can also install it simply downloading the Python file somewhere into `"c:\Python\Lib\site-packages"`

   http://isapi-wsgi.googlecode.com/svn/tags/isapi_wsgi-0.4.2/isapi_wsgi.py.

   `isapi_wsgi` runs on IIS 5.1, 6.0, and 7.0. But IIS 7.x must have **IIS 6.0 Management Compatability** installed.

   You may want to try running the following test to see that it was installed properly:

   ```
   cd C:\Python\Lib\site-packages
   C:\Python\Lib\site-packages> python isapi_wsgi.py install
   Configured Virtual Directory: isapi-wsgi-test
   Extension installed
   Installation complete.
   ```

2. Now go to http://localhost/isapi-wsgi-test/.

3. If you get a `500 error` that says `this is not a valid Win32 application`, then something is wrong and this is discussed here: http://support.microsoft.com/kb/895976/en-us.

4. If you see a normal `Hello` response, then the installation was successful, and you can remove the test:

   `C:\Python\Lib\site-packages> python isapi_wsgi.py remove`

   We are not yet ready to configure the web2py handler. You need to enable the 32-bits mode.

5. We are now ready to configure the web2py handler. Add your web2py installation to the `PYTHONPATH`:

   `set PYTHONPATH=%PYTHONPATH%;C:\path\to\web2py`

6. If it does not exist already, create the file `isapiwsgihandler.py` in the `C:\path\to\web2py` folder, which contains the following:

```python
import os
import sys
import isapi_wsgi

# The entry point for the ISAPI extension.
def __ExtensionFactory__():
    path = os.path.dirname(os.path.abspath(__file__))
    os.chdir(path)
    sys.path = [path]+[p for p in sys.path if not p==path]
    import gluon.main
    application = gluon.main.wsgibase
    return isapi_wsgi.ISAPISimpleHandler(application)

# ISAPI installation:
if __name__=='__main__':
    from isapi.install import ISAPIParameters
    from isapi.install import ScriptMapParams
    from isapi.install import VirtualDirParameters
    from isapi.install import HandleCommandLine
    params = ISAPIParameters()
    sm = [ScriptMapParams(Extension="*", Flags=0)]
```

```
vd = VirtualDirParameters(Name="appname",
  Description = "Web2py in Python",
  ScriptMaps = sm,
  ScriptMapUpdate = "replace")
params.VirtualDirs = [vd]
HandleCommandLine(params)
```

Recent versions of web2py may already contain this file, or even a better version.

7. The first part is the handler, and the second part will allow an automatic installation from the command line:

   **cd c:\path\to\web2py**

   **python isapiwsgihandler.py install --server=sitename**

   By default, this installs the extension for virtual directory `appname` under `Default Web Site`.

## There's more...

Check the current mode for Web Applications (32 bits or 64 bits):

**cd C:\Inetpub\AdminScripts**

**cscript.exe adsutil.vbs get W3SVC/AppPools/Enable32BitAppOnWin64**

**cscript %systemdrive%\inetpub\AdminScripts\adsutil.vbs get w3svc/\
AppPools/Enable32bitAppOnWin64**

If answer is `The parameter "Enable32BitAppOnWin64" is not set at this node` or `Enable32BitAppOnWin64         : (BOOLEAN) False`, then you must switch from 64 bits to 32 bits mode for the Web Server. ISAPI does not wok on IIS in 64 bits mode. You can switch with the command:

**cscript %systemdrive%\inetpub\AdminScripts\adsutil.vbs set w3svc/\
AppPools/Enable32bitAppOnWin64 1**

Then restart application pool, as follows:

**IIsExt /AddFile %systemroot%\syswow64\inetsrv\httpext.dll 1 ^
WEBDAV32 1 "WebDAV (32-bit)"**

Or set up a separate pool, as follows:

**system.webServer/applicationPool/add@enable32BitAppOnWin64.**

# 2
# Building Your First Application

In this chapter, we will cover the following recipes:

- Improving the scaffolding application
- Building a simple contacts application
- Building a Reddit clone
- Building a Facebook clone
- Using `crud.archive`
- Converting an existing static site into a web2py application
- Creating semi-static pages (flatpages)
- Adding your custom logo
- Creating menus and submenus
- Customizing menus with icons
- Creating a navigation bar
- Using cookies to set the language
- Designing modular applications
- Speeding up downloads

# Introduction

Now that you have web2py installed and running, you are ready to start building your first application. The recipes in this chapter will provide examples of complete applications, comprising models, views, and controllers. They range from simple **contacts** applications to a more complex **Facebook** clone. Other recipes in this chapter will show you how to solve some recurrent problems that new users typically encounter, from adding a logo to creating a navigation bar.

# Improving the scaffolding application

In this recipe, we discuss how to create your own scaffolding application and add your own configuration file. The **scaffolding application** is the collection of files that come with any new web2py application.

## How to do it...

The scaffolding app includes several files. One of them is `models/db.py`, which imports four classes from `gluon.tools` (`Mail`, `Auth`, `Crud`, and `Service`), and defines the following global objects: `db`, `mail`, `auth`, `crud`, and `service`.

The scaffolding application also defines tables required by the `auth` object, such as `db.auth_user`.

The default scaffolding application is designed to minimize the number of files, not to be modular. In particular, the model file, `db.py`, contains the configuration, which in a production environment, is best kept in separate files.

Here, we suggest creating a configuration file, `models/0.py`, that contains something like the following:

```
from gluon.storage import Storage
settings = Storage()

settings.production = False

if settings.production:
   settings.db_uri = 'sqlite://production.sqlite'
   settings.migrate = False
else:
   settings.db_uri = 'sqlite://development.sqlite'
   settings.migrate = True

settings.title = request.application
```

```
settings.subtitle = 'write something here'
settings.author = 'you'
settings.author_email = 'you@example.come'
settings.keywords = ''
settings.description = ''
settings.layout_theme = 'Default'
settings.security_key = 'a098c897-724b-4e05-b2d8-8ee993385ae6'
settings.email_server = 'localhost'
settings.email_sender = 'you@example.com'
settings.email_login = ''
settings.login_method = 'local'
settings.login_config = ''
```

We also modify `models/db.py`, so that it uses the information from the configuration file, and it defines the `auth_user` table explicitly (this makes it easier to add custom fields):

```
from gluon.tools import *                  Auth, Mail, Crud + Service

db = DAL(settings.db_uri)
if settings.db_uri.startswith('gae'):
  session.connect(request, response, db = db)

mail = Mail()                       # mailer
auth = Auth(db)                     # authentication/authorization
crud = Crud(db)                     # for CRUD helpers using auth
service = Service()                 # for json, xml, jsonrpc, xmlrpc, amfrpc
plugins = PluginManager()

# enable generic views for all actions for testing purpose
response.generic_patterns = ['*']

mail.settings.server = settings.email_server
mail.settings.sender = settings.email_sender
mail.settings.login = settings.email_login
auth.settings.hmac_key = settings.security_key

# add any extra fields you may want to add to auth_user
auth.settings.extra_fields['auth_user'] = []

# user username as well as email
auth.define_tables(migrate=settings.migrate,username=True)
auth.settings.mailer = mail
auth.settings.registration_requires_verification = False
```

*Building Your First Application*

```
auth.settings.registration_requires_approval = False

auth.messages.verify_email = 'Click on the link http://' \
  + request.env.http_host + URL('default','user',
  args=['verify_email']) \
  + '/%(key)s to verify your email'

auth.settings.reset_password_requires_verification = True

auth.messages.reset_password = 'Click on the link http://' \
  + request.env.http_host + URL('default','user',
  args=['reset_password']) \
  + '/%(key)s to reset your password'

if settings.login_method=='janrain':
  from gluon.contrib.login_methods.rpx_account import RPXAccount
  auth.settings.actions_disabled=['register', 'change_password',
     'request_reset_password']
  auth.settings.login_form = RPXAccount(request,
      api_key = settings.login_config.split(':')[-1],
      domain = settings.login_config.split(':')[0],
      url = "http://%s/%s/default/user/login" % \
      (request.env.http_host, request.application))
```

Normally, after a web2py installation or upgrade, the welcome application is tar-gzipped into `welcome.w2p`, and is used as the scaffolding application. You can create your own scaffolding application from an existing application using the following commands from a `bash` shell:

```
cd applications/app
tar zcvf ../../welcome.w2p *
```

## There's more...

The web2py wizard uses a similar approach, and creates a similar `0.py` configuration file. You can add more settings to the `0.py` file as needed.

The `0.py` file may contain sensitive information, such as the `security_key` used to encrypt passwords, the `email_login` containing the password of your smtp account, and the `login_config` with your Janrain password (http://www.janrain.com/). You may want to write this sensitive information in a read-only file outside the web2py tree, and read them from your `0.py` instead of hardcoding them. In this way, if you choose to commit your application to a version-control system, you will not be committing the sensitive information.

The scaffolding application includes other files that you may want to customize, including `views/layout.html` and `views/default/users.html`. Some of them are the subject of upcoming recipes.

## Building a simple contacts application

When you start designing a new web2py application, you go through three phases that are characterized by looking for the answer to the following three questions:

- What data should the application store?
- Which pages should be presented to the visitors?
- How should the page content, for each page, be presented?

The answer to these three questions is implemented in the **models**, the **controllers**, and the **views** respectively.

It is important for a good application design to try answering those questions exactly in this order, and as accurately as possible. Such answers can later be revised, and more tables, more pages, and more bells and whistles can be added in an iterative fashion. A good web2py application is designed in such a way that you can change the table definitions (add and remove fields), add pages, and change page views, without breaking the application.

A distinctive feature of web2py is that everything has a default. This means you can work on the first of those three steps without the need to write code for the second and third step. Similarly, you can work on the second step without the need to code for the third. At each step, you will be able to immediately see the result of your work; thanks to `appadmin` (the default database administrative interface) and generic views (every action has a view by default, until you write a custom one).

Here we consider, as a first example, an application to manage our business contacts, a CRM. We will call it `Contacts`. The application needs to maintain a list of companies, and a list of people who work at those companies.

### How to do it...

1. First of all we create the model.

   In this step we identify which tables are needed and their fields. For each field, we determine whether they:
   - Must contain unique values (`unique=True`)
   - Contain empty values (`notnull=True`)
   - Are references (contain a list of a record in another table)
   - Are used to represent a record (format attribute)

## Building Your First Application

From now on, we will assume we are working with a copy of the default scaffolding application, and we only describe the code that needs to be added or replaced. In particular, we will assume the default `views/layout.html` and `models/db.py`.

Here is a possible model representing the data we need to store in `models/db_contacts.py`:

```
# in file: models/db_custom.py

db.define_table('company',
    Field('name', notnull=True, unique=True),
    format='%(name)s')

db.define_table('contact',
    Field('name', notnull=True),
    Field('company', 'reference company'),
    Field('picture', 'upload'),
    Field('email', requires=IS_EMAIL()),
    Field('phone_number', requires=IS_MATCH('[\d\-\(\) ]+')),
    Field('address'),
    format='%(name)s')

db.define_table('log',
    Field('body', 'text',notnull=True),
    Field('posted_on', 'datetime'),
    Field('contact', 'reference contact'))
```

*[handwritten note: Alle Tabellen mit führendem "c"]*

Of course, a more complex data representation is possible. You may want to allow, for example, multiple users for the system, allow the same person to work for multiple companies, and keep track of changes in time. Here, we will keep it simple.

The name of this file is important. In particular, models are executed in alphabetical order, and this one must follow `db.py`.

2. After this file has been created, you can try it by visiting the following url: `http://127.0.0.1:8000/contacts/appadmin`, to access the web2py database administrative interface, `appadmin`. Without any controller or view, it provides a way to insert, select, update, and delete records.

3. Now we are ready to build the controller. We need to identify which pages are required by the application. This depends on the required workflow. At a minimum we need the following pages:

    - An index page (the home page)
    - A page to list all companies
    - A page that lists all contacts for one selected company
    - A page to create a company

- A page to edit/delete a company
- A page to create a contact
- A page to edit/delete a contact
- A page that allows to read the information about one contact and the communication logs, as well as add a new communication log

4. Such pages can be implemented as follows:

```
# in file: controllers/default.py

def index():
    return locals()

def companies():
    companies = db(db.company).select(orderby=db.company.name)
    return locals()

def contacts():
    company = db.company(request.args(0)) or
        redirect(URL('companies'))
    contacts = db(db.contact.company==company.id).select(
        orderby=db.contact.name)
    return locals()

@auth.requires_login()
def company_create():
    form = crud.create(db.company, next='companies')
    return locals()

@auth.requires_login()
def company_edit():
    company = db.company(request.args(0)) or
        redirect(URL('companies'))
    form = crud.update(db.company, company, next='companies')
    return locals()

@auth.requires_login()
def contact_create():
    db.contact.company.default = request.args(0)
    form = crud.create(db.contact, next='companies')
    return locals()

@auth.requires_login()
def contact_edit():
```

```
        contact = db.contact(request.args(0)) or
            redirect(URL('companies'))
        form = crud.update(db.contact, contact, next='companies')
        return locals()

    @auth.requires_login()
    def contact_logs():
        contact = db.contact(request.args(0)) or
            redirect(URL('companies'))
        db.log_contact.default = contact.id
        db.log_contact.readable = False
        db.log_contact.writable = False
        db.log_posted_on.default = request.now
        db.log_posted_on.readable = False
        db.log_posted_on.writable = False
        form = crud.create(db.log)
        logs = db(
            db.log_contact==contact.id).select(orderby=db.log_posted_on)
        return locals()

    def download(): return response.download(request, db)

    def user(): return dict(form=auth())
```

5. Make sure that you do not delete the existing `user`, `download`, and `service` functions in the scaffolding `default.py`.
6. Notice how all pages are built using the same ingredients: **select queries** and **crud forms**. You rarely need anything else.
7. Also notice the following:
    - Some pages require a `request.args(0)` argument (a company ID for contacts and `company_edit`, a contact ID for `contact_edit`, and `contact_logs`).
    - All selects have an `orderby` argument.
    - All crud forms have a next argument that determines the redirection after form submission.
    - All actions return `locals()`, which is a Python dictionary containing the local variables defined in the function. This is a shortcut. It is of course possible to return a dictionary with any subset of `locals()`.
    - `contact_create` sets a default value for the new contact company to the value passed as `args(0)`.
    - The `contacts_logs` retrieves past logs after processing `crud.create` for a new log entry. This avoid unnecessarily reloading of the page, when a new log is inserted.

8. At this point our application is fully functional, although the look-and-feel and navigation can be improved.:
   - You can create a new company at:
     `http://127.0.0.1:8000/contacts/default/company_create`
   - You can list all companies at:
     `http://127.0.0.1:8000/contacts/default/companies`
   - You can edit company #1 at:
     `http://127.0.0.1:8000/contacts/default/company_edit/1`
   - You can create a new contact at:
     `http://127.0.0.1:8000/contacts/default/contact_create`
   - You can list all contacts for company #1 at:
     `http://127.0.0.1:8000/contacts/default/contacts/1`
   - You can edit contact #1 at:
     `http://127.0.0.1:8000/contacts/default/contact_edit/1`
   - And you can access the communication log for contact #1 at:
     `http://127.0.0.1:8000/contacts/default/contact_logs/1`

9. You should also edit the `models/menu.py` file, and replace the content with the following:

   ```
   response.menu = [['Companies', False, URL('default',
      'companies')]]
   ```

   The application now works, but we can improve it by designing a better look and feel for the actions. That's done in the views.

10. Create and edit file `views/default/companies.html`:

    ```
    {{extend 'layout.html'}}
    <h2>Companies</h2>
    <table>
      {{for company in companies:}}
      <tr>
        <td>{{=A(company.name, _href=URL('contacts',
          args=company.id))}}</td>
        <td>{{=A('edit', _href=URL('company_edit',
          args=company.id))}}</td>
      </tr>
      {{pass}}
      <tr>
        <td>{{=A('add company', _href=URL('company_create'))}}</td>
      </tr>
    </table>
    ```

Here is how this page looks:

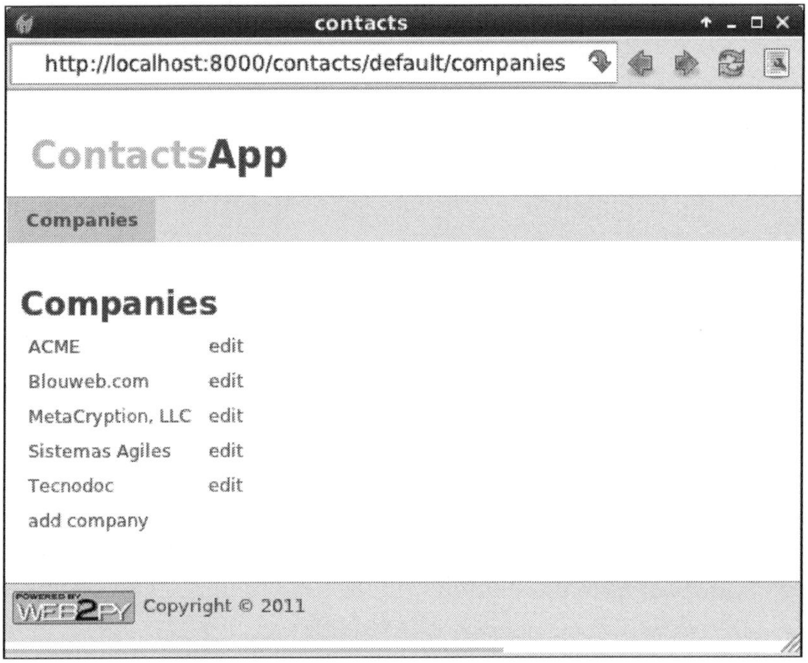
contacts
http://localhost:8000/contacts/default/companies
ContactsApp
Companies
Companies
ACME edit
Blouweb.com edit
MetaCryption, LLC edit
Sistemas Agiles edit
Tecnodoc edit
add company
POWERED BY WEB2PY
Copyright © 2011

11. Create and edit file `views/default/contacts.html`:

```
{{extend 'layout.html'}}
<h2>Contacts at {{=company.name}}</h2>
<table>
  {{for contact in contacts:}}
  <tr>
    <td>{{=A(contact.name, _href=URL('contact_logs',
      args=contact.id))}}</td>
    <td>{{=A('edit', _href=URL('contact_edit',
      args=contact.id))}}</td>
  </tr>
  {{pass}}
  <tr>
    <td>{{=A('add contact', _href=URL('contact_create',
      args=company.id))}}</td>
  </tr>
</table>
```

Here is how this page looks:

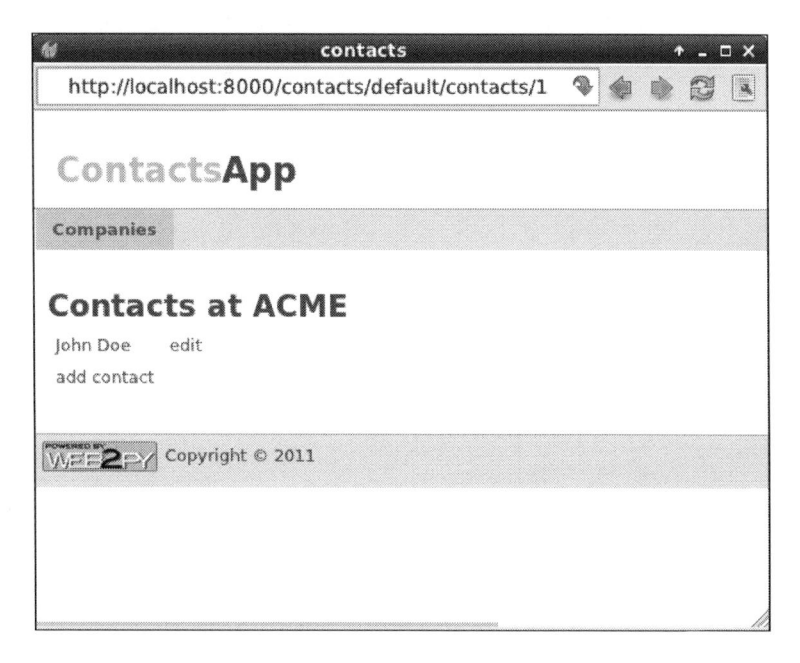

12. Create and edit file `views/default/company_create.html`:

    ```
    {{extend 'layout.html'}}
    <h2>New company</h2>
    {{=form}}
    ```

13. Create and edit file `views/default/contact_create.html`:

    ```
    {{extend 'layout.html'}}
    <h2>New contact</h2>
    {{=form}}
    ```

14. Create and edit file: `views/default/company_edit.html`:

    ```
    {{extend 'layout.html'}}
    <h2>Edit company</h2>
    {{=form}}
    ```

15. Create and edit file `views/default/contact_edit.html`:

    ```
    {{extend 'layout.html'}}
    <h2>Edit contact</h2>
    {{=form}}
    ```

**Building Your First Application**

16. Create and edit file `views/default/contact_logs.html`:

```
{{extend 'layout.html'}}
<h2>Logs for contact {{=contact.name}}</h2>
<table>
  {{for log in logs:}}
  <tr>
    <td>{{=log.posted_on}}</td>
    <td>{{=MARKMIN(log.body)}}</td>
  </tr>
  {{pass}}
  <tr>
    <td></td>
    <td>{{=form}}</td>
  </tr>
</table>
```

Here is how this page looks:

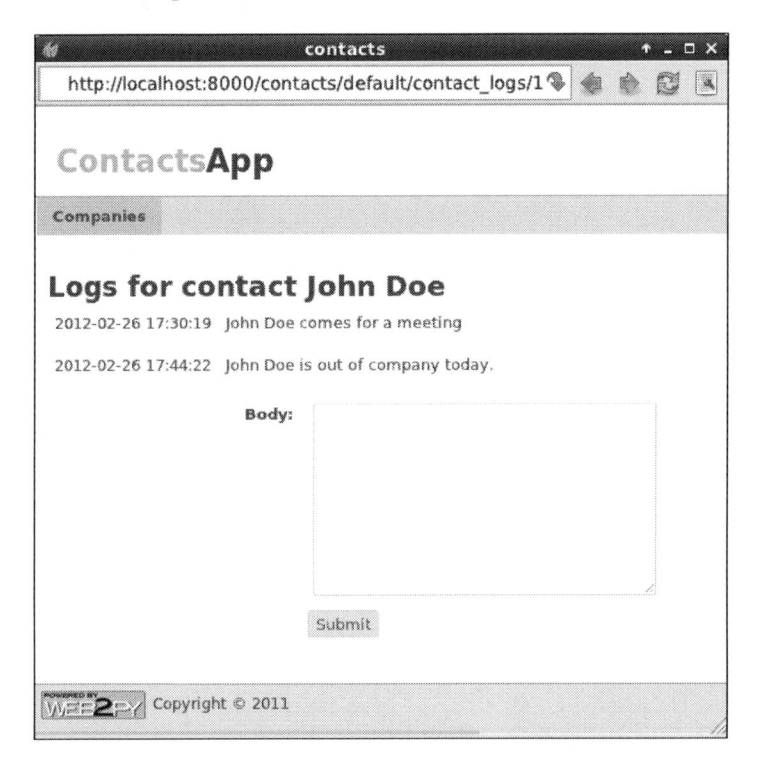

Notice that in the last view, we used the function `MARKMIN` to render the content of the `db.log.body`, using the `MARKMIN` markup. This allows embedding links, images, anchors, font formatting information, and tables in the logs. For details about the `MARKMIN` syntax we refer to: `http://web2py.com/examples/static/markmin.html`.

# Building a Reddit clone

Here we show how to build an application to post and rank links to online news items, similar to the `http://www.reddit.com/` website. The links are organized into categories, and users can post, vote, and comment on them. As in the previous recipe, the code only shows additions or changes to the default scaffolding application. We will call our application `reddit`.

In this recipe, we will not support threaded comments (as in the actual `http://www.reddit.com/` website), because it would be an unnecessary complication. We will discuss threaded comments in a subsequent recipe.

We will follow the same steps discussed in the previous recipe.

## How to do it...

This application is very similar to the `contacts` of the previous recipe. In fact, the data model is almost identical, provided that we map table `company` into a table `category`, and table `contact` into a table `news`. The main differences are that news items do not have a `name`, but they have a `title` and a `link` instead. Moreover, `news` items must be sorted by user votes, and not alphabetically. We also need to add a mechanism to allow users to vote, record votes, and prevent double counting. We need an extra table for this. We will also not deal with pagination, since this is discussed in a separate recipe.

Here is the complete model:

```
# in file: models/db_reddit.py
db.define_table('category',
   Field('name' ,notnull=True, unique=True),
   format='%(name)s')

db.define_table('news',
   Field('title', notnull=True),
   Field('link', requires=IS_URL()),
   Field('category', 'reference category', readable=False,
     writable=False),
   Field('votes', 'integer', readable=False, writable=False),
   Field('posted_on', 'datetime', readable=False, writable=False),
   Field('posted_by', 'reference auth_user', readable=False,
   writable=False),
   format='%(title)s')

db.define_table('comment',
   Field('news', 'reference news', readable=False, writable=False),
   Field('body', 'text', notnull=True),
```

## Building Your First Application

```
      Field('posted_on', 'datetime', readable=False, writable=False),
      Field('posted_by', 'reference auth_user', readable=False,
        writable=False))

  db.define_table('vote',
    Field('news', 'reference news'),
    Field('value', 'integer'),
    Field('posted_on', 'datetime', readable=False, writable=False),
    Field('posted_by', 'reference auth_user', readable=False,
      writable=False))
```

1. As discussed previously, many of the needed actions are equivalent to the `contacts` application of the previous recipe. In particular, we need actions to list categories, to list news for a given category, to create and edit categories, to create and edit news, to list comments, and vote for `news` items.

```
      def index():
        return locals()

      def categories():
        categories = db(db.category).select(orderby=db.category.name)
        return locals()

      def news():
        category = db.category(request.args(0)) or
          redirect(URL('categories'))
        news = db(db.news.category==category.id).select(
          orderby=~db.news.votes, limitby=(0, 25))
        return locals()

      @auth.requires_membership('manager')
      def category_create():
        form = crud.create(db.category, next='categories')
        return locals()

      @auth.requires_membership('manager')
      def category_edit():
        category = db.category(request.args(0)) or
          redirect(URL('categories'))
        form = crud.update(db.category, category, next='categories')
        return locals()

      @auth.requires_login()
      def news_create():
        db.news.category.default = request.args(0)
        db.news.votes.default = 0
        form = crud.create(db.news, next='news_comments/[id]')
        return locals()
```

```
@auth.requires_login()
def news_edit():
    news = db.news(request.args(0)) or redirect(URL('categories'))
    if not news.posted_by==auth.user.id:
        redirect(URL('not_authorized'))
    form = crud.update(db.news, category, next='news_comments/[id]')
    return locals()

def news_comments():
    news = db.news(request.args(0)) or redirect(URL('categories'))
    if auth.user:
        db.comment.news.default = news.id
        db.comment.posted_on.default = request.now
        db.comment.posted_by.default = auth.user.id
        form = crud.create(db.comment)
    comments = db(db.comment.news==news.id).select(
        orderby=db.comment.posted_on)
    return locals()

@auth.requires_login()
def vote():
    if not request.env.request_method=='POST': raise HTTP(400)
    news_id, mode = request.args(0), request.args(1)
    news = db.news(id=news_id)
    vote = db.vote(posted_by=auth.user.id, news=news_id)
    votes = news.votes
    value = (mode=='plus') and +1 or -1
    if vote and value*vote.value==1:
        message = 'you voted already'
    else:
        if vote:
            votes += value - vote.value
            vote.update_record(value=value)
        else:
            votes += value
            db.vote.insert(value=value, posted_by=auth.user.id,
                posted_on=request.now, news=news_id)
        news.update_record(votes=votes)
        message = 'vote recorded'
    return "jQuery('#votes').html('%s');jQuery('.flash').\
        html('%s').slideDown();" % (votes, message)
```

Most of these actions are very standard, and composed of the usual `select` and `crud` forms.

2. We used two types of decorators to make sure that only logged-in users can edit content, and only managers can create and edit categories. You can use `appadmin` to create a `manager` group and give membership to users:

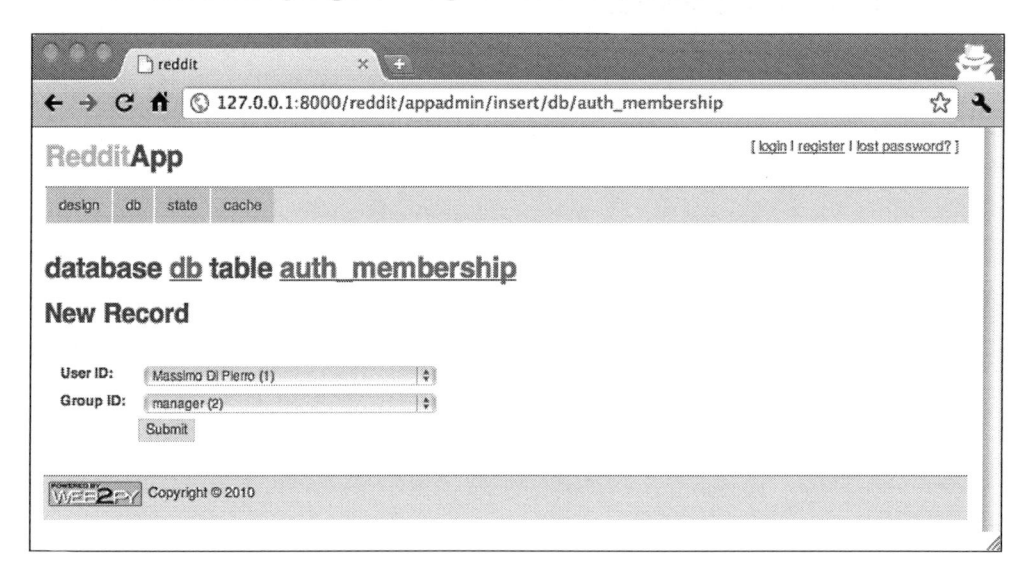

> The only special action is the last `vote`. The `vote` action is designed to be an Ajax callback. To avoid indirect reference attacks, the first line makes sure the action is called with a `POST` request. Then we parse the request `args`: it expects a news ID as `args(0)`, and `plus` or `minus` as `args(1)`, depending on whether we want to vote the news item up or down. If we vote up (`plus`), it creates a new `db.vote` entry with value equal to `+1`. If we vote down (`minus`), it creates a new `db.vote` entry with value equal to `-1`. The action also checks whether we voted already. We are allowed to change our vote, but not to vote twice.
>
> This action returns a JavaScript string that updates the `votes` HTML element with the latest `vote` count, and flashes a new message. The last line of the action is tightly coupled with the view that will perform the Ajax call (`views/default/news_comments.html`).

3. We also want to list all possible categories in the menu:

   ```
   # in file: models/menu.py"
   categories = db(db.category).select(orderby=db.category.name,
     cache=(cache.ram, 60))
   response.menu = [(c.name, False, URL('default', 'news',
     args=c.id)) for c in categories]
   ```

4. Finally, we need to create the following views:
    - views/default/categories.html:

```
{{extend 'layout.html'}}
<h2>Categories</h2>
<table>
  {{for category in categories:}}
  <tr>
    <td>{{=A(category.name, _href=URL('news',
      args=category.id))}}</td>
    <td>{{=A('edit', _href=URL('category_edit',
      args=category.id))}}
    </td>
  </tr>
  {{pass}}
  <tr>
    <td>{{=A('add category', _href=URL('category_create'))}}</td>
  </tr>
</table>
```

- views/default/news.html:

```
{{extend 'layout.html'}}
<h2>News at {{=category.name}}</h2>
<table>
  {{for news in news:}}
  <tr>
    <td>{{=A(news.title, _href=news.link)}}</td>
    <td>{{=A('comments', _href=URL('news_comments',
      args=news.id))}}
    </td>
    <td>{{=A('edit', _href=URL('news_edit', args=news.id))}}</td>
  </tr>
  {{pass}}
  <tr>
    <td>{{=A('post news item', _href=URL('news_create',
      args=category.id))}}
    </td>
    <td></td>
  </tr>
</table>
```

## Building Your First Application

Here is how this page looks:

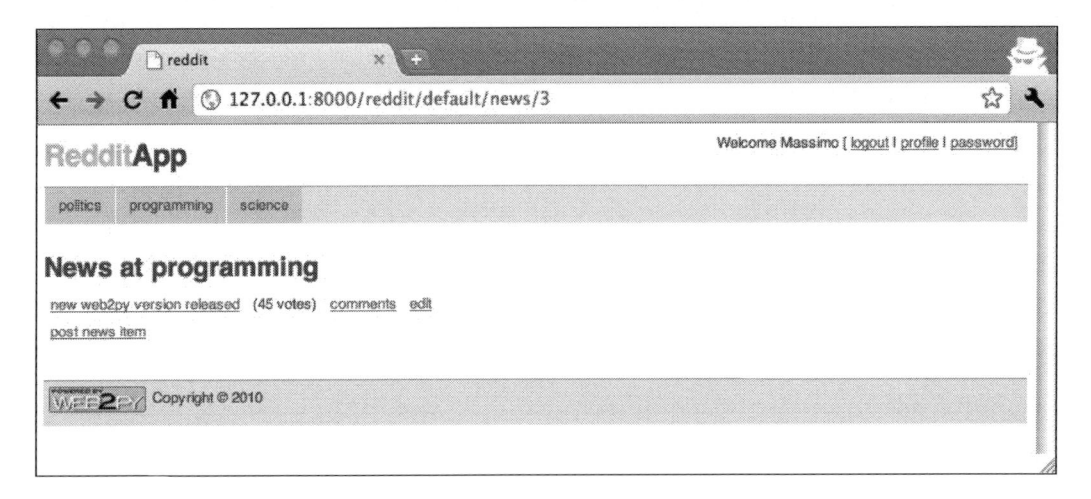

[Browser screenshot showing RedditApp at 127.0.0.1:8000/reddit/default/news/3, with tabs "politics | programming | science", heading "News at programming", a link "new web2py version released (45 votes) comments edit", and "post news item" link.]

- views/default/category_create.html:

```
{{extend 'layout.html'}}
<h2>New category</h2>
{{=form}}
```

- views/default/news_create.html:

```
{{extend 'layout.html'}}
<h2>Post news item</h2>
{{=form}}
```

- views/default/category_edit.html:

```
{{extend 'layout.html'}}
<h2>Edit category</h2>
{{=form}}
```

- views/default/categories.html:

```
{{extend 'layout.html'}}
<h2>Edit news item</h2>
{{=form}}
```

- views/default/news_comments.html:

```
{{extend 'layout.html'}}
<h2>Comments for {{=A(news.title, _href=news.link)}}</h2>
{{if auth.user:}}
  <span id="votes">{{=news.votes}}</span>
```

```
        <button id="plus"
          onclick="ajax('{{=URL('vote', args=(news.id, 'plus'))}}', [],
          ':eval')">
          plus
        </button>

        <button id="minus"
          onclick="ajax('{{=URL('vote', args=(news.id, 'minus'))}}', [],
          ':eval')">
          minus
        </button>
        {{=form}}
    {{pass}}
    <table>
      {{for comment in comments:}}
      <tr>
        <td>{{=comment.posted_on}}</td>
        <td>{{=comment.posted_by.first_name}} says </td>
        <td>{{=MARKMIN(comment.body)}}</td>
      </tr>
      {{pass}}
    </table>
```

Notice the code:

```
<button id="plus"
  onclick="ajax('{{=URL('vote', args=(news.id, 'plus'))}}', [],
  ':eval')">
  plus
</button>
```

On clicking, it performs an Ajax request that records our vote. The return value of the Ajax request is evaluated (`:eval`). The URL(`vote`) returns a JavaScript code that will be evaluated:

```
def vote():
    ...
    return
      "jQuery('#votes').html('%s');jQuery('.flash').
      html('%s').slideDown();" % (votes, message)
```

5. In particular, it will alter the content of the following code, and flash a new message (slidedown):

```
<span id="votes">{{=news.votes}}</span>
```

Here is how this page looks:

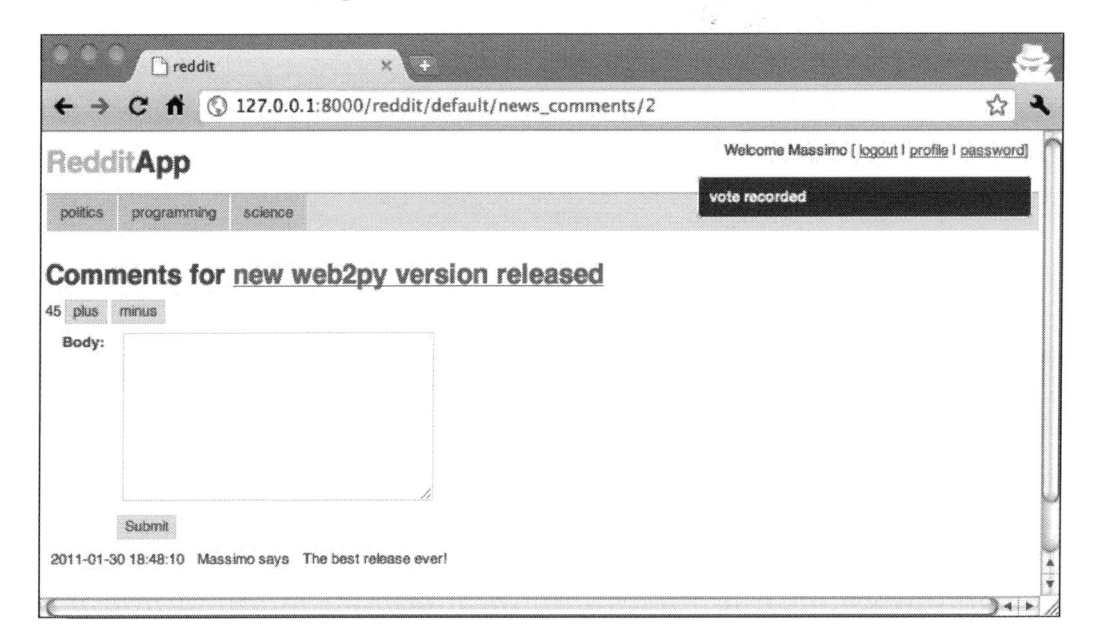

## Building a Facebook clone

At its fundamental level, Facebook handles friendship relations between users, and allows friends to see each other's posts. Users can register, log in, search for other users, request friendship, and accept friendship. When a user posts a message, the post will be visible on the wall (web page) of all his/her friends.

Of course, the real Facebook application is quite complex, and our version is greatly simplified, but it captures the most important features. In particular, we will omit the ability to attach comments after posts, and we will omit e-mail notification features. We will also omit the code to handle photos, videos, and chat. We are only interested in the friendship relations and display wall posts, based on friendship. We will call our application `friends`.

### How to do it...

The core of our design is a table to link two people: a `source` and a `target` of a friendship relation. The friendship relation is requested by a `source`, and must be approved by a `target`. When approved, the `source` user can see the posts and profile info of the `target`. While the real Facebook friendship relations are bi-directional (although friends can be hidden/blocked), in our case we assume unidirectional friendship (two users must give friendship to each other to see each other's posts).

1. The model is therefore quite simple, and we only need two tables:

   ```
   # in file: models: db.py
   # a table to store posted messages
   db.define_table('post',
     Field('body', 'text', requires=IS_NOT_EMPTY(), label='What is on
     your mind?'),
     Field('posted_on', 'datetime', readable=False, writable=False),
     Field('posted_by', 'reference auth_user', readable=False,
       writable=False))

   # a table to link two people
   db.define_table('link',
     Field('source', 'reference auth_user'),
     Field('target', 'reference auth_user'),
     Field('accepted', 'boolean', default=False))

   # and define some global variables that will make code more
   compact
   User, Link, Post = db.auth_user, db.link, db.post
   me, a0, a1 = auth.user_id, request.args(0), request.args(1)
   myfriends = db(Link.source==me)(Link.accepted==True)
   alphabetical = User.first_name|User.last_name
   def name_of(user): return '%(first_name)s %(last_name)s' % user
   ```

   The last five lines define various shortcuts that will make our controllers and views more compact. For example, they allow the user to use `User` instead of `db.user`, and `orderby=alphabetical` instead of the more verbose equivalent.

   `myfriends` is the set of people that have accepted our friendship, which means we can see their posts.

   The following list line allows us to print the first name followed by last name of a user, given a user object or a user reference:

   `{{=name_of(user)}}`

2. We are going to need the following pages:
   - An **index** page that, if we are logged in, redirects to our home page
   - A **private** home page that shows our messages, the posts of our friends, and allows us to post a new post
   - A page to search for new friends by name
   - A page to check who our current friends are, check pending friend requests, and approve or deny friendship
   - A wall page to see the status of one particular friend (or our own)

3. We also need a callback action ~~to implement~~ to allow users to **request** friendship, to **accept** friendship, to **deny** a friendship request, and to **cancel** a previous request for friendship. We implement these through a single Ajax callback in a function called `friendship`:

```
# in file: controllers/default.py
def index():
  if auth.user: redirect(URL('home'))
  return locals()

def user():
  return dict(form=auth())

def download():
  return response.download(request, db)

def call():
  session.forget()
  return service()

# our home page, will show our posts and posts by friends
@auth.requires_login()
def home():
  Post.posted_by.default = me
  Post.posted_on.default = request.now
  crud.settings.formstyle = 'table2cols'
  form = crud.create(Post)
  friends = [me]+[row.target for row in
    myfriends.select(Link.target)]
  posts = db(Post.posted_by.belongs(friends))\
    .select(orderby=~Post.posted_on, limitby=(0, 100))
  return locals()

# our wall will show our profile and our own posts
@auth.requires_login()
def wall():
  user = User(a0 or me)
  if not user or not (user.id==me or \
    myfriends(Link.target==user.id).count()):
      redirect(URL('home'))
  posts = db(Post.posted_by==user.id)\
    .select(orderby=~Post.posted_on, limitby=(0, 100))
  return locals()
```

```
# a page for searching friends and requesting friendship
@auth.requires_login()
def search():
  form = SQLFORM.factory(Field('name', requires=IS_NOT_EMPTY()))
  if form.accepts(request):
    tokens = form.vars.name.split()
    query = reduce(lambda a,b:a&b,
    [User.first_name.contains(k)|User.last_name.contains(k) \
    for k in tokens])
      people = db(query).select(orderby=alphabetical)
    else:
      people = []
  return locals()

# a page for accepting and denying friendship requests
@auth.requires_login()
def friends():
  friends = db(User.id==Link.source)(Link.target==me)\
    .select(orderby=alphabetical)
  requests = db(User.id==Link.target)(Link.source==me)\
    .select(orderby=alphabetical)
  return locals()

# this is the Ajax callback
@auth.requires_login()
def friendship():
  """Ajax callback!"""
  if request.env.request_method != 'POST': raise HTTP(400)
  if a0=='request' and not Link(source=a1, target=me):
    # insert a new friendship request
    Link.insert(source=me, target=a1)
  elif a0=='accept':
    # accept an existing friendship request
    db(Link.target==me)(Link.source==a1).update(accepted=True)
  if not db(Link.source==me)(Link.target==a1).count():
    Link.insert(source=me, target=a1)
  elif a0=='deny':
    # deny an existing friendship request
    db(Link.target==me)(Link.source==a1).delete()
  elif a0=='remove':
    # delete a previous friendship request
    db(Link.source==me)(Link.target==a1).delete()
```

4. We also include the **home**, **wall**, **friends**, and **search** pages in the menu:

```
# in file: models/menu.py
response.menu = [
   (T('Home'), False, URL('default', 'home')),
   (T('Wall'), False, URL('default', 'wall')),
   (T('Friends'), False, URL('default', 'friends')),
   (T('Search'), False, URL('default', 'search')),
]
```

Most of the views are straightforward.

- Here is `views/default/home.html`:

```
{{extend 'layout.html'}}
{{=form}}
<script>jQuery('textarea').css('width','600px').
   css('height','50px');</script>
{{for post in posts:}}
<div style="background: #f0f0f0; margin-bottom: 5px; padding:
   8px;">
   <h3>{{=name_of(post.posted_by)}} on {{=post.posted_on}}:</h3>
   {{=MARKMIN(post.body)}}
</div>
{{pass}}
```

Notice the jQuery script that resizes the input message box, and the use of MARKMIN for rendering message markup.

- Here is `views/default/wall.html`, which is very similar to the previous view (the difference is that there is no form, and the posts are relative to a single user, specified by `request.args(0)`):

```
{{extend 'layout.html'}}
<h2>Profile</h2>
{{=crud.read(db.auth_user, user)}}
<h2>Messages</h2>
{{for post in posts:}}
<div style="background: #f0f0f0; margin-bottom: 5px; padding:
   8px;">
   <h3>{{=name_of(post.posted_by)}} on {{=post.posted_on}}:</h3>
   {{=MARKMIN(post.body)}}
</div>
{{pass}}
```

Here is what this page looks like:

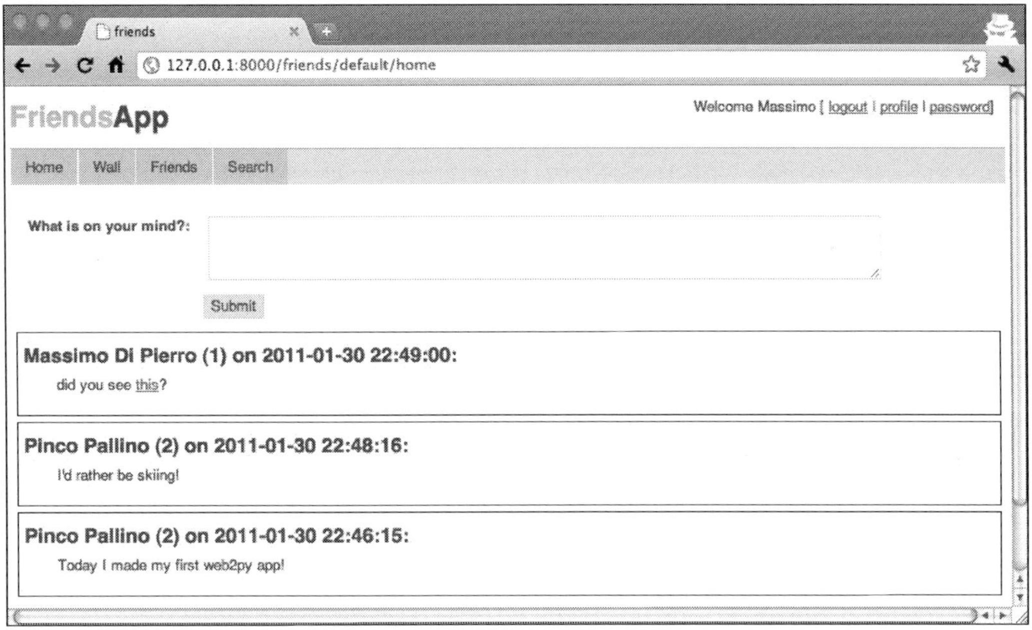


- Here is `views/default/search.html`:

```
{{extend 'layout.html'}}
<h2>Search for friends</h2>
{{=form}}
{{if people:}}
<h3>Results</h3>
<table>
  {{for user in people:}}
  <td>
    {{=A(name_of(user), _href=URL('wall', args=user.id))}}
  </td>
  <td>
    <button onclick="ajax(
      '{{=URL('friendship', args=('request', user.id))}}',
      [], null);
      jQuery(this).parent().html('pending')">
      request friendship
    </button>
  </td>
  {{pass}}
</table>
{{pass}}
```

Here is what this page looks like:

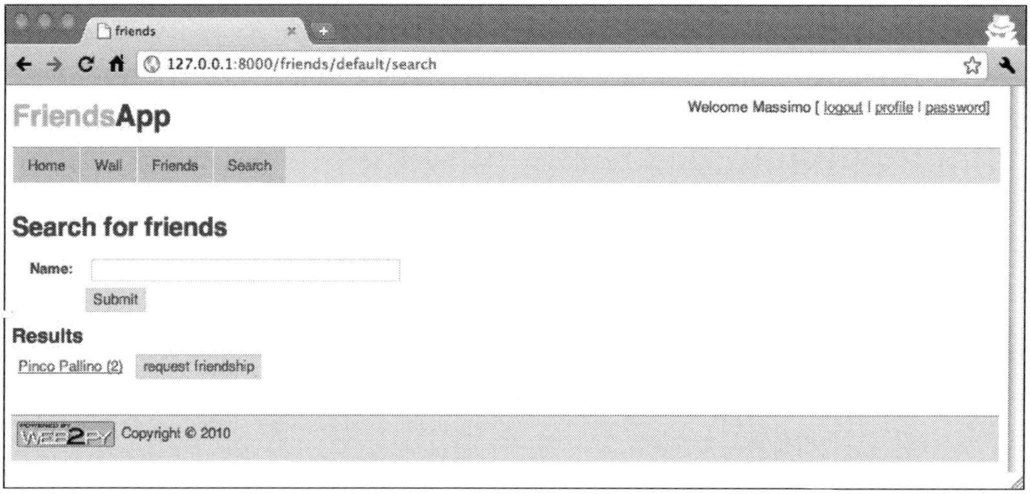
friends
127.0.0.1:8000/friends/default/search
FriendsApp
Welcome Massimo [ logout | profile | password]
Home
Wall
Friends
Search
Search for friends
Name:
Submit
Results
Pinco Pallino (2)
request friendship
Copyright © 2010

Notice how the buttons perform Ajax calls to `request` friendship to `user.id`. Upon click, the button is replaced by a message that says **pending**.

- Below is `views/default/friends.html`. It lists current friends and pending friendship requests:

```
{{extend 'layout.html'}}
<h2>Friendship Offered</h2>
<table>
  {{for friend in friends:}}
  <tr>
    <td>
      {{=A(name_of(friend.auth_user), _href=URL('wall',
        args=friend.auth_user.id))}}
    </td>
    <td>
      {{if friend.link.accepted:}}accepted{{else:}}
        <button onclick="ajax(
          '{{=URL('friendship', args=('accept',
          friend.auth_user.id))}}',
          [], null);
          jQuery(this).parent().html('accepted')">
          accept
        </button>
      {{pass}}
    </td>
    <td>
      <button onclick="ajax(
        '{{=URL('friendship', args=('deny',
```

```
                    friend.auth_user.id))}}',
                  [], null);
                  jQuery(this).parent().html('denied')">
                  deny
                </button>
              </td>
            </tr>
            {{pass}}
          </table>
          <h2>Friendship Requested</h2>
          <table>
            {{for friend in requests:}}
            <tr>
              <td>
                {{=A(name_of(friend.auth_user), _href=URL('wall',
                  args=friend.auth_user.id))}}
              </td>
              <td>
                {{if friend.link.accepted:}}accepted{{else:}}
          pending{{pass}}
              </td>
              <td>
                <button onclick="ajax(
                  '{{=URL('friendship', args=('deny',
                  friend.auth_user.id))}}',
                  [], null);
                  jQuery(this).parent().html('removed')">
                  remove
                </button>
              </td>
            </tr>
            {{pass}}
          </table>
```

Here is what this page looks like:

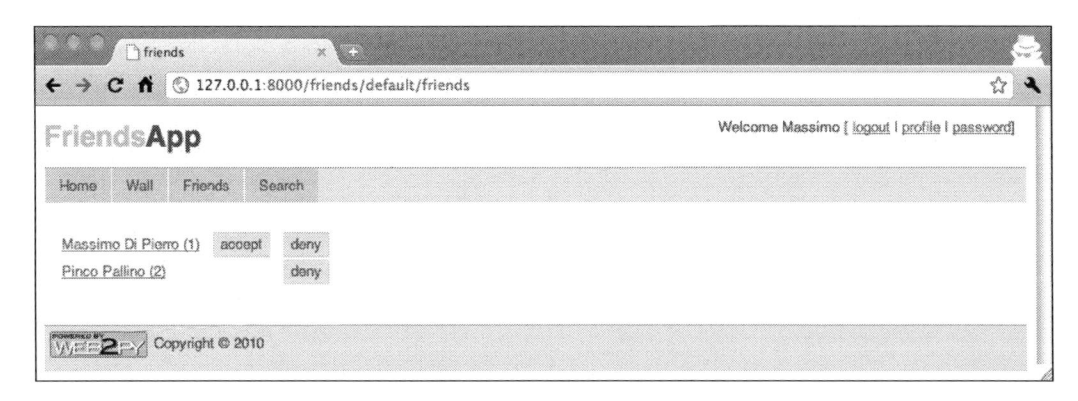

*Building Your First Application*

This view displays two tables: a list of friendships **offered** to us (by accepting, we give them the permission to see our profile and posts), and friendship **requests** that we sent (people we want to see profile and posts of). For each user in the first table, there are two buttons. A button that performs an Ajax call to **accept** a pending friendship request, and a button to **deny** friendship. For each user in the second table, there is a column that informs us of whether our request was accepted, and a column with a button to cancel the friendship relation (whether pending or established).

Notice how `{{=name_of(user)}}` and `{{=name_of(message.posted_by)}}` require a database lookup. Our application can be sped up by caching the output of this function.

# Using crud.archive

In this recipe, we discuss how to create full versioning for records in any application.

## How to do it...

If you have any table, for example, `db.mytable`, that needs versioning, and you use `crud.update`, you can store a full revision history for your records, by passing `onaccept=crud.archive` to `crud.update`. Here is an example:

```
form = crud.update(db.mytable, myrecord,
   onaccept=crud.archive,
   deletable=False)
```

`crud.archive` will create a hidden table `db.mytable_archive`, and store the old record, before update, in the newly created table, including a reference to the current record.

Normally, this new table is hidden and only visible to web2py internals, but you can have access to it by defining it explicitly in the model. If the original table was called `db.mytable`, the archive table must be called `db.mytable_archive` (postfix the original one with `_archive`), and it must extend the original table with a reference field called `current_record`. Here is a concrete example:

```
db.define_table('mytable_archive',
   Field('current_record', db.mytable),
   db.mytable)
```

For a different table, just replace `mytable` with the actual table name. Everything else stays the same.

Notice such table includes all fields of `db.mytable` plus one `current_record`.

## There's more...

Let's take a look at other features of `crud.archive`.

### Timestamping the stored record

`crud.archive` does not timestamp the stored record, unless your original table has a timestamp and signature. For example:

```
db.define_table('mytable',
   ...
   auth.signature)
```

By adding `auth.signature` to the table, we are adding the following fields:

```
Field('is_active', 'boolean', default=True),
Field('created_on', 'datetime', default=request.now,
   writable=False, readable=False),
Field('created_by', db.auth_user, default=auth.user_id,
   writable=False, readable=False),
Field('modified_on', 'datetime',
   update=default.now, default=request.now,
   writable=False, readable=False),
Field('modified_by', db.table_user,
   default=auth.user_id, update=auth.user_id,
   writable=False, readable=False)
```

You can also do this manually (without `auth.signature`), and give any name to the signature and timestamp fields. `crud.archive` handles them transparently. They are filled by the `SQLFORM.accepts` function.

### Storing the history of each record

The main idea behind `crud.archive` is that of storing the history of each record that is edited, and storing previous revisions in a separate table. This allows you to edit the record without breaking references to it. Moreover, if you alter (migrate) the original table, the archive table will migrate as well. The only catch is that deleting a record in the original table will cause a cascade delete in the archive table, and the entire previous history for the record is deleted. Hence, probably, you do not want to ever delete records, but just make them **disabled**, by unchecking the `is_active` field.

You will also have to change the query in some `select` statements to hide records that are disabled, by filtering records with the following:

```
db.mytable.is_active==True
```

## Converting an existing static site into a web2py application

We will assume that you have a collection of static HTML files, CSS files, JavaScript files, and images in one folder, and that you wish to turn them into a web2py application. There are two ways to do it: a naive way, in which existing HTML files continue to be treated as static, and a more complex way, in which HTML files are associated to controller actions, so that one can add some dynamic content later on.

### How to do it...

1. A naive way consists simply of creating a new web2py application (or using an existing one), and using a static folder. For example, create a new application called `app`, and copy the entire directory structure of your existing site under `applications/app/static/`.

   In this way, a static file, `applications/app/static/example.html` can be accessed at the URL:
   `http://127.0.0.1:8000/app/static/example.html`.

   While this process does not break relative URLs (URLs that do not start with a forward slash), such as:
   `<a href="../path/to/example2.html">click me</a>`, it may break absolute URLs (which start with a forward slash) such as:
   `<a href="/path/to/example2.html">click me</a>`.

   This is not a web2py-specific problem, but rather an indication of poor design of those HTML files, since the absolute links break every time the folder structure is moved into another folder.

2. The proper way to solve this problem, in case it occurs, consists of replacing all absolute URLS with relative ones. Here is an example.

   If a file, `static/path1/example1.html`, contains a link like
   `<a href="/path/to/example2.html">click me</a>`, and the file `example2.html`, appears under `static/path2/example2.html`, then the link should be replaced by
   `<a href="../path2/example2.html">click me</a>`.

   Here the `../` moves out of the `static/path1` folder into the `static` folder, and the rest of the path (`path2/example2.html`) correctly identifies the desired file.

3. A simple search for `href`, `src`, and `url` should allow you to locate all the URLS in the HTML, CSS, and JavaScript files. All the URLS starting with a `/` need to be fixed.

4. A more sophisticated approach consists of moving all images, movies, CSS, and JavaScript files into the static folder, and converting HTML files into views.

We proceed in five steps:

- We move all static files (except those ending in `html`) to the application `static/` folder.
- We create a new controller (for example, one called `controllers/legacy.py`), and a new `views` folder (for example `views/legacy`).
- We move all the HTML files (for example, `page.html`) under the new views folder.
- For each `view` file, we create a controller action with the same name returning `dict()`.
- We replace all internal links and references with `URL(...)`.

5. Let's consider a concrete example consisting of the following files:

```
page.html
image.png
```

Here, `page.html` contains `<img src="image.png" />`. We end up with the following file structure in our web2py application folder:

```
controllers/legacy.py
views/legacy/page.html
static/image.png
```

Here, `legacy.py` contains

```
def page(): return dict()
```

and `<img src="image.png"/>` in `page.html` is replaced by

```
<img src="{{=URL('static', 'image.png')}}"/>
```

The page is now accessible at the following URL:

`http://127.0.0.1:8000/app/legacy/page.html`.

# Creating semi-static pages (flatpages)

Any web application contains pages that are static, and whose content does not change very often. They are called **flatpages**. They can be handled by embedding a CMS into the application (for example `plugin_wiki`) or using the explicit mechanism described in this recipe.

Examples of flatpages are:

- Basic home and indexes
- About us
- License and disclaimer

Building Your First Application

With web2py, for these pages, we could set up simple controllers such as:

```
def about(): return dict()
```

And you can then code the page in the view directly, or store the page content in the database. This second approach is better, because it would allow easy in-place user editing, multiple-language internationalization support, log change history for audits, and much more.

The idea of this recipe is to store the flatpages in the database, and display them according the user request (controller, function, args, preferred language, and so on.)

## How to do it...

1. First, define a flatpage table to store the page contents, create a file in models called `flatpages.py`, and add the following definition:

    ```
    LANGUAGES = ('en', 'es', 'pt', 'fr', 'hi', 'hu', 'it', 'pl', 'ru')
    FLATPAGES_ADMIN = 'you@example.com'
    DEFAULT_FLATPAGE_VIEW = "flatpage.html"
    db.define_table('flatpage',
      Field('title', notnull=True),
      Field('subtitle', notnull=True),
      Field('c', label='controller'),
      Field('f', label='function'),
      Field('args', label='arguments'),
      Field('view', default=DEFAULT_FLATPAGE_VIEW),
      Field('lang', requires=IS_IN_SET(LANGUAGES), default='en'),
      Field('body', 'text', default=''),
      auth.signature,
    )
    ```

    The fields are:
    - `title`: This is the main title
    - `subtitle`: This is the optional subtitle
    - `c`: This is the controller for who this page belongs to (see URL helper)
    - `f`: This is the function for who this page belongs to (see URL helper)
    - `args`: This is the string argument to add several pages to a function (see URL helper)
    - `lang`: This is the language to match user preferences
    - `body`: This is the the page HTML body

    Notice that the FLATPAGES_ADMIN will be used to limit the edit access to the flatpages. This variable contains the e-mail of the user that will be allowed to edit.

2. At this point, you should be able to populate this table using the `appadmin` administrative interface, or you can do it programmatically, that is, creating a `setup_flatpage` function in a controller, such as the following: *default.py*

```
if not db(db.flatpage).count():
   db.flatpage.insert(title="Home", subtitle="Main Index",
      c="default", f='index', body="<h3>Hello world!</h3>")
   db.flatpage.insert(title="About us", subtitle="The company",
      c="company", f='about_us', body="<h3>My company!</h3>")
   db.flatpage.insert(title="Mision & Vision", subtitle="The
      company", c="company", f='mision_vision', body="<h3>
      Our vision is...</h3>")
   db.flatpage.insert(title="Our Team", subtitle="Who we are",
      c="company", f='our_team', body="<h1>We are...</h1>")
   db.flatpage.insert(title="Contact Us", subtitle="Where we are",
      c="company", f='contact_us', body="<h3>Contact form:...</h3>")
```

   This example page will look as follows:

```
Home: Hello world
About Us
   The Company : My company!
Mission & Vision: Our vision is...
Our Team: We are...
Contact Us: Contact Form:...
```

3. To be able to render a page, add to the previously created file `models/flatpage.py` the following function flatpage:

```
def flatpage():
   # define languages that don't need translation:
   T.current_languages = ['en', 'en-en']

   # select user specified language (via session or browser config)
   if session.lang:
      lang = session.lang
   elif T.accepted_language is not None:
      lang = T.accepted_language[:2]
   else:
      lang = "en"
      T.force(lang)

   title = subtitle = body = ""
   flatpage_id = None
   form = ''
   view = DEFAULT_FLATPAGE_VIEW

   if request.vars and auth.user and
      auth.user.email==FLATPAGES_ADMIN:
```

## Building Your First Application

```
    # create a form to edit the page:
    record = db.flatpage(request.get_vars.id)
    form = SQLFORM(db.flatpage, record)
if form.accepts(request, session):
    response.flash = T("Page saved")
elif form.errors:
    response.flash = T("Errors!")
else:
    response.flash = T("Edit Page")

if not form:
    # search flatpage according to the current request
    query = db.flatpage.c==request.controller
    query &= db.flatpage.f==request.function
if request.args:
    query &= db.flatpage.args==request.args(0)
else:
    query &= (db.flatpage.args==None)|(db.flatpage.args=='')
    query &= db.flatpage.lang==lang
    # execute the query, fetch one record (if any)
    flatpage = \
       db(query).select(orderby=~db.flatpage.created_on,
    limitby=(0, 1), cache=(cache.ram, 60)).first()
if flatpage:
    flatpage_id = flatpage.id
    title = flatpage.title
    subtitle = flatpage.subtitle
    body = flatpage.body
    view = flatpage.view
else:
    response.flash = T("Page Not Found!")
if auth.user and auth.user.email==FLATPAGES_ADMIN:
    # if user is authenticated, show edit button:
    form = A(T('edit'),
      _href=URL(vars=dict(id=flatpage_id)))

# render the page:
response.title = title
response.subtitle = subtitle
response.view = view
body = XML(body)
return dict(body=body, form=form)
```

This function:

- Checks user language preferences (or session setting)
- Checks action URL (according to request controller, function, and args)
- Fetches stored flatpage
- Renders the page HTML

If the user `FLATPAGES_ADMIN` is logged in, the function flatpage:

- Prepares/processes an `SQLFORM` if editing the page
- Or shows an **EDIT** button to edit the page

4. Finally, you should create a `flatpage.html` view, so that web2py can render the page, for example:

```
{{extend 'layout.html'}}
<h1>{{=response.title}}</h1>
<h2>{{=response.subtitle}}</h2>
{{=form}}
{{=body}}
```

The placeholders are:

- `form`: This is the edit `FORM` (or the link to edit)
- `body`: These are the actual page contents (stored in the database as HTML)

5. To tell web2py to show a flatpage in the desired controller (that is, `index` in `default.py`), write the following:

```
def index(): return flatpage()
```

This will render the flatpage for the home page.

`company.py` sample controller will look as follows:

```
def about_us(): return flatpage()
def mision_vision(): return flatpage()
def our_team(): return flatpage()
```

When you go to `default/index.php` or `company/about_us`, you should get a flatpage with an `EDIT` button, if you are logged in.

Remember that, for performance reasons, flatpages are cached. So, changes may not be seen immediately (you can change this by clearing the cache or removing the cache parameter at the database query).

*Building Your First Application*

## How it works...

With web2py, you can completely choose what content will be displayed, what view will be used, and so on.

In this case, when web2py executes your controller, the function `flatpage()` will try to fetch the stored page in the database according the request variables.

An `SQLFORM` will be rendered if the **Edit** button is pressed, to allow page editing by normal authenticated users. Page updates are inserted, so you'll get a history of page changes. It shows the latest record of the page, trying to match the preferred language (for example, use `session.lang = 'es'` to change the language).

You can add a `view` field to flatpage table, so you could have multiple views to show this kind of content. You can even add a `format` field, so that you can render the page body in other markup languages other than HTML (wiki, ReST, and so on).

## Adding your custom logo

We are going to change the default logo that came with web2py, and add our logo instead. We need an image editor; use your preferred one, or use the ones that come with the operating system. Paint, GIMP, or Photoshop are appropriate.

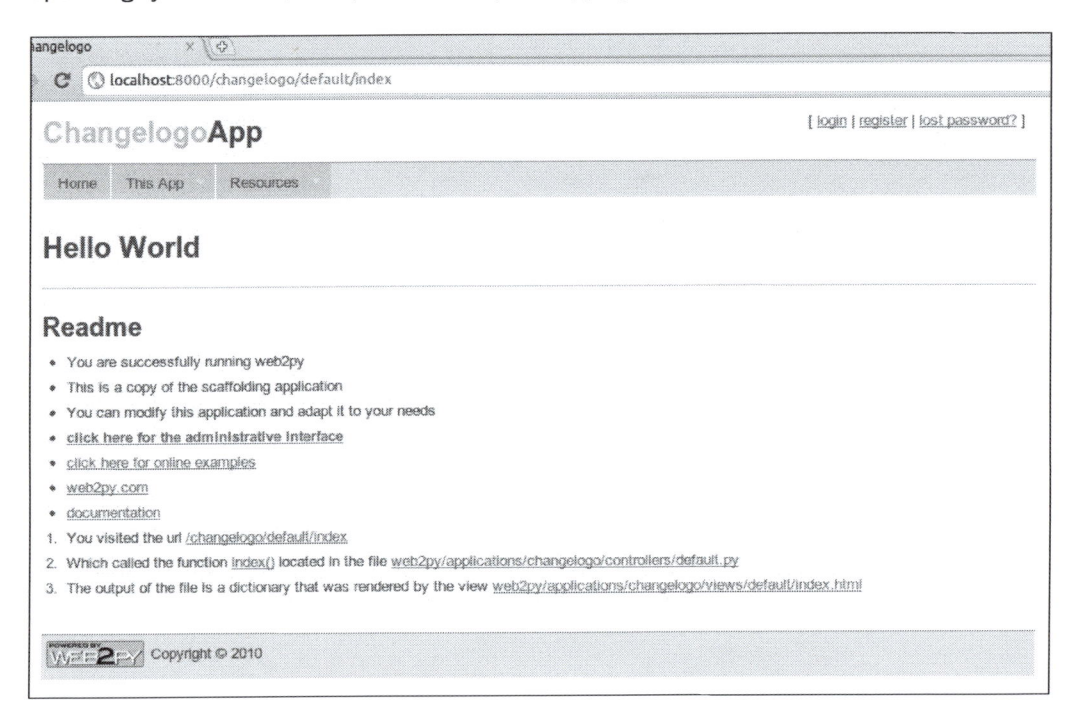

This is the look of the default application:

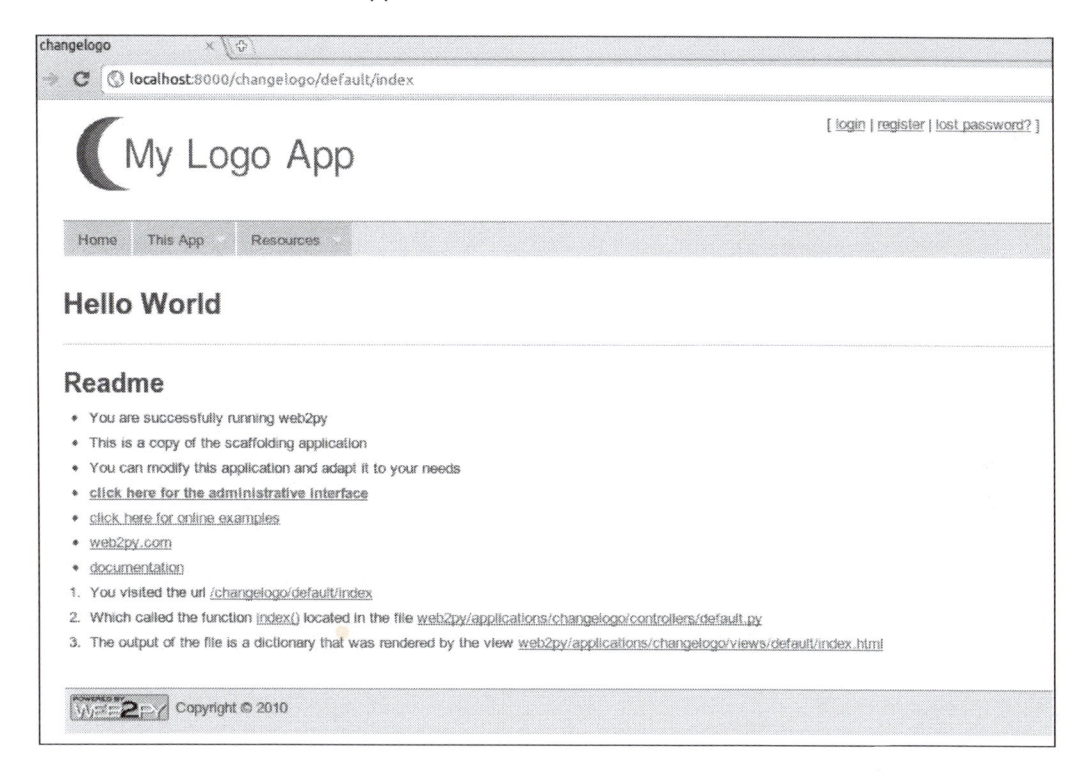

This is the result of customizing the logo.

## How to do it...

1. First, we need to create a new application. You can do that through the `admin` application. Choose **Create a new application**, and name it. The name of my application is `changelogo`. By default, the new application is a copy of the `welcome` scaffolding application. Now, if you run your application, you will see at the top of the application the title of your application followed by the word `App`, in my case `changelogoApp`.

2. Fire up your image editor, and make your logo, if you are going to start a new one. Choose a pixel dimension, according to the layout you are using. I chose a dimension of `300x90` pixels for my new logo. When you finish editing it, save it in PNG or JPEG format. Name it (for example, `mylogoapp.png`), and copy to the `static/images` directory inside your application.

## Building Your First Application

3. The next step is to edit `views/layout.html` of your application. You can use the admin or your own editor. Scroll down to the header section looking for the following:

   ```
   <div id="header"> <!-- header and login nav -->
     {{block header}} <!-- this is default header -->
     {{try:}}{{=auth.navbar(action=URL('default',
       'user'))}}{{except:pass}}
     <h1>
       <span id="appname">
         {{=request.application.capitalize()}}
       </span>
       App
     </h1>
     <div style="clear: both;"></div><!-- Clear the divs -->
     {{end}}
   </div><!-- header     -->
   ```

4. Let me explain the code a bit.

   The following code prints the user actions, such as login, register, and lost-password:

   ```
   {{try:}}{{=auth.navbar(action=URL('default',
     'user'))}}{{except:pass}}
   ```

   The following code prints the application name followed by `App`:

   ```
   <h1>
     <span id="appname">
       {{=request.application.capitalize()}}
     </span>
     App
   </h1>
   ```

   We need to change this to show the new logo. We will replace the `<h1>...</h1>` with the following:

   ```
   {{=IMG(_src=URL('static', 'images/mylogoapp.png'), _style="width:
     100%;")}}
   ```

   This will print the logo image instead of the title.

   The header section now looks as follows:

   ```
   <div id="header"> <!-- header and login nav -->
     {{block header}} <!-- this is default header -->
     {{try:}}{{=auth.navbar(action=URL('default',
       'user'))}}{{except:pass}}
     {{=IMG(_src=URL('static', 'images/mylogoapp.png'))}}
     <div style="clear: both;"></div><!-- Clear the divs -->
     {{end}}
   </div><!-- header     -->
   ```

5. Finally, it's a good practice that the logo links to the main page, so we will make a link to `default/index`:

   ```
   {{=A(IMG(_src=URL('static', 'images/mylogoapp.png')),
       _href=URL('default', 'index'))}}
   ```

## Creating menus and submenus

web2py handles menus in a transparent way, as follows:

- A list of menu items is stored, by convention, in `response.menu`
- The menu is embedded in a view with `{{=MENU(response.menu)}}`

You can have more than one menu in different places of the same view, or in different views. The value of `response.menu` is a list of menu items. Normally, each menu item is a list of tuple containing the following elements: **title**, **status**, **link**, and **submenu**.

Where title is the title of the menu, status is a Boolean that can be used to determine whether the menu link is the current page, link is the link to be redirected to when selecting the menu item, and submenu is a list of menu items.

Here is an example of code that one would normally put in the file `models/menu.py`:

```
response.menu = [
   ('Home', URL()==URL('default', 'home'), URL('default', 'home'),
      []),
   ('Search', URL()==URL('default', 'search'), URL('default',
      'search'), []),
]
```

The condition we used as the second argument checks whether the current page `URL()` is the page linked.

### How to do it...

1. Submenus can easily be built explicitly, as follows:

   ```
   response.menu = [
      ('Home', URL()==URL('default', 'home'), URL('default', 'home'),
         []),
      ('Search', False, None,
         [
            ('Local', URL()==URL('default', 'search'), URL('default',
               'search')),
            ('Google', False, 'http://google.com'),
            ('Bing', False, 'http://bing.com'),
         ]
      ),
   ]
   ```

*Building Your First Application*

2. The parent of a submenu may or may not have a link. In this example, we moved the link from `Search` to its `Local` submenu item. It is good practice to internationalize the menu titles.

   ```
   response.menu = [
       (T('Home'), URL()==URL('default', 'home'), URL('default',
           'home'), []),
   ]
   ```

3. It is also important to specify the controller name (`default` in the example) for each link; otherwise, menus break when there are multiple controllers (and that is almost always the case; think of `appadmin`).

## Customizing menus with icons

Sometimes, you want to customize a menu item more than the usual syntax seems to allow, for example, by adding icons to your menu items. This recipe shows you how.

### How to do it...

1. The first thing to realize is that the following:

   ```
   response.menu = [
       ('Home', False, URL('default', 'home'), []),
       ...]
   ```

   Is equivalent to the following:

   ```
   response.menu = [
       (A('Home', _href=URL('default', 'home')), False, None, []),
       ...]
   ```

   Here, `A` is the anchor (link) helper. You can use the latter syntax, and you can replace the `A` helper with any other combination of helpers. For example:

   ```
   response.menu = [
       (A(IMG(_src=URL('static', 'home.png'), _href=URL('default',
           'home'))), False, None, []),
       ...
   ]
   ```

   Or:

   ```
   response.menu = [
       (SPAN(IMG(_src=URL('static', 'home.png')),
           A('home', _href=URL('default', 'home'))), False, None, []),
       ...
   ]
   ```

2. You can create functions that build your menu items:

```
def item(name):
    return SPAN(IMG(_src=URL('static', name+'.png')), A(name,
    _href=URL('default', name)))

response.menu = [
    (item(home), False, None, []),
    ...
```

# Creating a navigation bar

web2py includes built-in support for menus, rendering using basic Python structures. In most cases, this is enough, but for more complex menus, it is difficult to maintain them using Python code exclusively. This recipe shows how to make a more dynamic menu, storing the menu entries in the database, and building the menu tree automatically.

## How to do it...

1. First, let's define a navigation bar table to store the menu entries. Create a file in `models` called `navbar.py`, and add the following definition:

```
db.define_table('navbar',
    Field("title", "string"),
    Field("url", "string", requires=IS_EMPTY_OR(IS_URL())),
    Field("c", label="Controller"),
    Field("f", label="Function"),
    Field("args", label="Arguments"),
    Field("sortable", "integer"),
    Field("parent_id", "reference navbar"),
    format="%(title)s",
)
```

The fields are:

- `title`: This is the text shown to the user
- `url`: This is the optional URL to link to
- `c`: This is the controller to build a link (see URL helper)
- `f`: This is the function to build a link (see URL helper)
- `args`: This is the string argument to build a link (see URL helper)
- `sortable`: This is a numeric value to sort the entries
- `parent_id`: This is the reference (`navbar.id`) of the higher-level menu ancestor (whose item is a submenu)

## Building Your First Application

2. At this point, you should be able to populate this table using the `appadmin` administrative interface, or you can do it programmatically by creating a `setup_navbar` function in a controller, such as the following:

```python
if not db(db.navbar).count():
    # create default index entry:
    home_id = db.navbar.insert(title="Home", c="default")

    # create a "Company" leaf with typical options:
    company_id = db.navbar.insert(title="Company", c="company")
    db.navbar.insert(title="About Us", f='about_us',
        parent_id=company_id)
    db.navbar.insert(title="Mision & Vision", f='mision_vision',
        parent_id=company_id)
    db.navbar.insert(title="Our Team", f='our_team',
        parent_id=company_id)

    products_id = db.navbar.insert(title="Products", c="products")
    # Add some "Computers models" to products entry:
    computers_id = db.navbar.insert(title="Computers",
        f='computers', parent_id=products_id)
    for model in 'basic', 'pro', 'gamer':
        db.navbar.insert(title="Model %s" % model, args=model,
            parent_id=computers_id)
```

This example menu looks like the following:

```
Home
Company
    About Us
    Mission & Vision
    Our Team
Products
    Computers
        Model basic
        Model pro
        Model gamer
```

Each top-level menu links to a specific controller, second-level submenus link to functions on that controller, and third-level entries supply arguments to those functions (note that you can use the same defaults for URL parameters `c` and `f`, which will be used hierarchically, using the inherited value).

3. Now, to show the menu, add to the previously created file `navbar.py` in `models` the following functions of `get_sub_menus`:

```python
def get_sub_menus(parent_id, default_c=None, default_f=None):
    children = db(db.navbar.parent_id==parent_id)
    for menu_entry in children.select(orderby=db.navbar.sortable):
        # get action or use defaults:
        c = menu_entry.c or default_c
        f = menu_entry.f or default_f
        # is this entry selected? (current page)
        sel = (request.controller==c and request.function==f and
          (request.args and request.args==menu_entry.args or True))
        # return each menu item
        yield (T(menu_entry.title),
        sel, menu_entry.url or URL(c, f, args=menu_entry.args),
        get_sub_menus(menu_entry.id, c, f)
    )
```

This function recursively builds the Python structure needed to render the menu in the HTML page, and does the following:

- Fetches the `navbar` menu entries for the solicited level
- Checks action destination or uses defaults (for `URL` helper)
- Calculates if this entry is the current selected one
- Makes and gives back the item to be used with the `MENU` helper

4. To tell web2py to build the menu, use the following in the same `navbar` model:

```python
response.menu = get_sub_menus(parent_id=None)
```

This will build the menu each time a page is viewed.

5. If you have a complex menu that doesn't change often, you can reuse it several times, using a cache to keep it in memory:

```python
response.menu = cache.ram('navbar_menu', lambda:
    get_sub_menus(parent_id=None), time_expire=60)
```

The menu is usually rendered in a page with the `MENU` helper that interprets this structure (see `views`, `layout.html`):

```
{{=MENU(response.menu, _class='sf-menu')}}
```

## Using cookies to set the language

By default, web2py determines the preferred user language from the **HTTP Accept-Language header**.

Here is an example of the normal workflow:

- A user sets the browser preferences to `en` (English), `en-us` (English spoken in US), and `fr-fr` (French spoken in France)
- When visiting our website, the browser sends the list of accepted languages in the HTTP header `Accept-Language`
- web2py parses the HTTP headers, validates the `Accept-Language` list, and loops over its languages
- web2py stops looping when a language appears in `T.current_languages`, or when a corresponding language file (for example `fr-fr.py`) is found in the language subfolder of the request application (`applications/app/languages`)

If web2py stops looping because a language, for example `en-en`, appears in `T.current_languages`, it means that the language does not need translation. If, instead, web2py stops looping because a language file if found, that language file will be used for translation. If neither of the two conditions are met for all of the languages in `Accept-Language`, there is no translation.

Normally, this selection is performed by web2py before calling the application code.

Within the application code (for example, in a model), you can override default settings. You can change the list of current languages:

```
T.set_current_languages('en', 'en-en')
```

You can also force web2py to pick a language from a different list than the one provided in the HTTP header:

```
T.force('it-it')
```

Often, you do not want the web application to rely on the browser to determine the language preference, but you want to ask the visitor explicitly through buttons, links, or a drop-down box. When this happens, the application needs to remember the selection as the user browses through the application pages.

If the application requires a login, this preference can be stored in the user profile, for example, in a custom field of the `auth_user` table.

But not all applications require a login, and often, the language preference is expressed before registration. A convenient and transparent way to set and remember the language that does not require a database, is to store the preference in a cookie. This can be achieved in the following way.

## How to do it...

1. Create a `model` file, for example `0_select_language.py`, that contains the following code:

   ```
   if 'all_lang' in request.cookies and not
     (request.cookies['all_lang'] is None):
     T.force(request.cookies['all_lang'].value)
   ```

2. Insert the following somewhere in `views/layout.html`:

   ```
   <span>
     <script>
       function set_lang(lang) {
         var date = new Date();
         cookieDate=date.setTime(date.getTime()+(100*24*60*60*1000));
         document.cookie='all_lang='+lang+';expires='+cookieDate+';
           path=/{{=request.application}}';
         window.location.reload();
       };
     </script>
     <select name="adminlanguage"
       onchange="set_lang(jQuery(this).val())">
       {{for language in T.get_possible_languages():}}
       <option {{=T.accepted_language==language and 'selected' or
         ''}}>
         {{=T(language)}}
       </option>
       {{pass}}
     </select>
   </span>
   ```

The previous code produces a select-language drop-down box, listing all languages for which web2py can find a translation file. When the value of the drop-down box changes, it forces a reload of the page. Upon reload, the code sets a cookie called `all_lang` that contains the selected language. When another page is loaded, if the code above finds the cookie, it uses the information in the cookie to choose and force the language selection.

## Building Your First Application

3.  The same can be achieved more explicitly using links instead of a drop-down box:

    ```
    <span>
      <script>
        function set_lang(lang) {
          var date = new Date();
          cookieDate=date.setTime(date.getTime()+(100*24*60*60*1000));
          document.cookie='all_lang='+lang+';expires='+cookieDate+';
            path=/{{=request.application}}';
          window.location.reload();
          return false;
        };
      </script>
        {{for language in T.get_possible_languages():}}
        {{if not T.accepted_language==language:}}
          <a href="#" onclick="set_lang('{{=language}}')">
            {{=T(language)}}
          </a>
          {{else:}}{{=T(language)}}{{pass}}{{pass}}
      </select>
    </span>
    ```

    This solution works even if the application does not use `sessions`.

Notice that the name of the language is itself translated, that is `{{=T(language)}}`, because it should be listed in the current selected language.

Also notice the following string is inside the cookie, which makes sure the preference applies only to the current application. This line is interpreted by the client-side, and may need to be changed, if custom URLs are enabled through routes:

```
path=/{{=request.application}}
```

In this case, a simple solution is to replace it with the following, and the preference will apply to all the applications under the same web2py installation, regardless of the URL:

```
path=/
```

## Designing modular applications

In this recipe, we will show you how to create a modular application using web2py components.

In particular, we will consider, as an example, an application that will allow you to create items, list items, and have the list updated dynamically when new items are created/updated.

## Getting ready

We will consider the scaffolding application with the following additional model `models/db_items.py`:

```
db.define_table('mytable',
  Field('name'),
  Field('quantity','integer'))
```

Notice that there is nothing specific about this table or its field structure, but we will use the `db.mytable` in the following example.

## How to do it...

1. In `controllers/default.py`, create a base action to load the components in the view and the controllers, to actually list and edit items:

   ```
   def index():
     "index will load the list and the create/edit forms as
     components"
     return dict()

   def list_items():
     """ shows a list of items that were created
     each items is clickable and can be edited """
    rows = db(db.mytable.id>0).select()
     return dict(rows=rows)

   def edit_item():
     """ return a creation form if no item is specified,
     return an edit form if the item is known """
     def display_changed(data):
       response.ajax = \
       'web2py_component("%s","show_itemlist")' % URL('showitems')
     form = crud.update(db.mytable,
                       request.args(0),onaccept=display_changed)
     return form
   ```

2. In the view `views/default/index.html`, just load the component to list the items and link the edit function (using a placeholder that will be used to insert the form to create or edit items):

   ```
   {{=LOAD('default', 'list_items', ajax = True, target =
   'showitems')}}
   {{=A('create',component=URL('edit_item'),target='placeholder')}}
   <div id="placeholder"></div>
   ```

*Building Your First Application*

3. In the view `views/default/list_items.html`, each item on the item list will load the specified URL into the `div` with the ID `placeholder`.

```
<ul>
  {{for item in rows:}}
    {{=LI(A('edit %s' % item.name,
        component=URL('edit_item',args=item.id),
        target='placeholder'))}}
  {{pass}}
</ul>
```

A view for the action `edit_item` is not necessary, since it returns a helper, not a dict.

## How it works...

The view index loads a list of items through Ajax into `div#showitems`. It also displays a link and a `div#placeholder`. Clicking on the link causes an Ajax request to `edit_item`, without `args` to return a `create form` that is rendered inside `div#placeholder`. The list also contains a link to `edit_item`, which also displays an `update form` into the `div#placeholder`. The form is not just displayed tharough Ajax. The component is always loaded by clicking an `A(...,component=URL(...),target="placeholder")`.

This ensures that the component is loaded through Ajax, and the forms in the component will be submitted through Ajax, thus refreshing the component only. Any form submission will return a `response.ajax`, which refreshes the other component `div@list_items`.

Notice that all the logic is generated at the server-side, translated under the hood in the JS code that is embedded in the page, and executed at the client-side. Clicking on a link causes a form to be displayed. Submitting a form causes a form to be processed, and, if accepted, the list of items is refreshed.

## Speeding up downloads

By default, the download function in the scaffolding controller sets the following HTTP response headers, preventing client-side caching:

```
Expires: Thu, 27 May 2010 05:06:44 GMT
Pragma: no-cache
Cache-Control: no-store, no-cache, must-revalidate, post-check=0,
pre-check=0
```

This may be good for some dynamic content, but, for example, a client browsing a site with several non static images, will see how each image loads every time the page is shown, slowing down navigation.

Caching download with the `@cache` decorator does not help, because caching would be done at server-side, while we want client-side caching.

Moreover, the download function also performs some authorization checks, which, in some cases, are not necessary, and therefore cause an unwanted slow-down.

A better approach consists of using a custom download function, which allows client-side caching, and skips authorization.

## How to do it...

We need to write a custom download function. We could edit the scaffolding one, but it's preferable to simply add another one that is call `fast_download`, so we will have the choice to use one or the other in different parts of our application.

1. First of all, we want our application to return the following HTTP header:

    ```
    Last-Modified: Tue, 04 May 2010 19:41:16 GMT
    ```

2. But omit these ones:

    ```
    Expires removed
    Pragma removed
    Cache-control removed
    ```

    This can be done by explicitly removing the unwanted headers before streaming back the file:

    ```
    def fast_download():
      filename = request.args(0)
      if not qualify_for_fast_download(filename)
        return download()
      else:
        del response.headers['Cache-Control']
        del response.headers['Pragma']
        del response.headers['Expires']
        filepath = os.path.join(request.folder, 'uploads', filename)
        response.headers['Last-Modified'] = \
          time.strftime("%a, %d %b %Y %H:%M:%S +0000",
          time.localtime(os.path.getmtime(filename)))
        return response.stream(open(filepath, 'rb'))
    ```

3. Notice that `response.stream` will handle `Range requests` and `If-Modified-Since` for you. Also notice that such an action could be used to download more files than it is intended to, so we insert a check, as follows:

    ```
    qualify_for_fast_download(filename)
    ```

    We leave this for you to implement.

## Building Your First Application

> It will check if this function can be used, or the normal download function should be used.

4. In your view, remember to make URLs using `fast_download` instead of download:

   ```
   URL('fast_download', args='filename')
   ```

### There's more...

If the filename you want to make sure `fast-download` is stored in an **upload** type field, for example, `mytable.myfield`, then you can configure your web server to serve it directly, and by-pass web2py completely. For example, if you are using Apache:

```
AliasMatch ^/([^/]+)/static/(mytable\.myfield.*) \
   /home/www-data/web2py/applications/$1/static/$2
<Directory /home/www-data/web2py/applications/*/static/>
  Options -Indexes
  Order Allow,Deny
  Allow from all
</Directory>
```

This works, because all filenames stored in `mytable.myfield` are renamed by web2py upon upload, and their names start with `mytable.myfield`.

# 3
# Database Abstraction Layer

In this chapter, we will cover the following recipes:

- Creating a new model
- Creating a model from a csv file
- Batch upload of your data
- Moving your data from one database to another
- Creating a model from existing MySQL and PostgreSQL databases
- Efficiently searching by tag
- Accessing your database from multiple applications
- Hierarchical category tree
- Creating records on demand
- OR, LIKE, BELONGS, and more on Google App Engine
- Replacing slow virtual fields with DB views

## Introduction

The **Database Abstraction Layer** (**DAL**) is probably the major strength of web2py. The DAL exposes a simple **Applications Programming Interface** (**API**) to the underlying SQL syntax, and this may hide its true power. In the recipes of this chapter, we provide examples of non-trivial applications of the DAL, such as building queries to search by tags efficiently and building a hierarchical category tree.

Database Abstraction Layer

# Creating a new model

As shown in the recipes in the previous chapter, most applications require a database, and building the database model is the first step in the design of the application.

## Getting ready

Here we assume that you have a newly created application, and you will be putting the models in a file called `models/db_custom.py`.

## How to do it...

1. First of all, you need a database connection. This is created by the DAL object.
   For example:

   ```
   db = DAL('sqlite://storage.sqlite')
   ```

   Notice that this line is already in the file `models/db.py`, and therefore you may not need it, unless you deleted it or need to connect to a different database. By default, web2py connects to an `sqlite` database stored in file `storage.sqlite`. This file is located in the application's `databases` folder. If the file is not there, it is created by web2py when the application is first executed.

   SQLite is fast, and stores all data in one single file. This means that your data can be easily transferred from one application to another. In fact, the `sqlite` database(s) are packaged by web2py together with the applications. It provides full SQL support, including translations, joins, and aggregates. Moreover SQLite comes standard with Python 2.5 and later, and therefore, it is already available to your web2py installation.

   There are two disadvantages of SQLite. One is that it does not enforce column types, and there is no `ALTER TABLE` except for adding and dropping columns. The other disadvantage is that the entire database is locked by any transaction that requires write access. Therefore, the database cannot be accessed concurrently except for reading.

   These features make it a good option for development purposes and low-traffic websites, but not a viable solution for high-traffic sites.

   In the following recipe, we will show you how to connect to a different type of database.

2. Once we have a db object, we can use the `define_table` method to define new tables. For example:

   ```
   db.define_table('invoice',Field('name'))
   ```

The syntax is always the same. The first argument is the **table name**, and it is followed by a list of `Field`(s). The field constructor takes the following arguments:

- **The field name**
- **The field type**: This can take values having any of the following datatypes - `string` (default), `text`, `boolean`, `integer`, `double`, `password`, `date`, `time`, `datetime`, `upload`, `blob`, `reference other_table`, `list:string`, `list:integer`, and `list:reference other_table`. Internally, `upload`, `password`, and `list` types are equivalent to `string`, but at the web2py level, they are handled differently.
- `length=512`: This is the maximum length for string-based fields. It is ignored for non-text based fields.
- `default=None`: This is the default value when a new record is inserted. The value of this attribute can be a function that is called when a value is needed (for example, on record insert, if no value is specified).
- `update=None`: This works the same as default, but the value is used only on update, not on insert.
- `ondelete='CASCADE'`: This maps onto the corresponding SQL `ON DELETE` attribute.
- `notnull=False`: This specifies whether the field value can be `NULL` or not (enforced at database level).
- `unique=False`: This specifies whether the field value must be unique or not (enforced at database level).
- `requires=[]`: This is a list of web2py validators (enforced at the level of web2py forms). Most field types have default validators.
- `required=False`: This is not to be confused with requires, and it tells web2py that a value for this field must be specified during insert and update. For a `required` field, default and update values are ignored. Unless used together with `notnull=True`, the `None` value is an acceptable value, even if the field is required.
- `readable=True`: This specifies whether the field is readable in forms or not.
- `writable=True`: This specifies whether the field is writable in forms or not.
- `represent=(lambda value: value)`: This is a function that is used to display the value of the field in forms and tables.
- `widget=SQLHTML.widgets.string.widget`: This is a function that will build the input widget in forms.
- `label="Field Name"`: This is the label to be used for this field in forms.
- `comment="..."`: This is a comment to be added to this field in forms.

The `Field` constructor has other attributes that are specific to `upload` type fields. See the web2py book for further information.

3. The `define_table` method also takes three named arguments:

   ```
   db.define_table('....',
     migrate=True,
     fake_migrate=False,
     format='%(id)s')
   ```

   - `migrate=True`: This instructs web2py to create the table if it does not exist, or alter it if it does not match the model definition. This process is accompanied by the creation of metadata files. The metadata files have the form `databases/<hash>_<name>.table`, and will be used to keep track of changes in the model, and perform automatic migrations. Set `migrate=False` to disable automatic migrations.
   - `fake_migrate=False`: Sometimes the above metadata gets corrupt (or accidentally deleted), and needs to be re-created. If the model matches the database table content, then set `fake_migrate=True`, and web2py will rebuild the metadata.
   - `format='%(id)s'`: This is a format string that determines how records of this table should be represented when referenced by another table in forms (for example in select dropboxes). The format can be a function that takes a row object that returns a string.

## There's more...

In all databases, but SQLite and Google App Engine datastore, if you change a table definition, an `ALTER TABLE` is issued to make sure the database matches the model. In SQLite, the `ALTER TABLE` is only performed when a column is added or deleted, not when a field type changes (because SQLite does not enforce it). In Google App Engine datastore, there is no concept of `ALTER TABLE`, and columns can be added but not deleted; web2py will ignore columns not listed in the model.

Completely removing a `define_table` from the model does not result in a `DROP TABLE`. The table simply becomes inaccessible to web2py until the corresponding `define_table` is put back. This prevents accidental deletion of data. You can drop tables in web2py using the command `db.<name>.drop()`.

# Creating a model from a CSV file

Consider the scenario in which you have a CSV file and you do not know much about it. Yet you want to create a web application to access the data in the CSV file.

## Getting ready

I will assume you have the csv file in a folder

`/tmp/mydata.csv`

You will also need a program called `csvstudio`, which you can download from `http://csvstudio.googlecode.com/hg/csvstudio.py`.

## How to do it...

1. This first step consists of looking at the csv file:

   **python csvstudio.py -a < /tmp/mydata.csv**

   If the file is not corrupt, and it is in a standard csv format, then `csvstudio` will generate a report listing the CSV columns, data types, and data ranges.

   If the file is in a non-standard CSV format, or is, for example, in XLS, try importing it in Excel, and save it again in CSV.

   You may also want to try using **Google Refine** to clean up the CSV file.

2. Once you know that `csvstudio` can correctly read the file, run the following command:

   **python csvstudio.py -w mytable -i /tmp/mydata.csv > db1.py**

   `csvstudio` creates a file called `db1.py` that contains a web2py model that is compatible with the data. `mytable`, here, is the name you choose to give to the table.

3. Move this file into your application's `models` folder.

4. Now you need to clean up the data, so that you can import it in web2py.

   **python csvstudio.py -f csv -i /tmp/mydata.csv -o /tmp/mydata2.csv**

   The file, `mydata2.csv`, now contains the same data as the original file, but the column names have been cleaned up to be compatible with the generated model. The field values have been stripped of any leading and trailing spaces.

5. At this point, all you have to do is run your application and call `appadmin`.

   `http://.../app/appadmin`

6. You should see the model you generated. Click on the model name, and you will see an upload link at the bottom. Upload the `mydata2.csv` file to populate your table.

## There's more...

If you prefer to upload the csv file from a shell instead of using the `appadmin` interface, you can do so.

From insider the main web2py folder, run the following command:

```
python web2py.py -S app -M -N
```

You will get a web2py shell (`-S` app opens the shell in the application context, `-M` loads the models, and `-N` prevents cron jobs from running).

From inside the shell do the following:

```
>>> f = open('/tmp/mydata2.csv','rb')
>>> db.mytable.import_from_csv_file(f)
>>> db.commit()
```

Et voila, the data is in the database. When you use the shell do not forget to `db.commit()`.

If for any reason this does not work (perhaps because the CSV file is non-standard, and there is no way to normalize it), try following our next recipe.

# Batch upload of your data

Here, we will assume you have data in a flat file of known `structure`. You want to create a database model and import the data in the database.

## Getting ready

For same of the argument, we will assume the file is in `/tmp/data.txt`, and has the following structure:

```
Clayton Troncoso|234523
Malinda Gustavson|524334
Penelope Sharpless|151555
Serena Ruggerio|234565
Lenore Marbury|234656
Amie Orduna|256456
Margery Koeppel|643124
Loraine Merkley|234555
Avis Bosserman|234523
...
Elinor Erion|212554
```

Each row is a record ending in \n. The fields are separated by –. The first column contains `<first name> <last name>`. The second column contains an annual salary value.

As usual, we will assume you have a new application called `app`.

## How to do it...

1. The first thing you do is create a model in your `app` called `models/db1.py` containing the following data:

   ```
   db.define_table('employees',
      Field('first_name'),
      Field('last_name'),
      Field('salary','double'))
   ```

2. Then, you would write a script, for example:

   **applications/app/private/importer.py**

   This script can read the data, parse it, and put it into the `db`, as follows:

   ```
   for line in open('/tmp/data.txt','r'):
      fullname,salary = line.strip().split('|')
      first_name,last_name = fullname.split(' ')
      db.employees.insert(first_name=first_name,
         last_name=last_name,
         salary=float(salary))
   db.commit()
   ```

3. Finally, from the web2py folder run the following script:

   **python web2py.py -S app -M -N -R applications/app/private/importer.py**

Notice that the importer is a Python script, but not a module (that is why we put it in the `private` folder and not the `modules` folder. It is executed in our application context, as if it were a controller. In fact, you can copy the code into a controller, and run it from a browser as well.

## There's more...

The previous script works fine if the data is clean. You may need to validate each record before inserting it. This is again a two-step procedure. First you need to add validators to your model, for example:

```
db.define_table('employees',
   Field('first_name', requires=IS_NOT_EMPTY()),
   Field('last_name', requires=SI_NOT_EMPTY()),
   Field('salary','double', requires=IS_FLOAT_IN_RANGE(0,10**7)))
```

Then you need to call validators on import and check for errors:

```
for line in open('/tmp/data.txt','r'):
  fullname,salary = line.strip().split('|')
  first_name,last_name = fullname.split(' ')
  r = db.employee.validate_and_insert(
    first_name=first_name,
    last_name=last_name,
    salary=float(salary))
  if r.errors: print line, r.errors
  db.commit()
```

Records that cause errors will not be inserted, and you can deal with them manually.

## Moving your data from one database to another

So, at this point, you have built your application, and you have data in your SQLite database. But let's say you need to move to a production MySQL or PostgreSQL environment.

### Getting ready

Here we assume you have an application called `app`, data in the `sqlite://storage.sqlite` database, and you want to move your data to a different database:

```
mysql://username:password@hostname:port/dbname
```

### How to do it...

1. Edit your model `db.py`, and replace the following:

   ```
   db=DAL('sqlite://storage.sqlite')
   ```

   With the following:

   ```
   production=False
   URI = 'mysql://username:password@hostname:port/dbname'
   if production:
      db=DAL(URI, pool_size=20)
   else:
      db=DAL('sqlite://storage.sqlite')
   ```

2. Create a file called `applications/app/private/mover.py` that contains the following data:

   ```python
   def main():
     other_db = DAL(URI)
     print 'creating tables...'
     for table in db:
       other_db.define_table(table._tablename,*[field for field in
         table])
     print 'exporting data...'
     db.export_to_csv_file(open('tmp.sql','wb'))
     print 'importing data...'
     other_db.import_from_csv_file(open('tmp.sql','rb'))
     other_db.commit()
     print 'done!'

   if __name__() == "__main__":
     main()
   ```

3. Run this file with the following command (run it only once or you end up with duplicate records):

   `python web2py.py -S app -M -N -R applications/app/private/mover.py`

4. Change the model `db.py`, and change the following:

   `production=False`

   To the following:

   `production=True`

## There's more...

Actually, web2py comes with the following script:

`script/cpdb.py`

This script performs tasks and variations using command-line options. Read the file for more information.

# Creating a model from existing MySQL and PostgreSQL databases

It is often necessary to access an existing database from a web2py application. This is possible under some conditions.

Database Abstraction Layer

## Getting ready

In order to connect to an existing database, it must be one that's supported. At the time of writing, this includes **MySQL, PostgreSQL, MSSQL, DB2, Oracle, Informix, FireBase**, and **Sybase**. You must know the database type (for example `mysql` or `postgres`), the database name (for example, `mydb`), and the hostname and port where the database server is running (for example `127.0.0.1:3306` for `mysql` or `127.0.0.1:5432` for `postgres`). You must have a valid username and password to access the database. In summary, you must know the following URI strings:

- `mysql://username:password@127.0.0.1:3306/mydb`
- `postgres://username:password@127.0.0.1:5432/mydb`

Assuming you can connect to this database, you will only be able to access those tables that meet the following conditions:

- Each table to be accessed must have a unique auto-increment integer primary key (whether called `id` or not). For PostgreSQL, you can also have compound primary keys (comprised of several fields), and not necessarily of `SERIAL` type (see **keyed tables** on web2py book).
- Records must be referenced by their primary key.
- The web2py model must include a `define_table` statement for each table to be accessed, listing all fields and their types.

In the following, we will also assume your system supports the `mysql` command to access the database locally (to extract MySQL models), or your system has installed the `psycopg2` python module (to extract PostgreSQL models, see installation recipes).

## How to do it...

1. First you need to query the database and come up with a possible model compatible with the content of the database. This can be done by running the following scripts that comes with web2py:

    - To build web2py models from a MySQL database, use:

    ```
    python scripts/extract_mysql_models.py
      username:password@databasename > db1.py
    ```

    - To build web2py models from a PostgreSQL database, use:

    ```
    python scripts/extract_pgsql_models.py databasename localhost 5432
      username password > db1.py
    ```

    The scripts are not perfect, but they will generate a `db1.py` file that describes the database tables.

2. Edit this model to remove tables that you do not need to access. Improve the field types (for example, a string field may be a password), and add validators.
3. Then move this file into the `models/` folder of your application.
4. Finally, edit the original `db.py` model, and replace the URI string with the one for this database.

    ❑ For MySQL, write:

```
db = DAL('mysql://username:password@127.0.0.1:8000/databasename',
  migrate_enabled=False, pool_size=20)
```

    ❑ For PostgreSQL, write:

```
db = DAL(
  "postgres://username:password@localhost:5432/databasename",
  migrate_enabled=False, pool_size=10)
migrate = False  # you can control migration per define_table
```

We disable all migrations, because the table already exists and web2py should not attempt to create or alter it.

Unfortunately, accessing the existing database is one of the most tricky tasks in web2py, because the database was not created by web2py, and web2py needs to make some guesses. The only way to fix these problems is by manually editing the model file, and using independent knowledge of the database content.

## There's more...

Actually, the `extract_pgsql_models.py` has the following additional features:

- It uses ANSI Standard `INFORMATION_SCHEMA` (this might work with other RDBMS)
- It detects legacy keyed tables (not having an `id` as its primary key)
- It connects directly to running databases, so there's no need to do an SQL dump
- It handles `notnull`, `unique`, and referential constraints
- It detects the most common datatypes and default values
- It supports PostgreSQL columns comments (that is, for documentation)

If you have to use it against other RDBMS that support ANSI `INFORMATION_SCHEMA` (for example, MSSQL Server), import and use the proper Python connector, and remove the `postgreSQL` specific queries (`pg_ tables` for comments)

## Database Abstraction Layer

> You cannot mix references between normal auto-increment primary keys tables (type='id') and keyed tables (primarykey=['field1', 'field2']). If you use both in your database, you have to manually define auto-increment primary keys as keyed tables at the web2py model (removing id type, and adding the primary key parameter to define_table).

# Efficiently searching by tag

Whether you are building a social network, a content management system, or an ERP system, you eventually need the ability to tag records. This recipe shows you a way to efficiently search for records by tag.

## Getting ready

Here we assume the following two models:

1. A model for containing the data:
   ```
   db.define_table('data', Field('value'))
   ```

2. A model for storing the tags:
   ```
   db.define_table('tag', Field('record_id', db.data), Field('name'))
   ```

Here, name is the tag name.

## How to do it...

1. We want to search all records having at least one of the tags in the list:
   ```
   tags = [...]
   ```
   
   For this purpose, we create a search function:
   ```
   def search_or(data=db.data, tag=db.tag, tags=[]):
     rows = db(data.id==tag.record_id)\
       (tag.name.belongs(tags)).select(
         data.ALL,
         orderby=data.id,
         groupby=data.id,
         distinct=True)
     return rows
   ```

2. Similarly, if you want to search for records that have all the tags (as opposed to one of those in the list):

```
def search_and(data=db.data,tag=db.tag,tags=[]):
  n = len(tags):
  rows = db(data.id==tag.record_id)\
    (tag.name.belongs(tags)).select(
    data.ALL,
    orderby=data.id,
    groupby=data.id,
    having=data.id.count()==n)
  return rows
```

Notice that these two functions work for any table that is passed as first argument.

In both functions, the query involves two tables.

```
data.id==tag.record_id
```

web2py interprets this as join.

## There's more...

This system works great if users are free to choose the tag names. Sometimes, you want to restrict tags to a well defined set. In that case, the model needs to be updated:

```
db.define_table('data', Field('value'))
db.define_table('tag', Field('name', unique=True))
db.define_table('link', Field('record_id',db.data), Field('tag_id',db.tag))
```

Here, the link table implements a many-to-many relation between data records and tag items.

In this case, we need to modify our search functions, so first we convert a list of tag names (tags) into a list of tag IDs, and then perform the previous query. This can be done using a subquery:

```
def search_or(data=db.data, tag=db.tag,link=db.link,tags=[]):
  subquery = db(db.tag.name.belongs(tags)).select(db.tag.id)
  rows = db(data.id==link.record_id)\
    (link.tag_id.belongs(subquery)).select(
    data.ALL,
    orderby=data.id,
    groupby=data.id,
    distinct=True)
  return rows
```

```
def search_and(data=db.data, tag=db.tag, link=db.link, tags=[]):
  n = len(tags)
  subquery = db(db.tag.name.belongs(tags)).select(db.tag.id)
  rows = db(data.id==link.record_id)\
    (link.tag_id.belongs(subquery)).select(
      data.ALL,
      orderby=data.id,
      groupby=data.id,
      having=data.id.count()==n)
  return rows
```

The technique we implemented here is known as the **Toxi** method, and is described in a more general and abstract way at the following link:

http://www.pui.ch/phred/archives/2005/04/tags-database-schemas.html.

# Accessing your database from multiple applications

One way to build distributed applications, is by having the same database available to multiple applications. Unfortunately, this is more than a matter of connecting to the database. In fact, the different applications need to be aware of the table content and other metadata, which is stored in the model definition.

There are three ways to do this, and they are not equivalent. It depends on whether the applications share a file system, and the degree of autonomy you want to give to the two applications.

## Getting ready

We will assume you have two web2py applications, one called `app1`, and one called `app2`, where `app1` connects to a database through the following:

```
db = DAL(URI)
```

Here, URI is some connection string. It does not matter whether this is SQLite or a client/server database. We will also assume that the model used by `app1` is stored in `models/db1.py`, although the name is unimportant here.

Now we want `app2` to connect to the same database.

## How to do it...

It is also a common scenario that you want the two applications to be autonomous, although able to share data. **Autonomous** means that you want to be able to distribute each application without the other one.

If this is the case, each application needs its own copy of the model and its own database metadata. The only way to achieve this is by duplication of code.

You must follow these steps:

1. Edit the URI string of `app2` so that it looks the same as `app1`, but disable migrations:
   ```
   db = DAL(URI, migrate_enabled=False)
   ```
2. Copy the model file `models/d1.py` from `app1` into `app2`.

Notice that only `app1` will be able to perform migrations (if both were able to do it, the situation would get very confused). If you change the model in `app1`, you will have to copy the model file again.

Although this solution breaks the **Don't Repeat Yourself** (**DRY**) pattern, it guarantees complete autonomy to each application, and they can access the same database even if running on separate servers.

If the two applications are running on the same server, instead of copying the model file, you can just make a symbolic link:

```
ln applications/app1/models/db1.py applications/app2/models/db1.py
```

Now you have only one model file.

## There's more...

Sometimes you need a script (not a web application) to be able to access a web2py model. This can be done by accessing the metadata only, without executing the actual model file.

Here is a python script (not a web2py model) that can do it:

```
# file myscript.py
from gluon.dal import DAL
db = DAL(URI, folder='/path/to/web2py/applications/app1', auto_import=True)
print db.tables
# add your code here
```

Notice the `auto_import=True`. It tells the DAL to look in the specified folder for the meta-data associated to the URI connection, and rebuilds the models on the fly, in memory. Models defined in this way have the right names and field types, but they will not have the correct values of other attributes, such as readable, writable, default, validators, and so on. This is because those attributes cannot be serialized in the metadata, and are probably not needed in this scenario.

# Hierarchical category tree

Sooner or later, any application needs a way to categorize data, and categories must be stored in a tree, because each category has a parent and possibly subcategories. A category without a subcategory is a leaf of the tree. If there are categories without a parent, we create a fictitious root tree node, and append all of them as subcategories of the root.

The main issue is how to store categories with parent-child relations in a database table, and efficiently add nodes and queries for ancestors and descendants of a node.

This can be done using a modified pre-order tree traversal algorithm, described as follows.

## How to do it...

The key trick consists of storing each node in its own record with two integer attributes, left and right, so that all its ancestors have a left attribute lower than or equal to the left attribute of the current node, and a right attribute larger than the one of the current node. Similarly, all descendants will have a left larger or equal than the current left and a right smaller than the current right. In formula:

A is parent of B if `A.ileft<=B.ileft`, and `A.iright>B.iright`.

Notice that `A.iright - A.ileft` is always the number of descendants.

The following is a possible implementation:

```
from gluon.dal import Table

class TreeProxy(object):
    skeleton = Table(None,'tree',
                     Field('ileft','integer'),
                     Field('iright','integer'))
    def __init__(self,table):
        self.table=table
    def ancestors(self,node):
        db = self.table._db
        return
            db(self.table.ileft<=node.ileft)(self.table.iright>node.iright)
```

```
      def descendants(self,node):
         db = self.table._db
   return
      db(self.table.ileft>=node.ileft)(self.table.iright<node.iright)
      def add_leaf(self,parent_id=None,**fields):
         if not parent_id:
            nrecords = self.table._db(self.table).count()
            fields.update(dict(ileft=nrecords,iright=nrecords))
         else:
            node = self.table(parent_id)
            fields.update(dict(ileft=node.iright,iright=node.iright))
            node.update_record(iright=node.iright+1)
            ancestors = self.ancestors(node).select()
         for ancestor in ancestors:
            ancestor.update_record(iright=ancestor.iright+1)
            ancestors = self.ancestors(node).select()
         for ancestor in ancestors:
            ancestor.update_record(iright=ancestor.iright+1)
   return self.table.insert(**fields)

   def del_node(self,node):
      delta = node.iright-node.ileft
      deleted = self.descendants(node).delete()
      db = self.table._db
      db(self.table.iright>node.iright).
         update(iright=self.table.iright-delta)
      del self.table[node.id]
   return deleted + 1
```

This allows us to perform the following operations:

- Define your own tree table (`mytree`) and proxy object (`treeproxy`):

    ```
    treeproxy =
       TreeProxy(db.define_table('mytree',Field('name'),Tree.skeleton))
    ```

- Insert a new node:

    ```
    id = treeproxy.add_leaf(name="root")
    ```

- Append some nodes:

    ```
    treeproxy.add_leaf(parent_id=id,name="child1")
    treeproxy.add_leaf(parent_id=id,name="child2")
    ```

## Database Abstraction Layer

- Search ancestors and descendants:

  ```
  for node in treeproxy.ancestors(db.tree(id)).select():
      print node.name
  for node in treeproxy.descendants(db.tree(id)).select():
      print node.name
  ```

- Delete a node and all its descendants:

  ```
  treeproxy.del_node(db.tree(id))
  ```

# Creating records on demand

It is common that we need to get a record or update a record, based on a condition, yet the record may not exist. If the record does not exist, we want to create it. In this recipe, we will show two utility functions that can serve this purpose:

- get_or_create
- update_or_create

For this to work, we need to pass enough `field:value` pairs to create the missing record.

## How to do it...

1. Here is the code for `get_or_create`:

   ```
   def get_or_create(table, **fields):
       """
       Returns record from table with passed field values.
       Creates record if it does not exist.
       'table' is a DAL table reference, such as 'db.invoice'
       fields are field=value pairs
       """
       return table(**fields) or table.insert(**fields)
   ```

   Notice how `table(**fields)` selects a record from the table, matching the requested fields, and returns `None` if the record does not exist. In this latter case, the record is inserted. Then, `table.insert(...)` returns a reference to the inserted record, which, for practical purposes, gets the record just inserted.

2. Here is an example of usage:

   ```
   db.define_table('person', Field('name'))
   john = get_or_create(db.person, name="John")
   ```

3. The code for `update_or_create` is very similar, but we need two sets of variables— variables for the **search** (before update) and variables to be **updated**:

   ```
   def update_or_create(table, fields, updatefields):
     """
     Modifies record that matches 'fields' with 'updatefields'.
     If record does not exist then create it.

     'table' is a DAL table reference, such as 'db.person'
     'fields' and 'updatefields' are dictionaries
     """
     row = table(**fields)
     if row:
       row.update_record(**updatefields)
     else:
       fields.update(updatefields)
       row = table.insert(**fields)
     return row
   ```

4. And here is an example of usage:

   ```
   tim = update_or_create(db.person, dict(name="tim"),
   dict(name="Tim"))
   ```

# OR, LIKE, BELONGS, and more on Google App Engine

A major limitation of the **Google App Engine** (**GAE**) is the inability to perform queries that use the OR, BELONGS(IN), and LIKE operators.

The web2py DAL provides a system for abstracting database queries, and it works on **Relational Databases** (**RDBS**) as well as on GAE but, still, it is crippled by the limitations mentioned. Here we show some workarounds.

We have created an additional API that allows merging, filtering, and sorting records after they are extracted from the GAE storage, at the web2py level. They can be used to mimic the missing features, and will make your GAE code portable to RDBS too.

Current supported RDBS are SQLite, MySQL, PostgreSQL, MSSQL, DB2, Informix, Oracle, FireBird, and Ingres.

GAE is the only currently supported NoDB. Other adapters are under development.

## Database Abstraction Layer

### Getting ready

In the following recipe, we plan to develop an application to run on GAE, and we connect to the database using the following logic:

```
if request.env.web2py_runtime_gae:
    db = DAL('google:datastore')
else:
    db = DAL('sqlite://storage.sqlite')
```

We assume the following models, as an example:

```
product = db.define_table('product',
    Field('name'),
    Field('price','double'))

buyer = db.define_table('buyer',
    Field('name'))

purchase = db.define_table('purchase',
    Field('product',db.product),
    Field('buyer',db.buyer),
    Field('quantity','integer'),
    Field('order_date','date',default=request.now))
```

### How to do it...

After setting up the GAE model that we described previously, let's see how to do insert and update records, do joins and other manipulations in the following sections.

#### Record insert

To test the rest of the code, you may want to insert some records in the tables. You can do this with `appadmin` or programmatically. The following code will work fine on GAE with the caveats that the IDs returned by the `insert` method are not sequential on GAE:

```
icecream = db.product.insert(name='Ice Cream',price=1.50)
kenny = db.buyer.insert(name='Kenny')
cartman = db.buyer.insert(name='Cartman')
db.purchase.insert(product=icecream,buyer=kenny,quantity=1,
    order_date=datetime.datetime(2009,10,10))
db.purchase.insert(product=icecream,buyer=cartman,quantity=4,
    order_date=datetime.datetime(2009,10,11))
```

## Record update

The `update` on GAE works as you would normally expect. Both syntaxes are supported:

```
icecream.update_record(price=1.99)
```

And also:

```
icecream.price=1.99
icecream.update_record()
```

## Joins

On a relational database, you can do the following:

```
rows = db(purchase.product==product.id)
   (purchase.buyer==buyer.id).select()
for row in rows:
  print row.product.name, row.product.price,
  row.buyer.name, row.purchase.quantity
```

This produces the following:

```
Ice Cream 1.99 Kenny 1
Ice Cream 1.99 Cartman 4
```

This does not work on GAE. You have to perform the query without the join, using recursive `selects`.

```
rows = db(purchase.id>0).select()
for row in rows:
  print row.product.name, row.product.price, row.buyer.name,
  row.quantity
```

Here, `row.product.name` performs recursive `selects`, and gets you the name of the product referenced by `row.product`.

## Logical OR

On an RDBS, you can implement OR in queries using the — operator:

```
rows = db((purchase.buyer==kenny)|(purchase.buyer==cartman)).select()
```

This does not work on GAE, because OR is not supported (at the time of writing). If the queries involve the same field, you can use the IN operator:

```
rows = db(purchase.buyer.contains((kenny,cartman))).select()
```

## Database Abstraction Layer

This is a portable and efficient solution. In the most general case, you may need to perform the OR operation at the web2py level as opposed to at the database level.

```
rows_kenny = db(purchase.buyer==kenny).select()
rows_cartman = db(purchase.buyer==cartman).select()
rows = rows_kenny|rows_cartman
```

In this latter case, the − is not between queries, but between rows object, and it is performed after the records are fetched. This presents some problems because the original order is lost, and because of the increased memory and resource consumption penalty.

### OR with orderby

On a relational database you can do the following:

```
rows = db((purchase.buyer==kenny)|(purchase.buyer==cartman))\
   .select(orderby=purchase.quantity)
```

But, again on GAE, you have to perform the OR at web2py level. Therefore you also have to sort at the web2py level:

```
rows_kenny = db(purchase.buyer==kenny).select()
rows_cartman = db(purchase.buyer==cartman).select()
rows = (rows_kenny|rows_cartman).sort(lambda row:row.quantity)
```

The `sort` method of the `rows` objects take a function of the row, and must return an expression to sort about. They can also be used with RDBS to implement sorting, when the expression is too complex to implement at the database level.

### OR with more complex orderby

Consider the following query that involves a OR, a JOIN, and an ordering, and would only work on RDBS:

```
rows = db((purchase.buyer==kenny)|(purchase.buyer==cartman))\
   (purchase.buyer==buyer.id).select(orderby=buyer.name)
```

You can rewrite it for GAE using the `sort` method, and a recursive `select` in the `sort` argument:

```
rows = (rows_kenny|rows_cartman).sort( \
   lambda row:row.buyer.name)
```

This works, but it may be inefficient. You may want to cache the mapping of `row.buyer` into `buyer_names`:

```
buyer_names = cache.ram('buyer_names',
   lambda:dict(*[(b.id,b.name) for b in db(db.buyer).select()]),
   3600)
rows = (rows_kenny|rows_cartman).sort(
   lambda row: buyer_names.get(row.buyer,row.buyer.name))
```

Here, `buyer_names` is a mapping between `ids` and `names`, and it is cached every hour (3600 seconds). `sort` tries to pick the names from `buyer_names` if possible, or else it performs the recursive select.

## LIKE

On a relational database, you can, for example, search all records with a name starting with the letter C followed by anything (%):

```
rows = db(buyer.name.like('C%')).select()
print rows
```

But GAE neither supports full text search, nor anything that resembles the SQL LIKE operator. Once more, we have to select all records and perform the filtering at the web2py level. We can use the `find` method of the `rows` object:

```
rows = db(buyer.id>0).select().find(lambda
    row:row.name.startswith('C'))
```

Of course, this is expensive, and not recommended for large tables (more than a few hundred records). If this kind of search is critical for your application, perhaps you should not be using GAE.

### date and datetime manipulations

The same problem occurs for queries involving other expressions, such as date and datetime manipulations. Consider the following query that works on relational databases but not on GAE:

```
rows = db(purchase.order_date.day==11).select()
```

On GAE you would have to rewrite it as follows:

```
rows = db(purchase.id>0).select().find(lambda
    row:row.order_date.day==11)
```

# Replacing slow virtual fields with DB views

Consider the following table:

```
db.define_table('purchase',
   Field('product'),
   Field('price', 'double'),
   Field('quantity','integer'))
```

You need to add a field called `total_price` that is computed when records are retrieved, and is defined as the product of price by quantity for each record.

## Database Abstraction Layer

The normal way to do it is by using **virtual fields**:

```
class MyVirtualFields(object):
  def total_price(self):
    return self.purchase.price * self.purchase.quantity
db.purchase.virtualfields.append(MyVirtualFields())
```

Then you can do the following:

```
for row in db(db.purchase).select():
  print row.name, row.total_price
```

This is fine, but computing virtual fields at the web2py level can be slow. Moreover, you would not be used to involving the virtual fields in queries.

Here we propose an alternate solution that involves creating a database view for the table, which includes the column with computed fields, and provides a way for web2py to access it.

### How to do it...

Given the table, do the following:

```
if not db.executesql("select * from information_schema.tables where table_name='purchase_plus' limit 1;"):
  db.executesql("create view purchase_plus as select purchase.*,
    purchase.price * purchase.quantity as total_price from purchase")
db.define_table('purchase_plus', db.purchase, Field('total_price',
  'double'),
  migrate=False)
```

Now, you can use `db.purchase_plus` anywhere you would use `db.numbers_plus`, except for inserts, with a performance increase when compared to the `VirtualFields` solution.

### How it works...

The following line checks whether the view has been created already:

```
if not db.executesql("select ...")
```

If not, it instructs the database to create it:

```
db.executesql("create view ...")
```

Finally, it defines a new web2py model, which maps into the table:

```
db.define_table('purchase_plus',...)
```

This model includes all fields from the db.purchase table, the new field total_price, and sets migrate=False, so that web2py does not attempt to create the table (it should not because this is not a new table, it's a view, and has been already created).

## There's more...

Notice that not all supported databases support views, and not all of those that do have an information_schema.tables. Therefore, this recipe is not guaranteed to work on all supported databases, and will make your application not portable.

# 4
# Advanced Forms

In this chapter, we will cover the following recipes:

- Adding a cancel button to forms
- Adding confirmation on form submit
- Searching data dynamically
- Embedding multiple forms in one page
- Detecting and blocking concurrent updates
- Creating a form wizard
- De-normalizing data temporarily
- Removing form labels
- Using `fileuploader.js`
- Uploading files using a `LOADed` component
- Making image thumbnails from uploaded images
- Monitoring upload progress
- Auto tooltip in forms
- Color picker widget
- Shortening text fields
- Creating multi-table forms
- Creating a multi-table form with references
- Creating a multi-table update form
- Star rating widget

*Advanced Forms*

# Introduction

Web2py comes with powerful functions for form generation. In this chapter, we provide examples of customization of forms from adding buttons to creating custom form widgets. We also provide examples of complex forms, such as wizards and multi-table forms.

## Adding a cancel button to forms

This recipe explains a method to add cancel buttons to forms, that is, a button that does not submit the forms, ignores any changes, and goes back to the previous page (or moves on to the next, depending on settings). The cancel button is really just a special case of a more general mechanism described herein to add buttons to your form.

### Getting ready

Our recipe assumes a generic model.

### How to do it...

1. The controller builds the form and button with the following statements:

   ```
   form=SQLFORM(db.mytable,
     record=mytable_index,
     deletable=True,
     submit_button=T('Update'))
   ```

2. You can add a button using the following statement:

   ```
   form[0][-1][1].append(TAG.BUTTON('Cancel',
     _onclick="document.location='%s';"%URL('index')))
   ```

   The last line shows how adding a `Cancel` button to a form is as simple as appending to the form. The index of the `SQLFORM`, where you choose append (or insert) your cancel button, determines where your button will appear on your page.

   Here `form[0]` is the `TABLE` inside the form. `form[0][-1]` is the last `TR`. `form[0][-1][1]` is column number one (the second `TD` in the last `TR`). The `_onclick` argument takes the user to the URL specified in the right-hand-side of the `window.location=` statement.

3. An equivalent notation to put the `Cancel` button after the `Submit` button would be:

   ```
   form.element('input[type=submit]').parent.append(TAG.BUTTON(...))
   ```

   Here, the element method partially accepts CSS3 syntax.

4. In general, buttons of any type can be added into a form using this same mechanism.

   If you prefer more control and transparency over the creation of your `Cancel` button, or other buttons, then a custom view might be in order. However, you may not mix this method with a form that has been appended to. This example shows a custom form, where the form was created by the following:

   ```
   form=SQLFORM.factory(db.mytable)
   ```

The example assumes a generic table with fields numbered `1` to `N`.

```
{{=form.custom.begin}}
{{=form.custom.widget.field1}}
{{=form.custom.widget.field2}}
{{=form.custom.widget.field3}}
{{=form.custom.submit}}
{{=TAG.BUTTON(T('Cancel'), _onclick='...')}}
{{=form.custom.end}}
```

Here, cannot `field1...field3` must be actual field names. Once more, the `_onclick` action can be of any kind and flavor you like.

## Adding confirmation on form submit

Often, you want to double-check that the user is not accidentally submitting an incorrect form. You can do this by prompting the user for confirmation when he/she presses the submit button. This can be done in two ways.

## How to do it...

1. One way is by using `jQuery` to only edit the view that renders the form. In the view add the following code:

   ```
   <script>
     jQuery(function(){
       jQuery('input[type=submit]').click(
         function(){return confirm('Are you sure?');
       });
     });
   </script>
   ```

   Here, `confirm` is a JavaScript function that instructs the browser to create a confirmation dialog-box. If you press **[yes]** the `onclick` function returns `true`, and the form is submitted. If you press **[no]**, the `onclick` function returns `false`, and the form is not submitted.

## Advanced Forms

2. The same can be achieved by adding the string to the `onclick` attribute of the button when the form is created.

   ```
   return confirm('Are you sure?')
   ```

3. In web2py, there is an easy way to do it:

   ```
   def my_action():
     form = SQLFORM.factory(...)
     form.element('input[type=submit]')['_onclick'] = "return
       confirm('Are you sure?');"
     return dict(form=form)
   ```

Notice how we grab the `form.element(...)` using the `jQuery` syntax on the server-side (before the form is actually rendered in HTML), and we modify its `onclick` attribute (using the web2py notation with the preceding underscore).

# Searching data dynamically

Web2py comes with a `crud.search` mechanism that allows you to do the following:

```
def index():
  form, results = crud.search(db.things)
  return dict(form=form, results=results)
```

Here, `form` is a search form and `records` are the result of the search. To understand how this works, we present in this recipe a simplified implementation of this function that you can further customize depending on your needs. Here, `db.things` is a table containing our things. The actual name of the table or its structure are not relevant here.

## How to do it...

1. First of all crate a new model, for example `dynamic_search.py`, and add the following code to it:

   ```
   def build_query(field, op, value):
     if op == 'equals':
       return field == value
     elif op == 'not equal':
       return field != value
     elif op == 'greater than':
       return field > value
     elif op == 'less than':
       return field < value
     elif op == 'starts with':
       return field.startswith(value)
   ```

```python
        elif op == 'ends with':
           return field.endswith(value)
        elif op == 'contains':
           return field.contains(value)
    def dynamic_search(table):
      tbl = TABLE()
      selected = []
      ops = ['equals','not equal','greater than','less than',
            'starts with','ends with','contains']
      query = table.id > 0
      for field in table.fields:
        chkval = request.vars.get('chk'+field,None)
        txtval = request.vars.get('txt'+field,None)
        opval = request.vars.get('op'+field,None)
        row = TR(TD(INPUT(_type="checkbox",_name="chk"+field,
                      value=chkval=='on')),
                  TD(field),TD(SELECT(ops,_name="op"+field,
                                   value=opval)),
                  TD(INPUT(_type="text",_name="txt"+field,
                      _value=txtval)))
        tbl.append(row)
        if chkval:
          if txtval:
            query &= build_query(table[field], opval,txtval)
            selected.append(table[field])
      form = FORM(tbl,INPUT(_type="submit"))
      results = db(query).select(*selected)
      return form, results
```

2. Now, you can use `dynamic_search` as a replacement for `crud.search`.

   ```python
   def index():
     form,results = dynamic_search(db.things)
     return dict(form=form,results=results)
   ```

   We can render this with the following view:

   ```
   {{extend 'layout.html'}}
   {{=form}}
   {{=results}}
   ```

Advanced Forms

Here is how it looks like:

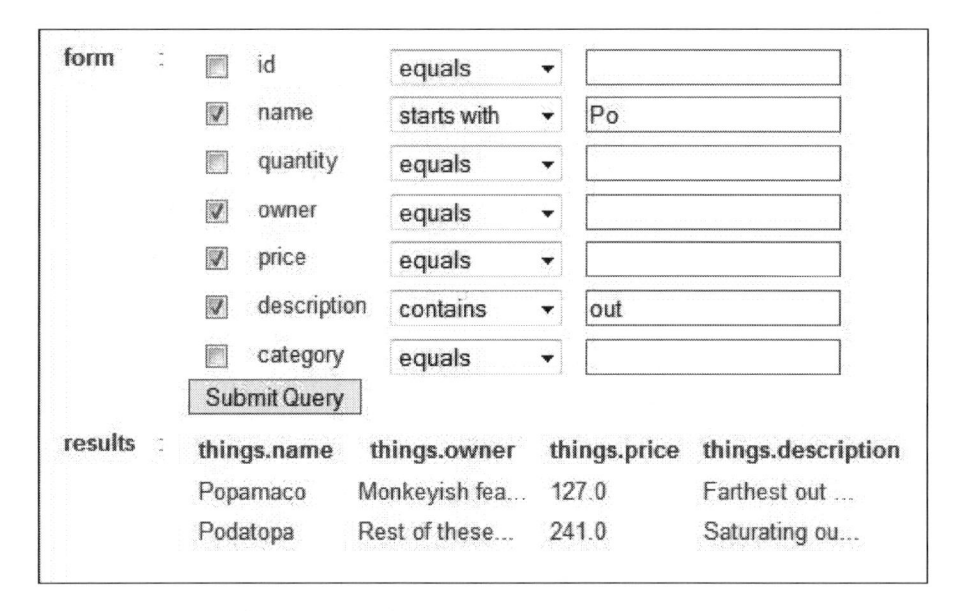

| form | | | |
|---|---|---|---|
| ☐ | id | equals ▼ | |
| ☑ | name | starts with ▼ | Po |
| ☐ | quantity | equals ▼ | |
| ☑ | owner | equals ▼ | |
| ☑ | price | equals ▼ | |
| ☑ | description | contains ▼ | out |
| ☐ | category | equals ▼ | |

[Submit Query]

| results | things.name | things.owner | things.price | things.description |
|---|---|---|---|---|
| | Popamaco | Monkeyish fea... | 127.0 | Farthest out ... |
| | Podatopa | Rest of these... | 241.0 | Saturating ou... |

# Embedding multiple forms in one page

This recipe explains how to embed more than one form in a page. Doing so can increase user productivity by reducing HTTP calls, but carries a risk of cluttering the page layout.

## How to do it...

1. To illustrate a page with multiple forms, we create a stripped-down system for storing a person's educational **Curriculum Vitae** (**CV**). We begin by defining tables for schools, students, and the degrees they received.

   ```
   YEARS = range(1910, 2011)
   DEGREES = ('BA', 'BS', 'MA', 'MS', 'MBA', 'JD', 'PhD')

   db.define_table('school',
     Field('name', 'string', unique=True),
     Field('address', 'string'),
     Field('established', 'integer', requires=IS_IN_SET(YEARS)),
     format='%(name)s')

   db.define_table('student',
     Field('name', 'string', unique=True),
   ```

```
        Field('birthday', 'date'),
        format='%(name)s')

    db.define_table('education',
        Field('student', db.student),
        Field('school', db.school),
        Field('degree', 'string', requires=IS_IN_SET(DEGREES)),
        Field('graduated', 'integer', requires=IS_IN_SET(YEARS)))
```

2. The `index()` controller creates a form for each of the tables:

   ```
   def index():

       student_form = SQLFORM(db.student)
       if student_form.accepts(request, session):
           response.flash = 'Student Form Accepted'
       elif student_form.errors:
           response.flash = 'Form has errors'

       school_form=SQLFORM(db.school)
       if school_form.accepts(request, session):
           redirect(URL('index'))
           response.flash = 'School Form Accepted'
       elif school_form.errors:
           response.flash = 'Form has errors'

       education_form=SQLFORM(db.education)
       if education_form.accepts(request, session):
           response.flash = 'Education Form Accepted'
       elif education_form.errors:
           response.flash = 'Form has errors'

       return locals()
   ```

3. In a typical web2py controller, you would see only one `form=SQLFORM(...)` statement, and one `if form.accepts(...)` clause. Since we have three forms to render and process, we need three `SQLFORM(...)` statements, and three `if specific_form.accepts(...)` statements. Each form must be given a unique name, so that when one of the forms is POSTed, its respective `form.accepts` clause will be triggered.

   Note that forms about tables that contain references to other tables must be defined and processed in the order of the dependences. So if a new `school` or a new `student` is added, it shows the `education` form drop-down menu.

## Advanced Forms

The simplest view to display all three forms on a single page is something like this:

```
{{extend 'layout.html'}}
<h2>Education CV</h2>
<div id='form1'>{{=education_form}}</div>

<h2>Student</h2>
<div id='form1'>{{=student_form}}</div>

<h2>School</h2>
<div id='form1'>{{=school_form}}</div>
```

If two or more forms are relative to the same table, the accepts must be passed a `formname` argument, and it must be different for the two forms.

### There's more...

Another option consists of implementing the different forms and components loaded in the main (index) page using the `LOAD` command. Also notice that a submission of the `education` form does not affect the other two, while the other two affect the drop-down in the `education` form. This allows us to create different actions for each of the forms:

```
def index():
    return dict()

def create_student():
    return crud.create(db.student, message='Student Form Accepted')

def create_school():
    return crud.create(db.school, message='School Form Accepted')

def create_education():
    return crud.create(db.education, message='Education Form Accepted')
```

A view `views/default/index.html` embeds the three forms and traps the `education` form, so that when this form is submitted, the other two are not processed and reloaded:

```
{{extend 'layout.html'}}
<h2>Education CV</h2>
<div id='form1'>
    {{=LOAD('default','create_eduction',ajax_trap=True)}}
</div>

<h2>Student</h2>
<div id='form1'>{{=LOAD('default', 'create_student')}}</div>

<h2>School</h2>
<div id='form1'>{{=LOAD('default', 'create_school')}}</div>
```

Multiple-form pages can also be created using the FORM, SQLFORM.factory, and crud statements, or a combination of all form-generating statements. Customized forms can be mixed with automatically-generated forms. There is no limit to the flexibility available to generating beautiful form-entry pages with web2py.

# Detecting and blocking concurrent updates

Consider for example a wiki page. You open the page, edit it, and save it. It is possible that while you edit your page, somebody accesses the same page, and saves a new version of the page before you do. Your save action will result in the previous edits being lost.

Of course, you can prevent concurrent edits by implementing a locking mechanism, but it is difficult to properly implement such a mechanism. What if a user opens a page for editing, leaves the browser open, and forgets about it? Everybody else would be prevented to edit the same page. Implementing a timeout re-introduces the original problem.

There is a simple solution. Every time you save a page (or any record for that matters) ask web2py to check whether the original record has been modified on the server since the moment when the record was originally retrieved.

This is easy in web2py, as we will explain in the this recipe.

## Getting ready

We will consider, as an example, an application with following model:

```
db.define_table('page', Field('title', notnull=True), Field('body'))
```

And the following edit form:

```
def edit():
    page = db.page(request.args(0))
    form = SQLFORM(db.page,page)
    if form.accepts(request,session):
        response.flash = "page saved"
    return dict(form=form)
```

## How to do it...

1. All you have to do is pass an extra attribute to form.accepts, detect_record_change, and check whether the record has changed:

   ```
   def edit():
       page = db.page(request.args(0))
       form = SQLFORM(db.page,page)
   ```

## Advanced Forms

```
        if form.accepts(request,session, detect_record_change=True):
            response.flash = "page saved"
        elif form.record_changed:
            response.flash = "page not saved because changed on server"
        return dict(form=form)
```

2. On `record-changed`, you can the write your own logic to deal with the conflict. The data on the server is always in the page (`page.title` and `page.body`); the submitted values are in `request.vars.title` and `request.vars.body`.

### There's more...

What about `crud` forms? It turns out that `crud.create` and `crud.update` forms have `detect_record_change=True`, by default (while it is `False` by default for normal SQLFORMs). Therefore, if a record is modified on the server, the newly submitted values are not saved. Yet crud forms do not provide any logic to deal with this situation, and leave it to the developer. For example, you can rewrite the previous example using `crud` as follows:

```
def edit():
    page = db.page(request.args(0))
    form = crud.update(db.page,page)
    if form.record_changed:
        response.flash = "page not saved; try resubmit"
    return dict(form=form)
```

Notice that when a submission is rejected because the record changed on the server, a second submission will succeed.

## Creating a form wizard

We often need to gather information from a user (for example, to populate a database or perform some other operation), yet we do not want to overwhelm the user with a very large form. A better approach consists of breaking the form into multiple pages that the user can navigate with a `[next]` button. Such an approach is a called a **wizard**.

### How to do it...

1. Here we assume we want to use a wizard to populate multiple fields in a table called `mytable`:

   ```
   db.define_table('mytable',
       Field('field1'),
       Field('field2'),
       ...
       Field('fieldN'))
   ```

   It does not matter how many fields you have.

2. We can handle the wizard with a single action. The action needs to know how many steps, which fields to query at each step, and where to go after the last step. Here is a possible implementation:

```
def wizard():
  STEPS = {0: ('field1','field2'), # fields for 1st page
    1: ('field3','field4'), # fields for 2nd page
    2: ('field5',''field6'), # fields for 3rd page
    3: URL('done')}          # url when wizard completed

  step = int(request.args(0) or 0)
  if not step in STEPS: redirect(URL(args=0))
  fields = STEPS[step]
  if step==0:
    session.wizard = {}
  if isinstance(fields,tuple):
    form = SQLFORM.factory(*[f for f in db.mytable if f.name in
      fields])
  if form.accepts(request,session):
    session.wizard.update(form.vars)
    redirect(URL(args=step+1))
  else:
    db.mytable.insert(**session.wizard)
    session.flash = T('wizard completed')
    redirect(fields)
  return dict(form=form,step=step)
```

3. You can render the wizard with the following:

```
{{extend 'layout.html'}}
<h1>Wizard Step {{=step}}</h1>
{{=form}}
```

## How it works...

It is pretty simple, actually. The wizard action gets its page number from `request.args(0)`, and looks up in `STEPS` which fields to display. It uses `SQLFORM.factory` to build the partial form. Completed data from `form.vars` are stored in `session.wizard`. The last page instead of a tuple for the list of fields, contains a `URL('done')`, which is a string. When the wizard encounters this condition, it knows that it is time to insert the `session.wizard` variables in a new table and redirect them to the said URL. Notice that validation is done at each step for the fields that are displayed.

*Advanced Forms*

# De-normalizing data temporarily

In this recipe, we consider the model described in the recipe *Efficient search by tag*, and we want to create insert, update forms, or a table `data` that allows the user to type in tags in a single input type text-box within the same form. In other words, we want to create a form that is automatically populated from the `data`, and all `tag` records referring to this `data` record. On submission, the form should update both the `data` and the `tag` tables.

## Getting ready

We assume our usual application, and the following model:

```
db.define_table('data',Field('value'))
db.define_table('tag',Field('record_id',db.data),Field('name'))
```

We will also assume the following function in `controllers/default.py`:

```
def edit():
  record = db.data(request.args(0))
  form = crud.update(db.data,record)
  return dict(form=form)
```

## How to do it...

We need to do this in two steps, each represented by a function. One function will assume we have new tags, delete old tags, and store the new tags. Another function will modify the crud form and add an input field containing the current tags. These two functions can then be used to modify our original form.

```
def update_tags(form):
  db(db.tag.record_id==form.record.id).delete()
  new_tags = [tag.strip() for tag in request.vars.tags.split(',')]
  for tag in new_tags:
    if tag:
      db.tag.insert(record_id=form.record.id,name=tag)

def make_taggable(form):
  tags = [tag.name for tag in db(db.tag.record_id==form.record.id).
select()]
  value = ', '.join(tags)
    form.element('table').insert(-2, TR(LABEL('Tags:'),
      INPUT(_name='tags', value=value)))
  return form

def edit():
```

```
record = db.data(request.args(1))
form = make_taggable(crud.update(db.data, record,
   onaccept=update_tags))
return dict(form=form)
```

## How it works...

The `make_taggable` function takes a form object (forms are always derivatives of the FORM class), and injects into the form table a new row containing a label (`Tags:`), and an INPUT element. The INPUT value defaults to a string containing the current tags for the record.

When the form is submitted and accepted, `crud.update` ignores the `request.vars.tags` because it is not a field of the `db.data` table. If the form is accepted, the `onaccept` function is called, which points to `update_tags`. This function deletes the current tags and updates them.

Notice that this mechanism is very general, and there is nothing specific to the table `db.data`. In fact, the two functions `update_tags` and `make_taggable` can be used with any table, as long as it is referenced by a `db.tags` table, and both by `crud.update` and `crud.create` forms.

## There's more...

We will need a minor tweak if the tags field needs validation. We will assume that each tag name needs validation and the validator is given by:

```
db.tag.name.requires=IS_MATCH('\w[\w\-\./]+')
```

That is, each tag must contain at least two characters. The first one must be alphanumeric (\w), while the subsequent ones can be alphanumeric (\w), or dash (\-), or dot (\.), or forward slash (/).

In order to perform the validation, we need a smart validation function:

```
def validate_tags(form):
   new_tags = [tag.strip() for tag in request.vars.tags.split(',')]
   if tag in new_tags:
      (value, error) = db.tag.name.validate(tag)
   if error:
      form.errors['tags'] = error + '(%s)' % value
```

Then we need to force its call on validation:

```
def edit():
   record = db.data(request.args(0))
   form = make_taggable(crud.update(db.data,record,
```

```
            onvalidation=validate_tags,
            onaccept=update_tags))
    return dict(form=form)
```

If all the other fields are validated, the `onvalidation` function is called. This function loops over all the tags, and validates them using the `db.tag.name` validator. If one of them does not pass, the error is stored in `form.errors`, which is a `Storage` object. The presence of form errors prevents the form from being accepted. When the form is rendered, the `INPUT(...,_name='tags')` object will pick up the error from the form, and display it appropriately.

## Removing form labels

When you use `SQLFORM` or crud, the generated form has labels. You can use the `formstyle` attribute of the form to decide how the labels should display:

- `table3cols` (on the left of the input widgets)
- `table2cols` (on the top of the input widgets)
- `divs` (on separate `divs` without a table, so you can position them by coordinates)
- `ul` (on the left of the input widgets but using unordered lists instead of a table)

Yet sometimes you just want to hide labels.

## How to do it...

There are two ways to do this:

1. One way consists of generating the form and removing them from the form:
   ```
   db.define_table('mytable',Field('myfield'))
   def index():
       form = SQLFORM(db.mytable)
       for row in form.element('table'): del row[0]
       return dict(form=form)
   ```

2. Another method consists of using a custom form in the view:
   ```
   {{=form.custom.begin}}
   <table>
     <tr>
       <td>{{=form.custom.widget.myfield}}</td>
       <td>{{=db.mytable.myfield.comment}}</td>
     </tr>
     <tr>
   ```

```
      <td>{{=form.custom.submit}}</td>
    </tr>
  </table>
  {{=form.custom.end}}
```

The net effect is the same.

## Using fileuploader.js

In this recipe, we will assume you have a database table to store uploaded files and you want to create an interface that allows users to upload multiple files using Ajax. `fileuploader.js` is a jQuery plugin that uses XHR for uploading multiple files, and displays a progress-bar. It works in Firefox 3.6+, Safari 4+, and Chrome, and falls back to the hidden iframe-based upload in other browsers.

### Getting ready

First you need to download the plugin from https://github.com/valums/file-uploader, and place the file `fileuploader.js` into the application `static/js/`. Also, place the `fileuploader.css` into the application `static/css`.

Second, we will assume you have a model, such as the following where you would store uploaded files:

```
db.define_table('document',
   Field('filename', 'upload'),
   Field('uploaded_by', db.auth_user))
```

### How to do it...

We need to create the following upload action in `controllers/default.py`:

```
@auth.requires_login()
def upload_callback():
  if 'qqfile' in request.vars:
    filename = request.vars.qqfile
    newfilename = db.document.filename.store(request.body, filename)
    db.document.insert(filename=newfilename,
       uploaded_by=auth.user.id)
  return response.json({'success': 'true'})

@auth.requires_login()
def upload():
  return dict()
```

## Advanced Forms

The `upload_callback` action will receive a file in the `request.body` with a name in `request.vars.qqfile`. It will rename it, store it, insert the new name in the database, and return success. The `upload` action, instead, does nothing but its view will display the jQuery plugin:

```
{{response.files.append(URL(request.application,'static','js/
fileuploader.js'))}}
{{response.files.append(URL(request.application,'static','css/
fileuploader.css'))}}
{{extend 'layout.html'}}

<script>
jQuery(document).ready(function() {
  var uploader = new qq.FileUploader({
    // pass the dom node (ex. jQuery(selector)[0] for jQuery users)
    element: document.getElementById('file-uploader'),
    // path to server-side upload script
    action: '{{=URL("upload_callback")}}',
    sizeLimit: 15000000,
    minSizeLimit: 0,
    allowedExtensions: ['xls','jpg','jpeg','pdf',
      'txt','doc','htm','html','xml','xmls','txt','ppt','png',
      'gif'],
    // set to true to output server response to console
    debug: true,

    // events
    // you can return false to abort submit
    onSubmit: function(id, fileName){},
    onProgress: function(id, fileName, loaded, total){},
    onComplete: function(id, fileName, responseJSON){},
    onCancel: function(id, fileName){},

    messages: {
      // error messages, see qq.FileUploaderBasic for content
      typeError: "{file} {{=T('has invalid extension.')}}
        {{=T('Only')}} {extensions} {{=T('are allowed.')}}",
      sizeError: "{file} {{=T('is too large, maximum file size
        is')}} {sizeLimit}.",
      minSizeError: "{file} {{=T('is too small, minimum file size
        is')}} {minSizeLimit}.",
      emptyError: "{file} {{=T('is empty, please select files again
        without it.')}}",
      onLeave: "{{=T('The files are being uploaded, if you leave now
        the upload will be cancelled.')}}"
```

```
      },
      showMessage: function(message){ alert(message); }
    });
  });
</script>

<div id="file-uploader">
  <noscript>
    <p>Please enable JavaScript to use file uploader.</p>
    <!-- or put a simple form for upload here -->
  </noscript>
</div>
```

This plugin is very powerful, and it has many configuration options. To learn more about it we refer to its website: `http://valums.com/ajax-upload/`.

A screenshot of the result can be seen here:

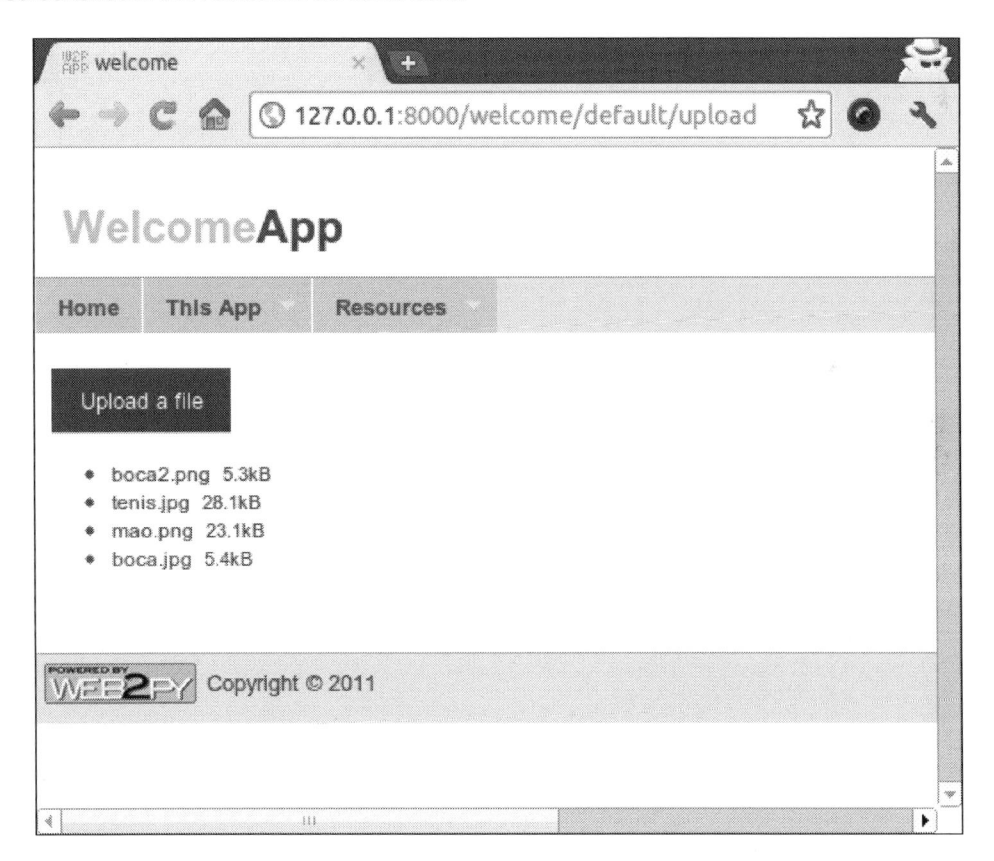

*Advanced Forms*

# Uploading files using a LOADed component

web2py allows you to design pages in a modular way and LOAD components in the page using Ajax. A component is a subset of the page served by its own action. The component may, for example, render a form. The component traps form submission, and only refreshes itself upon submission. This magic is possible, thanks to the `static/js/web2py_ajax.js` utilities, and the LOAD helper. The problem is that this mechanism breaks for multi-part forms, and it does not work when the form in a LOADed component includes a file `upload` field.

To fix the problem, we need a jQuery plugin called `jquery.form.js`.

## Getting ready

To start, you need to download the required jQuery plugin from `http://github.com/malsup/form/raw/master/jquery.form.js?v2.43`, and place it into the `static/js` folder as `jquery.form.js`.

We will also assume the following models (same as previous recipe), but we will ignore authentication:

```
db.define_table('document',
   Field('filename','upload',requires=IS_NOT_EMPTY()),
   Field('uploaded_by',db.auth_user))
```

The following controller:

```
def index():
   return dict()

@auth.requires_signature()
def component_list():
   db.document.filename.represent = lambda f,r: f and A('file',_href\
      =URL('download',args=f))
   return db(db.document).select()

@auth.requires_signature()
def component_form():
   db.document.uploaded_by.default = auth.user_id
   db.document.uploaded_by.writable = False
   form = SQLFORM(db.document)
   if form.accepts(request):
      response.flash = 'Thanks for filling the form'
      response.js = "web2py_component('%s','doc_list');" % \
      URL('component_list.load',user_signature=True)
```

```
    elif form.errors:
      response.flash = 'Fill the form correctly'
    else:
      response.flash = 'Please fill the form'
    return dict(form=form)
```

And `views/default/index.html`:

```
{{extend 'layout.html'}}

<h1>{{=T("Change the user's image!")}}</h1>

{{=LOAD('default', 'component_list.load', ajax=True,
  target='doc_list', user_signature=True)}}

{{=LOAD('default', 'component_form.load', ajax=True,
  user_signature=True)}}
```

For any form but the one we created, this would work fine. It would not work with our form, because it contains an `upload` field. Notice that, in this recipe, we have used `user_signature=True` and `auth.requires_signature()` decorator. This will make sure that all URLs are signed, and any authentication/authorization that we apply to the parent page `index` will propagate to the components.

## How to do it...

1. To fix the problem, we need two steps. First we need to include the plugins by adding this line in `views/web2py_ajax.html`:

   ```
   response.files.insert(2,URL('static','js/jquery.form.js'))
   ```

2. Then we need to modify `static/js/web2py_ajax.js`, by adding the logic to capture the form and handle the uploads using the `ajaxForm` function, defined in `jqeury.form.js`. To achieve this, edit `web2py_ajax.js` and replace the function `web2py_trap_form` with the following:

   ```
   function web2py_trap_form(action,target) {
     jQuery('#'+target+' form').each(function(i){
       var form=jQuery(this);
       if(!form.hasClass('no_trap'))
         if(form.find('.upload').length>0) {
           form.ajaxForm({
             url: action,
             success: function(data, statusText, xhr) {
               jQuery('#'+target).html(xhr.responseText);
               web2py_trap_form(action,target);
               web2py_ajax_init();
   ```

## Advanced Forms

```
          }
        });
      } else {
        form.submit(function(e){
          jQuery('.flash').hide().html('');
          web2py_ajax_page('post',action,form.serialize(),target);
          e.preventDefault();
        });
      }
    });
}
```

It will handle the form upload using `ajaxForm`, only if the form contains an input element of the `upload` class.

3. Then we need to create a view for the action `component_form` called `views/default/component_form.load` that contains the following:

```
{{=form}}

<script>
/* hack because jquery.form.js does not properly passes headers */
  jQuery('.flash').hide().html("{{=response.flash}}").slideDown();
  eval("{{=XML(response.js or '')}}");
</script>
```

The script should not be necessary, but the `ajaxForm` function does not properly pass the headers back-and-forth to the server. Therefore, we need to explicitly include in the view, the logic to show `response.flash`, and execute `response.js`.

## Making image thumbnails from uploaded images

The title says it all. We want to upload images, and dynamically make thumbnails images from them. We will store the thumbnail references in the same records as the uploaded images.

### Getting ready

To use the recipe, you must install the **Python Imaging Library** (**PIL**). You can find it at the following link:

`http://www.pythonware.com/products/pil/`

*Chapter 4*

That requires running web2py from source. As usual with Python, you can use `easy_install`:

`easy_install PIL`

Or from a Debian compatible distribution with the following:

`sudo apt-get install python-imaging`

## How to do it...

For this purpose, we will modify the model used in the two previous recipes by adding a field called `thumbnail`, and we will ignore authentication, since it is an orthogonal issue.

```
db.define_table('document',
  Field('filename','upload'),
  Field('thumbnail','upload', readable=False, writable=False))
```

Here is the controller:

```
def make_thumbnail(table, image_id, size=(150, 150)):
  import os
  from PIL import Image
  this_image = table(image_id)
  im = Image.open(os.path.join(request.folder, 'uploads',
    this_image.filename))
  im.thumbnail(size, Image.ANTIALIAS)
  thumbnail = 'document.thumbnail.%s.jpg' % \
    this_image.filename.split('.')[2]
  im.save(os.path.join(request.folder, 'uploads', thumbnail), 'jpeg')
  this_image.update_record(thumbnail=thumbnail)

def uploadimage():
  form = SQLFORM(db.document)
  if form.accepts(request, session):
    response.flash = 'form accepted'
    make_thumbnail(db.document,form.vars.id,(175,175))
  elif form.errors:
    response.flash = 'form has errors'
  docs = db(db.document).select()
  return dict(form=form,docs=docs)
```

Advanced Forms

# Monitoring upload progress

In this recipe, we will show how to create a JavaScript widget that displays a progress bar, and displays the upload progress. Our solution is server-based and more reliable than pure JavaScript solutions. Be aware that no browser can handle a file over 2GB.

This recipe is based on the following recipes adapted to web2py:

http://www.motobit.com/help/scptutl/pa98.htm

http://www.djangosnippets.org/snippets/679/

## How to do it...

1. The main idea consists of using `cache.ram` to store the progress server-side, and expose an action to query for the value of this variable.

   This is accomplished in two steps. In the first step, we choose an `X-Progress-ID` key, so that we can later retrieve the cache value:

   ```
   <form action="http://127.0.0.1:8000/example/upload/post?X-
     Progress-ID=myuuid">
   ```

2. Then we retrieve the upload total length from `cache.ram`:

   ```
   cache.ram("X-Progress-ID:myuuid:length",lambda:0,None)
   ```

   And the current uploaded length:

   ```
   cache.ram('X-Progress-ID:myuuid:uploaded',
       lambda: 0, None)
   ```

   Here `myuuid` has to be replaced everywhere with a server generated UUID.

3. Let's do it now in more detail with a concrete example. Consider this controller action in `controllers/default.py`:

   ```
   def post():
     if request.extension=='json' and 'X-Progress-ID' in
       request.get_vars:
       cache_key = 'X-Progress-ID:'+request.get_vars['X-Progress-ID']
       length=cache.ram(cache_key+':length', lambda: 0, None)
       uploaded=cache.ram(cache_key+':uploaded', lambda: 0, None)
       from gluon.serializers import json
       return json(dict(length=length, uploaded=uploaded))
     form = FORM(INPUT(_type='file',
       _name='file',requires=IS_NOT_EMPTY()),
       INPUT(_type='submit', _value='SUBMIT'))
     return dict(form=form, myuuid = "[server generated uuid]")
   ```

Note that this action servers two purposes:

- It creates and processes the form
- If called with .json, and passed an X-Progress-ID, it returns the length and uploaded variables in json

4. Now we need to customize the form in views/default/post.html:

```
{{extend 'layout.html'}}
<script type="text/javascript">
  // Add upload progress for multipart forms.
  jQuery(function() { jQuery('form[enctype="multipart/form-
    data"]').submit(function(){
  // Prevent multiple submits
  if (jQuery.data(this, 'submitted')) return false;
  // freqency of update in ms
  var freq = 1000;
  // id for this upload so we can fetch progress info.
  var uuid = ''+Math.floor(Math.random() * 1000000);
  // ajax view serving progress info
  var progress_url = '{{ =URL( extension= "json" )}}';
  // Append X-Progress-ID uuid form action
  this.action += ((this.action.indexOf('?') == -1)?'?':'&') +
    'X-Progress-ID=' + uuid;
  var progress = jQuery('<div id="upload-progress"
    class="upload-progress"></div>').insertAfter(
    jQuery('input[type="submit"]')).append('<div
    class="progress-container">
    <span class="progress-info">uploading 0%</span>
    <div class="progress-bar"></div></div>');
  jQuery('input[type="submit"]').remove();
  // style the progress bar
  progress.find('.progress-bar').height('1em').width(0);
  progress.css("background-color", "red");

  // Update progress bar
  function update_progress_info() {
    progress.show();
    jQuery.getJSON(progress_url,
    {'X-Progress-ID': uuid, 'random': Math.random()},
    function(data, status){ if (data) {
      var progress_coefficient=
        parseInt(data.uploaded)/parseInt(data.length);
      var width=progress.find('.progress-container').width();
      var progress_width = width * progress_coefficient;
```

## Advanced Forms

```
            progress.find('.progress-bar').width(progress_width);
            progress.find('.progress-info').text('uploading '
              + progress_coefficient*100 + '%');
        }
        window.setTimeout(update_progress_info, freq);
      });
    };
    window.setTimeout(update_progress_info, freq);
    // mark form as submitted.
    jQuery.data(this, 'submitted', true);
    });
  });
</script>

{{=form}}
```

### How it works...

The important part in this is the following:

```
this.action += (this.action.indexOf('?') == -1 ? '?' : '&')
  + 'X-Progress-ID=' + uuid;
```

It passes the `uuid` variable as a `GET` variable. The rest of the magic is done automatically by web2py, which reads this variables, computes the upload programs, and stores it in `cache.ram`.

These lines is also important:

```
var progress_url = '{{=URL(extension='json')}}';
jQuery.getJSON(progress_url,
  {'X-Progress-ID': uuid, 'random': Math.random()},
  ...)
```

They tell web2py to use the same URL, but with the `.json` extension to get the length and uploaded values necessary to update the progress bar.

## Auto tooltips in forms

This recipe shows you how to display tooltips in forms created through Crud or SQLFORM, using the field's `comment` attribute.

## Getting ready

First of all, you have to fill the `comment` attribute in the `field` definition where you want the tooltip to appear. For example:

```
db.define_table('board',
  Field('message', comment='Let your message here.'))
```

If you do only this, the tip will appear on the right side of the field when the form is generated through Crud or SQLFORM.

Remember that you can put HTML code in a comment using helpers:

```
db.define_table('recados',
  Field('message', comment=SPAN('Let here your ',B('message'))))
```

## How to do it...

You will need a jQuery plugin to show the tip, so you may Google it and pick one. Or you can use this link: `http://jquery.bassistance.de/tooltip/jquery.tooltip.zip`. See what it looks like here: `http://jquery.bassistance.de/tooltip/demo/`.

1. Extract `jquery.tooltip.min.js` in `static/js`, and `jquery.tooltip.css` to `static/css` respectively.

2. Edit your layout file, and in the head, before `{{include 'web2py_ajax.html'}}` add the following:

    ```
    {{
      response.files.append(URL('static','js/jquery.tooltip.min.js'))
      response.files.append(URL('static','css/jquery.tooltip.css'))
    }}
    ```

3. Now you have this script on every page you want tooltips:

    ```
    <script type="text/javascript">
      jQuery(function() {
        // iterates over all form widgets
        jQuery(".w2p_fw").each(function (){
          // set title for the widget taken from the comment column
          jQuery(this).attr('title',jQuery(this).next().html());
          // clear the comment (optional)
          jQuery(this).next().html('');
          // create the tooltip with title attribute set
          jQuery(this).tooltip();
        });
      });
    </script>
    ```

    Your comment column will be converted into nice tooltips.

*Advanced Forms*

You can also include this script in `web2py_ajax.html` or `layout.html`, to reuse the code. Or you may put this code in another file, and include it when needed; maybe this is a better way.

# Color picker widget

If you have a table field that is supposed to contain a color (red, green, #ff24dc, and so on.) you may want to a widget to represent the feild that allows you to change/select the color by picking it from a color canvas. Here we show you how to build a widget to do just that.

## Getting ready

You need to download `mColorPicker` from `http://www.bertera.it/software/web2py/mColorPicker-w2p.tgz`, and uncompress it in the `static/` folder of your application.

## How to do it...

1. Define the widget in the file `models/plugin_colorpicker.py`:

```
class ColorPickerWidget(object):
    """
    Colorpicker widget based on
    http://code.google.com/p/mcolorpicker/
    """
    def __init__ (self, js = colorpicker_js, button=True, style="",
                  transparency=False):
        import uuid
        uid = str(uuid.uuid4())[:8]
        self._class = "_%s" % uid
        self.style = style
        if transparency == False:
            self.transparency = 'false'
        else:
            self.transparency = 'true'
        if button == True:
            self.data = 'hidden'
        if self.style == "":
            self.style = "height:20px;width:20px;"
        else:
            self.data = 'display'
        if not js in response.files:
            response.files.append(js)
```

```
      def widget(self, f, v):
        wrapper = DIV()
        inp = SQLFORM.widgets.string.widget(f,v, _value=v,\
        _type='color',\
        _data_text='hidden', _style=self.style, _hex='true',\
        _class=self._class)
        scr = SCRIPT("jQuery.fn.mColorPicker.init.replace = false; \
        jQuery.fn.mColorPicker.init.allowTransparency=%s; \
        jQuery('input.%s').mColorPicker(\
                 {'imageFolder': '/%s/static/mColorPicker/'});"\
        % (self.transparency, self._class, request.application))
        wrapper.components.append(inp)
        wrapper.components.append(scr)
        return wrapper

color_widget = ColorPickerWidget()
```

2. To test it, create a table, and set the widget to our new `colorpicker` widget:

   ```
   db.define_table('house',
       Field('color', widget = color_widget.widget))
   ```

3. Finally, create the form in your controller:

   ```
   def index():
     form = SQLFORM(db.house)
     if form.accepts(request, session):
       response.flash = T('New house inserted')
     return dict(form=form)
   ```

# Shortening text fields

In this recipe, we assume we have a table like the following, and we want to display a list of selected post bodies, but shortened.

```
db.define_table('post', Field('body', 'text'))
```

## How to do it...

How to do this depends on whether the post contains HTML or wiki syntax.

1. We'll consider HTML first.

   This is done in three steps. In the controller we select the rows:

   ```
   def index():
     posts = db(db.post).select()
     return dict(posts=posts)
   ```

*Advanced Forms*

2. Then we shorten by serializing and truncating the HTML:

    ```
    def index():
       posts = db(db.post).select()
       for post in posts:
           post.short = TAG(post.body).flatten()[:100]+'...'
       return dict(posts=posts)
    ```

3. Then we display in the associated view:

    ```
    {{for post in posts:}}<div
       class="post">{{=post.short}}</div>{{pass}}
    ```

    Notice that `TAG(post.body)` parses the HTML, and then `flatten()` serializes the parsed HTML into text, omitting tags. We then extract the first 100 characters and add `'...'`.

4. If the body contained wiki syntax instead of HTML, then things are simpler, because we do not need to parse, and we could render the shortened text. Here we assume `MARKMIN` wiki syntax:

    ```
    def index():
       posts = db(db.post).select()
       for post in posts:
           post.short = post.body[:100]+'...'
       return dict(posts=posts)
    ```

5. And in the view:

    ```
    {{for post in posts:}}<div
       class="post">{{=MARKMIN(post.short)}}</div>{{pass}}
    ```

## There's more...

In the latter case, if you are using a relational database, the truncation can be done in the database server, thus reducing the amount of data transferred from `db` server to `db` client.

```
def index():
   posts = db(db.post).select(db.post.body[:100]+'...')
   for post in posts:
      post.short = post(db.post.body[:100]+'...')
   return dict(posts=posts)
```

An even better approach is to store the shortened text in a different database field instead of shortening every time it is needed. This will result in a faster application.

# Creating multi-table forms

Let us consider the example case of a database table called bottles with fields representing guests bringing a bottle of wine to a tasting party. Each bottle can have one or two tasters. Rest assured, there is also a one-to-many relation for the tasting, but here we assume only two testers. Our goal is to create a custom form that allows inserting a description of the bottle, and fill in the names of the two tasters, even if the one-to-may relation is implemented through a separate table.

## Getting ready

We will assume the following minimalist model, where the latter table implements the one-to-many relation:

```
db.define_table('bottle', Field('name'), Field('year', 'integer'))
db.define_table('taster', Field('name'), Field('bottle', db.bottle))
```

## How to do it...

1. First, we ask the `factory` to make us a form that contains a description of the bottle and a list field for the tasters:

    ```
    form=SQLFORM.factory(
      db.bottle,
      Field('tasters', type='list:string', label=T('Tasters')))
    ```

2. Now, we can handle the `accept` in the following two steps:

    - We insert the `bottle` into the `db.bottle` table
    - We insert each of the `tasters` into the `db.taster` table

    ```
    def register_bottle():
      form=SQLFORM.factory(
        db.bottle, Field('tasters', type='list:string',
        label=T('Tasters')))
      if form.accepts(request,session):
        bottle_id =
          db.bottle.insert(**db.bottle._filter_fields(form.vars))
        if isinstance(form.vars.tasters, basestring):
          db.taster.insert(name=form.vars.tasters, bottle=bottle_id)
        else:
          for taster in form.vars.tasters:
            db.taster.insert(name=taster, bottle=bottle_id)
    ```

```
        response.flash = 'Wine and guest data are now registered'
        return dict(form=form, bottles = db(db.bottle).select(), \
        tasters = db(db.taster).select())
```

Notice that we have to filter fields from `form.vars`, before we can perform a `db.bottle.insert`, because the form contains fields that do not belong to the table.

## Creating a multi-table form with references

Now we want to modify the previous example, so that tasters must be registered users in the system, and we want to select them using drop-boxes. One easy way to do this is by setting a maximum number of tasters (here we choose `10`).

### How to do it...

1. First we need to modify the model, so that tasters is now a many-to-many link table (a bottle can have many tasters, and a taster can taste multiple bottles):

    ```
    db.define_table('bottle', Field('name'), Field('year', 'integer'))
    db.define_table('taster', Field('auth_user', db.auth_user),
        Field('bottle', db.bottle))
    ```

2. Now we change the action accordingly:

    ```
    def register_bottle():
        tasters = range(10)
        form=SQLFORM.factory(
          db.bottle,
            *[Field('taster%i'%i, db.auth_user,label=T('Taster #%i'%i))
            for i in tasters])
        if form.accepts(request,session):
          bottle_id = \
            db.bottle.insert(**db.bottle._filter_fields(form.vars))
          for i in tasters:
            if 'taster%i'%i in form.vars:
              db.taster.insert(auth_user=
                form.vars['taster%i'%i],bottle=bottle_id)
          response.flash='Wine and guest data are now registered'
        return dict(form=form)
    ```

### There's more...

A naive way to render this form is the following:

```
{{extend 'layout.html'}}
{{=form}}
```

But, it is possible to make it smarter using JavaScript. The idea consists of hiding all rows of the form related to tasters, but showing only the first one and then letting the following rows appear as needed. jQuery is a fantastic tool for this kind of manipulation:

```
{{extend 'layout.html'}}
{{=form}}
<script>
  var taster_rows = new Array();
  for(var i=0; i<10; i++){
  taster_rows[i] = new Array();
  taster_rows[i][0] = '#no_table_taster'+i;
  taster_rows[i][1] = '#no_table_taster'+(i+1)+'__row';
}
  jQuery(function(){
    for(var i=1; i<10; i++){
      jQuery('#no_table_taster'+i+'__row').hide();
    }
    for(var i=0; i<9; i++){
      jQuery('#no_table_taster'+i).change(
        function(){
          for(var i=0; i<10; i++){
            if(taster_rows[i][0] == ("#" + $(this).attr("id"))){
              jQuery(taster_rows[i][1]).slideDown();
            }
          }
        });
    }
  }
  );
</script>
```

## How it works...

First of all, we hide all rows, but `taster0`. Then we register `js` actions to events. When a field value changes, for example, `taster2`, we make the next one, `taster3`, appear (i+1). Notice that if `taster3` is a field name, then `#no_table_taster3` is the ID of the input/select tag, and `#no_table_taster3__row` is the ID of the row in the table. This is a web2py convention. `no_table` comes from the fact that the form is generated by a `SQLFORM.factory`, and is not uniquely associated to a database table.

*Advanced Forms*

# Creating a multi-table update form

What we now want is to update a record of the `db.bottle` table and its associated `db.tasters` in one single form. This can be done using a mechanism similar to the one explained in the previous recipe. We need to do a little more work.

## How to do it...

First, we will retain the same model structure as in the previous example, but we change the controller action:

```
def edit_bottle():
  bottle_id = request.args(0)
  bottle = db.bottle(bottle_id) or redirect(URL('error'))
  bottle_tasters = db(db.taster.bottle==bottle_id).select()
  tasters, actual_testers = range(10), len(bottle_tasters)
  form=SQLFORM.factory(
    Field('name', default=bottle.name),
    Field('year', 'integer', default=bottle.year),
    *[Field('taster%i'%i,db.auth_user,
      default=bottle_tasters[i].auth_user \
      if i<actual_testers else '', label=T('Taster #%i'%i)) for
 i in tasters])
  if form.accepts(request,session):
    bottle.update_record(**db.bottle._filter_fields(form.vars))
    db(db.taster.bottle==bottle_id).delete()
  for i in tasters:
    if 'taster%i'%i in form.vars:
      db.taster.insert(auth_user=
        form.vars['taster%i'%i],bottle=bottle_id)
  response.flash = 'Wine and guest data are now updated'
  return dict(form=form)
```

## How it works...

Very much like the previous form, but the bottle fields are passed explicitly to the `SQLFORM.factory`, so that they can be pre-populated. The `tasters%i` fields are also pre-populated with existing tasters. When the form is submitted, the corresponding bottle record is updated, the past tasters are deleted, and new relations between the bottle and new tasters are inserted.

## There's more...

There is always more. The problem is that the JS code that hides empty rows, is now more complex. This is because, when editing the custom form, we do not want to hide rows that have a selected value. Here is a possible solution:

```
{{extend 'layout.html'}}
{{=form}}
<script>
  var taster_rows = new Array();
  for(var i=0; i<10; i++){
    taster_rows[i] = new Array();
    taster_rows[i][0] = '#no_table_taster'+i;
    taster_rows[i][1] = '#no_table_taster'+(i+1)+'__row';
  }
  jQuery(function(){
    for(var i=1; i<10; i++){
      if(!jQuery('#no_table_taster'+i).val()){
        jQuery('#no_table_taster'+i+'__row').hide();
      }
    }
    for(var i=0; i<9; i++){
      jQuery('#no_table_taster'+i).change(
        function(){
          for(var i=0; i<10; i++){
            if(taster_rows[i][0] == ("#" + $(this).attr("id"))){
              jQuery(taster_rows[i][1]).slideDown();
            }
          }
        });
    }
  }
  );
</script>
```

Can you figure out what it does?

Advanced Forms

# Star rating widget

In this recipe, we show you how to use the `jquery` star rating plugin, and integrate it with web2py.

## Getting ready

You need to download the jQuery star rating widget from the following link:

`http://orkans-tmp.22web.net/star_rating/index.html`

Extract the files under a new `static/stars` folder, so that `stars/ui.stars.js`, `stars/ui.stars.css`, and the necessary images provided by the plugin are in it.

## How to do it...

1. Create a model file called `models/plugin_rating.py`, and in the file write the following:

    ```
    DEPENDENCIES = [
      'http://ajax.googleapis.com/ajax/libs/jqueryui/1.8.9/jquery-
         ui.js',
      'http://ajax.googleapis.com/ajax/libs/jqueryui/1.8.9/themes/ui-
         darkness/jquery-ui.css',
      URL(c='static/stars',f='jquery.ui.stars.js'),
      URL(c='static/stars',f='jquery.ui.stars.css')]

    def rating_widget(f,v):
      from gluon.sqlhtml import OptionsWidget
      import uuid
      id = str(uuid.uuid4())
      for path in DEPENDENCIES:
        response.files.append(path)
      return DIV(SPAN(_id="stars-cap"),
        DIV(OptionsWidget.widget(f,v),_id=id),
        SCRIPT("jQuery(function(){jQuery('#%s').stars({inputType:
          'select'});});" % id))
    ```

2. Then, create a model. For example:

    ```
    db.define_table('song',
      Field('title'),
      Field('rating', 'integer'))
    ```

3. Set the widget to the `rating_widget`, as follows:

    ```
    db.song.rating.requires = IS_IN_SET(range(0, 6))
    db.song.rating.widget = rating_widget
    ```

4. The plugin model must be executed before the above two lines or the `rating_widget` function will be undefined.
5. It is important here that the field represented by the star rating be an integer with `IS_IN_SET(range(0,6))`.

Notice how the `rating_plugin` uses a `UUID` to define the `id` attribute of the `DIV` that renders the widget. In this way, you can have more than one field using the `rating` plugin at once.

# 5
# Adding Ajax Effects

In this chapter, we will cover the following recipes:

- Using `jquery.multiselect.js`
- Creating a `select_or_add` widget
- Using an autocompletion plugin
- Creating a drop-down date selector
- Improving the built-in `ajax` function
- Using a slider to represent a number
- Using jqGrid and web2py
- Improving data tables with WebGrid
- Ajaxing your search functions
- Creating sparklines

## Introduction

In this chapter, we discuss examples of integration of jQuery plugins with web2py. These plugins help in making forms and tables more interactive and friendly to the user, thus improving the usability of your application. In particular, we provide examples of how to improve the multi-select drop-down with an interactive **add option** button, how to replace an input field with a slider, and how to display tabular data using `jqGrid` and `WebGrid`.

Adding Ajax Effects

# Using jquery.multiselect.js

The default rendering of `<select multiple="true">..</select>` is quite ugly and not intuitive to use, in particular, when you need to select multiple non-contiguous options. This is not an HTML shortcoming, but a poor design of most browsers. Anyway, the presentation of the multiple `select` can be overwritten using JavaScript. Here, we will be using a jQuery plugin called `jquery.multiselect.js`. Notice that this jQuery plugin comes as standard and enabled with PluginWiki, but we assume that you are not using PluginWiki.

## Getting ready

You will need to download `jquery.muliselect.js` from `http://abeautifulsite.net/2008/04/jquery-multiselect`, and place the corresponding files into `static/js/jquery.multiselect.js` and `static/css/jquery.multiselect.css`.

## How to do it...

1. In your view, simply add the following before `{{extend 'layout.html}}`:

    ```
    {{
      response.files.append('http://ajax.googleapis.com/ajax\
         /libs/jqueryui/1.8.9/jquery-ui.js')
      response.files.append('http://ajax.googleapis.com/ajax\
         /libs/jqueryui/1.8.9/themes/ui-darkness/jquery-ui.css')
      response.files.append(URL('static','js/jquery.multiSelect.js'))
      response.files.append(URL('static','css/jquery.\
         multiSelect.css'))
    }}
    ```

2. Place the following after `{{extend 'layout.html'}}`:

    ```
    <script>
      jQuery(document).ready(function(){jQuery('[multiple]').
         multiSelect();});
    </script>
    ```

    That is all. All your multiple `select` will be nicely styled.

3. Consider the following action:

    ```
    def index():
      is_fruits = 
        IS_IN_SET(['Apples','Oranges','Bananas','Kiwis','Lemons'],
          multiple=True)
      form = SQLFORM.factory(Field('fruits','list:string',
        requires=is_fruits))
    ```

```
      if form.accepts(request,session):
         response.flash = 'Yummy!'
      return dict(form=form)
```

This action can be tried with the following view:

```
{{
   response.files.append('http://ajax.googleapis.com/ajax\
      /libs/jqueryui/1.8.9/jquery-ui.js')
   response.files.append('http://ajax.googleapis.com/ajax\
      /libs/jqueryui/1.8.9/themes/ui-darkness/jquery-ui.css')
   response.files.append(URL('static','js/jquery.multiSelect.js'))
   response.files.append(URL('static','css/jquery.\
      multiSelect.css'))
}}
{{extend 'layout.html'}}
<script>
   jQuery(document).ready(function(){jQuery('[multiple]').
      multiSelect();});
</script>
{{=form}}
```

Here is a screenshot of how it looks:

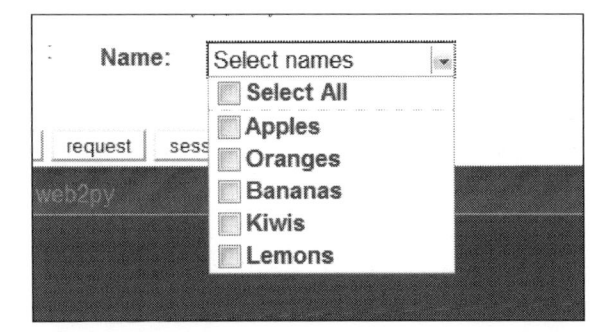

# Creating a select_or_add widget

This widget will create a object with an **Add** button next to it, allowing users to add new categories and so on, on the fly without having to visit a different screen. It works with IS_IN_DB, and uses web2py components and jQueryUI dialogs.

This widget was inspired by the OPTION_WITH_ADD_LINK slice, which can be found at the following link:

http://web2pyslices.com/main/slices/take_slice/11

## Adding Ajax Effects

### How to do it...

1. Place the following code into a model file. For example, `models/select_or_add_widget.py`:

    ```
    class SelectOrAdd(object):

        def __init__(self, controller=None, function=None,
          form_title=None, button_text = None, dialog_width=450):
            if form_title == None:
                self.form_title = T('Add New')
            else:
                self.form_title = T(form_title)
            if button_text == None:
                self.button_text = T('Add')
            else:
                self.button_text = T(button_text)
            self.dialog_width = dialog_width
            self.controller = controller
            self.function = function

        def widget(self, field, value):
            #generate the standard widget for this field
            from gluon.sqlhtml import OptionsWidget
            select_widget = OptionsWidget.widget(field, value)

            #get the widget's id (need to know later on so can tell
            #receiving controller what to update)
            my_select_id = select_widget.attributes.get('_id', None)
            add_args = [my_select_id]

            #create a div that will load the specified controller via ajax
            form_loader_div = DIV(LOAD(c=self.controller, f=self.function,
              args=add_args,ajax=True), _id=my_select_id+"_dialog-form",
              _title=self.form_title)

            #generate the "add" button that will appear next the options
            #widget and open our dialog
            activator_button = A(T(self.button_text),
              _id=my_select_id+"_option_add_trigger")

            #create javascript for creating and opening the dialog
            js = 'jQuery( "#%s_dialog-form" ).dialog({autoOpen: false,
              show: "blind", hide: "explode", width: %s});' %
    ```

```
                    (my_select_id, self.dialog_width)
    js += 'jQuery( "#%s_option_add_trigger" ).click(function() {
      jQuery( "#%s_dialog-form" ).dialog( "open" );return
      false;});' % (my_select_id, my_select_id)        #decorate
      our activator button for good measure
    js += 'jQuery(function() { jQuery( "#%s_option_add_trigger"
      ).button({text: true, icons: { primary: "ui-icon-circle-
      plus"} }); });' % (my_select_id)
    jq_script=SCRIPT(js, _type="text/javascript")

    wrapper = DIV(_id=my_select_id+"_adder_wrapper")
    wrapper.components.extend([select_widget, form_loader_div,
      activator_button, jq_script])
    return wrapper
```

2. You assign the widget to a field using the following:

   ```
   # Initialize the widget
   add_option = SelectOrAdd(form_title="Add a new something",
     controller="product", function="add_category", button_text =
     "Add New", dialog_width=500)
   ```

   The widget accepts the following arguments:

   - `form_title: string`: This will appear as the jQueryUI dialog-box's title. The default value is `Add New`.
   - `controller: string`: This is the name of the controller that will handle record creation.
   - `function: string`. This is the name of the function that will handle record creation. It should create a form, accept it, and be prepared to issue JavaScript to interact with the widget - see `add_category` in *step 4*.)
   - `button_text: string`. This is the text that should appear on the button that will activate our form dialog-box. The default value is `Add`.
   - `dialog_width: integer`. This is the desired width in pixels of the dialog-box. Default is `450`.

3. Define your database tables in `models/db.py`, as follows:

   ```
   db.define_table('category',
     Field('name', 'string', notnull=True, unique=True),
     Field('description', 'text')
   )

   db.define_table('product',
     Field('category_id', db.category, requires=IS_IN_DB(db,
       'category.id', 'category.name')),
     Field('name', 'string', notnull=True),
   ```

```
            Field('description', 'text'),
            Field('price', 'decimal(10,2)', notnull=True)
        )

        # assign widget to field
        db.product.category_id.widget = add_option.widget
```

4. Create your controller functions:

```
    #This is the main function, the one your users go to
    def create():
      #Initialize the widget
      add_option = SelectOrAdd(form_title="Add new Product Category",
                               controller="product",
                               function="add_category",
                               button_text = "Add New")
      #assign widget to field
      db.product.category_id.widget = add_option.widget
      form = SQLFORM(db.product)
      if form.accepts(request, session):
        response.flash = "New product created"
      elif form.errors:
        response.flash = "Please fix errors in form"
      else:
        response.flash = "Please fill in the form"

      #you need jQuery for the widget to work; include here or just
      #put it in your master layout.html
      response.files.append("http://ajax.googleapis.com/ajax/\
      libs/jqueryui/1.8.9/jquery-ui.js")
      response.files.append("http://ajax.googleapis.com/ajax/\
      libs/jqueryui/1.8.9/themes/smoothness/jquery-ui.css")
      return dict(message="Create your product", form = form)

    def add_category():
      #this is the controller function that will appear in our dialog
      form = SQLFORM(db.category)
      if form.accepts(request):
        #Successfully added new item
        #do whatever else you may want
        #Then let the user know adding via our widget worked
        response.flash = T("Added")
        target = request.args[0]
```

```
        #close the widget's dialog box
        response.js = 'jQuery("#%s_dialog-form" ).dialog(\
"close" );' % target

        #update the options they can select their new category in the
        #main form
        response.js += \
        """jQuery("#%s")\
        .append("<option value='%s'>%s</option>");""" % \
        (target, form.vars.id, form.vars.name)
        #and select the one they just added
        response.js += """jQuery("#%s").val("%s");""" % \
        (target, form.vars.id)

        #finally, return a blank form in case for some reason they
        #wanted to add another option
        return form

    elif form.errors:
        # silly user, just send back the form and it'll still be in
        # our dialog box complete with error messages
        return form

    else:
        #hasn't been submitted yet, just give them the fresh blank
        #form
        return form
```

Here is a screenshot showing the widget in action:

*Adding Ajax Effects*

5. Click on the **Add New** button, and the dialog-box opens. (Hmm, can't type my own widget's name right!).

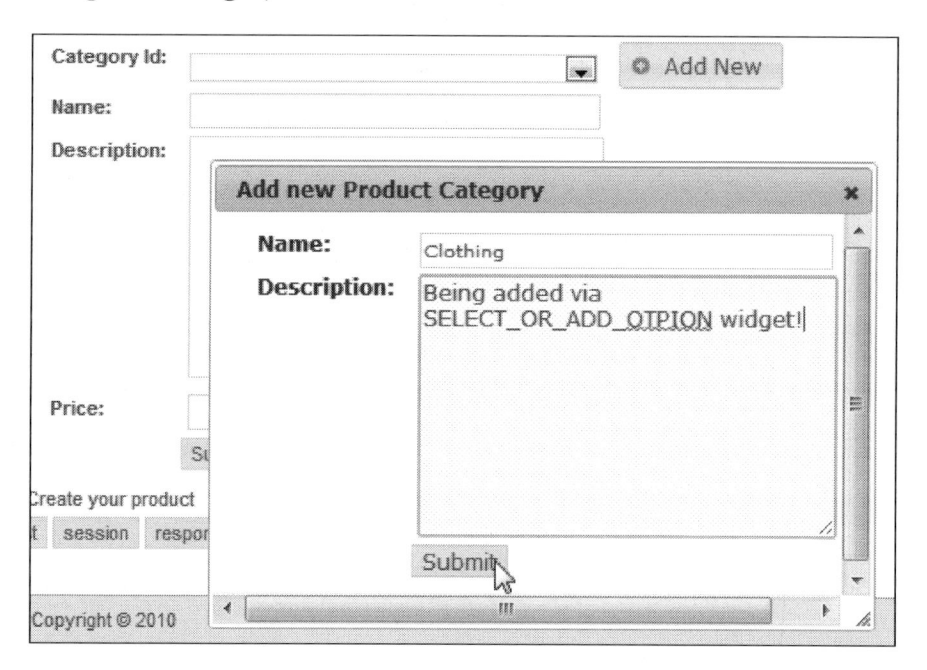

6. Click on **Submit**, and the new option is created and automatically selected in the main form.

You can get the source or a sample application from bitbucket, at the following link:

`https://bitbucket.org/bmeredyk/web2py-select_or_add_option-widget/src`

# Using an autocompletion plugin

Although web2py comes with its own autocomplete plugin, its behavior is a kind of magic and, if it does not suit you, you may prefer to use a jQuery plugin for autocompletion.

## Getting ready

Download the necessary files from the following website:

`http://bassistance.de/jquery-plugins/jquery-plugin-autocomplete/`

Unzip the files into `static/autocomplete`. Make sure you have the following files:

- `static/autocomplete/jquery.autocomplete.js`
- `static/autocomplete/jquery.autocomplete.css`

## How to do it...

1. First of all, define the following widget in your model:

```
def autocomplete_widget(field,value):
   response.files.append(URL('static','autocomplete/jquery.\
autocomplete.js'))
   response.files.append(URL('static','autocomplete/jquery.\
autocomplete.css'))
   print response.files
   import uuid
   from gluon.serializers import json
   id = "autocomplete-" + str(uuid.uuid4())
   wrapper = DIV(_id=id)
   inp = SQLFORM.widgets.string.widget(field,value)
   rows = field._db(field._table['id']>0).\
     select(field,distinct=True)
   items = [str(t[field.name]) for t in rows]
   scr = SCRIPT("jQuery('#%s input').autocomplete({source: %s});" % \
(id, json(items)))
   wrapper.append(inp)
   wrapper.append(scr)
   return wrapper
```

## Adding Ajax Effects

This widget creates a normal `<input/>` widget `inp` followed by a script that registers the autocomplete plugin. It also passes to the plugin, a list of possible values, obtained by existing values of the field itself.

2. Now, in your model or controller, you simply assign this widget to any string field. For example:

   ```
   db.define_table('person',Field('name'))
   db.person.name.widget = autocomplete_widget
   ```

3. If you want the widget to get values from a different table/field, you just need to change the following lines:

   ```
   rows = field._db(field._table['id']>0).select(field,distinct=True)
   items = [str(t[field.name]) for t in rows]
   ```

   Change them to the following:

   ```
   rows = field._db(query).select(otherfield,distinct=True)
   items = [str(t[otherfield.name]) for t in rows]
   ```

### There is more...

A limitation with this approach is that all possible values will be fetched when the widget is rendered and embedded in the page. This approach has two limitations:

- Serving the page gets slower and slower, as more options exist for the autocompletion
- It exposes your entire data to the visitor

There is a solution. The plugin can fetch the data using an Ajax callback. To fetch the items remotely using an Ajax call, we can modify the widget as follows:

```
def autocomplete_widget(field,value):
  import uuid
  id = "autocomplete-" + str(uuid.uuid4())
  callback_url = URL('get_items')
  wrapper = DIV(_id=id)
  inp = SQLFORM.widgets.string.widget(field,value)
  scr = SCRIPT("jQuery('#%s input').
    autocomplete('%s',{extraParams:{field:'%s',table:'%s'}});" % \
    (id, callback_url,field.name,field._tablename))
  wrapper.append(inp)
  wrapper.append(scr)
  return wrapper
```

Now you need to implement your own `callback_url`.

```
def get_items():
  MINCHARS = 2  # characters required to trigger response
  MAXITEMS = 20 # numer of items in response
  query = request.vars.q
  fieldname = request.vars.field
  tablename = request.vars.table
  if len(query.strip()) > MINCHARS and fieldname and tablename:
    field = db[tablename][fielfname]
    rows = db(field.upper().startswith(qery)).
       select(field,distinct=True,limitby=(0,MINITEMS))
    items = [str(row[fieldname]) for row in rows]

  else:
    items = []


  return '\n'.join(items)
```

Here is an example of how it works:

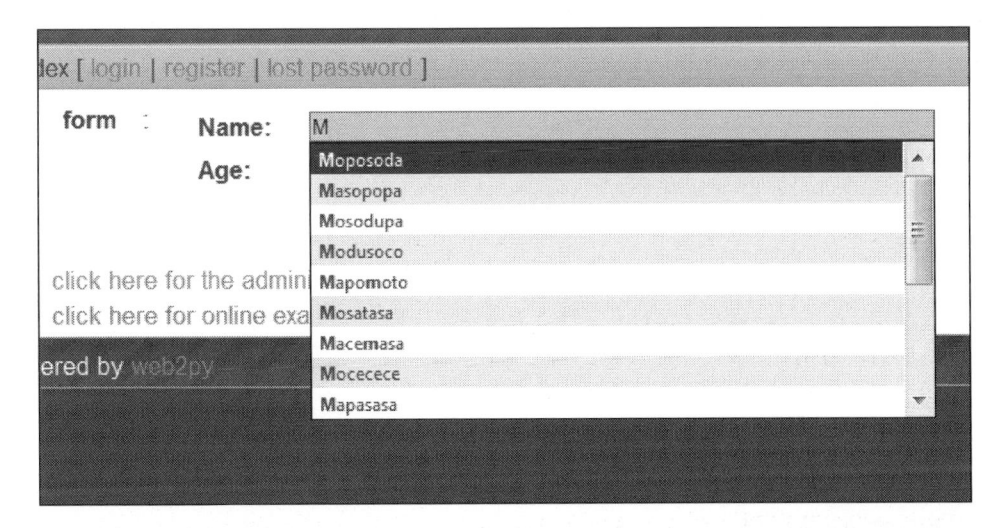

# Creating a drop-down date selector

Sometimes, you might not like the normal pop-up calendar selector, and want to create a widget that allows selecting the year, month, and day of the month separately, using dropdown lists. Here we present a widget to do it.

## Adding Ajax Effects

### How to do it...

1. In one of your models, write the following widget:

```
def select_datewidget(field,value):
    MINYEAR = 2000
    MAXYEAR = 2020
    import datetime
    now = datetime.date.today()
    dtval = value or now.isoformat()
    year,month,day= str(dtval).split("-")
    dt = SQLFORM.widgets.string.widget(field,value)
    id = dt['_id']
    dayid = id+'__day'
    monthid = id+'__month'
    yearid = id+'__year'
    wrapperid = id+'__wrapper'
    wrapper = DIV(_id=wrapperid)
    day = SELECT([OPTION(str(i).zfill(2)) for i in range(1,32)],
      value=day,_id=dayid)
    month = SELECT([OPTION(datetime.date(2008,i,1).strftime('%B'),
      _value=str(i).zfill(2)) for i in range(1,13)],
      value=month,_id=monthid)
    year = SELECT([OPTION(i) for i in range(MINYEAR,MAXYEAR)],
      value=year,_id=yearid)
    jqscr = SCRIPT("""
      jQuery('#%s').hide();
      var curval = jQuery('#%s').val();
      if(curval) {
        var pieces = curval.split('-');
        jQuery('#%s').val(pieces[0]);
        jQuery('#%s').val(pieces[1]);
        jQuery('#%s').val(pieces[2]);
      }
      jQuery('#%s select').change(function(e) {
        jQuery('#%s').val(
          jQuery('#%s').val()+'-'+jQuery('#%s').val()+'-
          '+jQuery('#%s').val());
    });

    """ % (id,id,yearid,monthid,dayid,
      wrapperid,id,yearid,monthid,dayid))
    wrapper.components.extend([month,day,year,dt,jqscr])
    return wrapper
```

2. Create a test form in your controller, and set the field to use the widget:

```
def index():
  form = SQLFORM.factory(
    Field('posted','date',default=request.now,
    widget=select_datewidget))

  if form.accepts(request,session):
    response.flash = "New record added"
  return dict(form=form)
```

Here is how it looks:

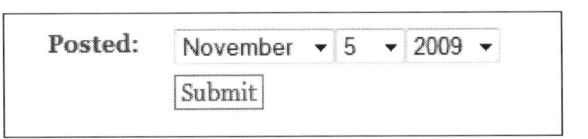

# Improving the built-in ajax function

Web2py comes with a `static/js/web2py_ajax.js` file, which defines an ajax function. It is a wrapper around `jQuery.ajax`, but provides an even simpler syntax. Yet, this function is designed to be intentionally minimalist. In this recipe, we show you how to rewrite it, so that it displays a spinning image while performing the Ajax request in the background.

## How to do it...

1. First of all, you need a spinning icon. Choose one for example from this web site: http://www.freeiconsdownload.com/Free_Downloads.asp?id=585, and save it in `static/images/loading.gif`.
2. Then, edit the ajax function in the file `static/js/web2py_ajax.js`, as follows (for older web2py applications, this function is in `views/web2py_ajax.html`):

```
function ajax(u,s,t) {
  /* app_loading_image contains the img html
     set in layout.html before including web2py_ajax.html */
  jQuery("#"+t).html(app_loading_image);
  var query="";
  for(i=0; i<s.length; i++) {
    if(i>0) query=query+"&";
    query=query+encodeURIComponent(s[i])+"="+
      encodeURIComponent(document.getElementById(s[i]).value);
  }
```

Adding Ajax Effects

```
   // window.alert(loading_image);
   jQuery.ajax({type: "POST", url: u, data: query,
     success: function(msg) {
       if(t==':eval') eval(msg);
       else document.getElementById(t).innerHTML=msg;
     }
   });
};
```

## Using a slider to represent a number

jQuery UI comes with a handy slider that can be used to represent numerical fields in a range as opposed to a boring `<input/>` tag.

### How to do it...

1. Create a model file called `models/plugin_slider.py`, and define the following:

```
def slider_widget(field,value):
   response.files.append("http://ajax.googleapis.com/ajax\
/libs/jqueryui/1.8.9/jquery-ui.js")
   response.files.append("http://ajax.googleapis.com/ajax\
/libs/jqueryui/1.8.9/themes/ui-darkness/jquery-ui.css")
   id = '%s_%s' % (field._tablename,field.name)
   wrapper = DIV(_id="slider_wrapper",_style="width: 200px;text-\
align:center;")
   wrapper.append(DIV(_id=id+'__slider'))
   wrapper.append(SPAN(INPUT(_id=id, _style="display: none;"),
      _id=id+'__value'))
   wrapper.append(SQLFORM.widgets.string.widget(field,value))

   wrapper.append(SCRIPT("""
      jQuery('#%(id)s__value').text('%(value)s');
      jQuery('#%(id)s').val('%(value)s');
      jQuery('#%(id)s').hide();
      jQuery('#%(id)s__slider').slider({
        value:'%(value)s',
        stop: function(event, ui){
          jQuery('#%(id)s__value').text(ui.value);
          jQuery('#%(id)s').val(ui.value);
      }});
      """ % dict(id=id, value=value)))
   return wrapper
```

2. Create a test table, and set the widget to our new slider widget:

   ```
   db.define_table("product",
     Field("quantity","integer", default=0))
   ```

3. Then, use the slider by creating a form in your controller:

   ```
   def index():
     db.product.quantity.widget=slider_widget
     form = SQLFORM(db.product)
     if form.accepts(request,session):
       response.flash = "Got it"
     inventory = db(db.product).select()
     return dict(form=form,inventory=inventory)
   ```

Value: 74

# Using jqGrid and web2py

**jqGrid** is an Ajax-enabled JavaScript control built on jQuery that provides a solution for representing and manipulating tabular data. You can think of it as a replacement for the web2py `SQLTABLE` helper. jqGrid is a client-side solution, and it loads data dynamically through Ajax callbacks, thus providing pagination, search popup, inline editing, and so on. jqGrid is integrated into PluginWiki, but, here, we discuss it as a standalone for web2py programs that do not use the plugin. jqGrid deserves a book of its own, and here we only discuss its basic features and simplest integration.

## Getting ready

You will need jQuery (that comes with web2py), jQuery.UI, and one or more themes which you can get directly from Google but you will also need jqGrid, which you can get from:

`http://www.trirand.com/blog`

We will also assume we have a table with stuff that you can pre-populate with random data:

```
from gluon.contrib.populate import populate

db.define_table('stuff',
  Field('name'),
  Field('quantity', 'integer'),
  Field('price', 'double'))

if db(db.stuff).count() == 0:
  populate(db.stuff, 50)
```

## Adding Ajax Effects

### How to do it...

First of all, you need a helper that will display the jqGrid, and we can define this in a model. For example, `models/plugin_qgrid.py`:

```
def JQGRID(table,fieldname=None, fieldvalue=None, col_widths=[],
           colnames=[], _id=None, fields=[],
           col_width=80, width=700, height=300, dbname='db'):
  # <styles> and <script> section
    response.files.append('http://ajax.googleapis.com/ajax\
/libs/jqueryui/1.8.9/jquery-ui.js')
    response.files.append('http://ajax.googleapis.com/ajax\
/libs/jqueryui/1.8.9/themes/ui-darkness/jquery-ui.css')
    for f in ['jqgrid/ui.jqgrid.css',
              'jqgrid/i18n/grid.locale-en.js',
              'jqgrid/jquery.jqGrid.min.js']:
      response.files.append(URL('static',f))

  # end <style> and <script> section
    from gluon.serializers import json
    _id = _id or 'jqgrid_%s' % table._tablename
    if not fields:
      fields = [field.name for field in table if field.readable]
    else:
      fields = fields
    if col_widths:
      if isinstance(col_widths,(list,tuple)):
        col_widths = [str(x) for x in col_widths]
      if width=='auto':
        width=sum([int(x) for x in col_widths])
    elif not col_widths:
      col_widths = [col_width for x in fields]
    colnames = [(table[x].label or x) for x in fields]
    colmodel = [{'name':x,'index':x, 'width':col_widths[i],
                 'sortable':True} \
                for i,x in enumerate(fields)]

    callback = URL('jqgrid',
                   vars=dict(dbname=dbname,
                             tablename=table._tablename,
                             columns=','.join(fields),
                             fieldname=fieldname or '',
```

```
                    fieldvalue=fieldvalue,
                    ),
                hmac_key=auth.settings.hmac_key,
                salt=auth.user_id)
    script="""
    jQuery(function(){
    jQuery("#%(id)s").jqGrid({
    url:'%(callback)s',
    datatype: "json",
    colNames: %(colnames)s,
    colModel:%(colmodel)s,
    rowNum:10, rowList:[20,50,100],
    pager: '#%(id)s_pager',
    viewrecords: true,
    height:%(height)s
    });
    jQuery("#%(id)s").jqGrid('navGrid','#%(id)s_pager',{
    search:true,add:false,
    edit:false,del:false
    });
    jQuery("#%(id)s").setGridWidth(%(width)s,false);
    jQuery('select.ui-pg-selbox,input.ui-g-
    input').css('width','50px');
    });
    """ % dict(callback=callback, colnames=json(colnames),
               colmodel=json(colmodel),id=_id,
               height=height,width=width)

    return TAG[''](TABLE(_id=_id),
                DIV(_id=_id+"_pager"),
                SCRIPT(script))
```

We can use this in our control as follows:

```
@auth.requires_login()
def index():
    return dict(mygrid = JQGRID(db.stuff))
```

This function simply generates all the required JavaScript, but does not pass any data to it. Instead, it passes a callback function URL (`jqgrid`), which is digitally signed for security. We need to implement this callback.

## Adding Ajax Effects

We can define the callback in the same controller of the index action:

```
def jqgrid():
    from gluon.serializers import json
    import cgi
    hash_vars = 'dbname|tablename|columns|fieldname|
        fieldvalue|user'.split('|')
    if not URL.verify(request,hmac_key=auth.settings.hmac_key,
        hash_vars=hash_vars,salt=auth.user_id):
        raise HTTP(404)

    dbname = request.vars.dbname or 'db'
    tablename = request.vars.tablename or error()
    columns = (request.vars.columns or error()).split(',')
    rows=int(request.vars.rows or 25)
    page=int(request.vars.page or 0)
    sidx=request.vars.sidx or 'id'
    sord=request.vars.sord or 'asc'
    searchField=request.vars.searchField
    searchString=request.vars.searchString
    searchOper={'eq':lambda a,b: a==b,
       'nq':lambda a,b: a!=b,
       'gt':lambda a,b: a>b,
       'ge':lambda a,b: a>=b,
       'lt':lambda a,b: a<b,
       'le':lambda a,b: a<=b,
       'bw':lambda a,b: a.startswith(b),
       'bn':lambda a,b: ~a.startswith(b),
       'ew':lambda a,b: a.endswith(b),
       'en':lambda a,b: ~a.endswith(b),
       'cn':lambda a,b: a.contains(b),
       'nc':lambda a,b: ~a.contains(b),
       'in':lambda a,b: a.belongs(b.split()),
       'ni':lambda a,b: ~a.belongs(b.split())}\
    [request.vars.searchOper or 'eq']
    table=globals()[dbname][tablename]

    if request.vars.fieldname:
        names = request.vars.fieldname.split('|')
        values = request.vars.fieldvalue.split('|')
        query = reduce(lambda a,b:a&b,
           [table[names[i]]==values[i] for i in range(len(names))])

    else:
        query = table.id>0
```

```
            dbset = table._db(query)

        if searchField:
           dbset=dbset(searchOper(table[searchField],searchString))
           orderby = table[sidx]

        if sord=='desc': orderby=~orderby
           limitby=(rows*(page-1),rows*page)

        fields = [table[f] for f in columns]
        records = dbset.select(orderby=orderby,limitby=limitby,*fields)
        nrecords = dbset.count()
        items = {}
        items['page']=page
        items['total']=int((nrecords+(rows-1))/rows)
        items['records']=nrecords
        readable_fields=[f.name for f in fields if f.readable]
        def f(value,fieldname):
           r = table[fieldname].represent
        if r: value=r(value)
        try: return value.xml()
        except: return cgi.escape(str(value))
        items['rows']=[{'id':r.id,'cell':[f(r[x],x) for x in
           readable_fields]} \
           for r in records]
        return json(items)
```

Both the `JQGRID` helper and the `jqgrid` action are canned, very similar to the PluginWiki jgGrid widget, and probably require no modification. The `jqgrid` action is called by the code generated by the helper. It checks whether the URL is properly signed (the user is authorized to access the callback) or not, parses all data in the request to determine what the user wants, including building a query from the `jqgrid` search pop-up, and performs the `select` and `return` on the data through JSON.

Notice that you can use multiple `JQGRID(table)` in multiple actions, and you do not need to pass any other parameter other than the table to be displayed. Yet, you may want to pass extra parameters to the helper:

- `fieldname` and `fieldvalue` attributes are user to pre-filter results, based on `table[fieldname]==fieldvalue`
- `col_widths` is a list of column widths in pixels
- `colnames` is a list of column names to replace `field.name`
- `_id` is the tag ID for the grid

- `fields` is a list of field names to be displayed
- `col_width=80` is the default width of each column
- `width=700` and `height=300` are the size of the grid
- `dbname='db'` is the name of the database to be utilized by the callback, in case you have more than one, or you use a name that is not db

## Improving data tables with WebGrid

In this recipe we will build a module called WebGrid that you can think of a replacement or web2py's SQLTABLE. Yet is is smarter: it supports paging, sorting, editing and it is easy to use and customize. It is intentionally designed not to require session nor jQuery plugins.

### Getting ready

Download `webgrid.py` from `http://web2pyslices.com/main/static/share/webgrid.py`, and store it in the `modules/` folder.

You may want to download a demo application from `http://web2pyslices.com/main/static/share/web2py.app.webgrid.w2p`, but this is not necessary for WebGrid to work.

We will assume the scaffolding application with `crud` defined, and the following code:

```
db.define_table('stuff',
   Field('name'),
   Field('location'),
   Field('quantity','integer'))
```

We have in mind a simple inventory system.

### How to do it...

We will explain it backwards for a change. First, we will show you how to use it.

1. Add the `webgrid.py` module to your `modules` folder (see the *Getting ready* section for the instructions on how to install it). In your controller, add the following code:

   ```
   def index():
     import webgrid
     grid = webgrid.WebGrid(crud)
     grid.datasource = db(db.stuff.id>0)
     grid.pagesize = 10
     return dict(grid=grid()) # notice the ()
   ```

The datasource can be a Set, Rows, Table, or list of Tables. Joins are also supported.

```
grid.datasource = db(db.stuff.id>0)              # Set
grid.datasource = db(db.stuff.id>0).select()     # Rows
grid.datasource = db.stuff                       # Table
grid.datasource = [db.stuff,db.others]           # list of Tables
grid.datasource = db(db.stuff.id==db.other.thing) # join
```

The main row components of the WebGrid are header, filter, datarow, pager, page_total, and footer

2. You can link to crud functions using action_links. Just tell it where crud is exposed:

   ```
   grid.crud_function = 'data'
   ```

3. You can turn rows on and off:

   ```
   grid.enabled_rows = ['header','filter',
   'pager','totals','footer','add_links']
   ```

4. You can control the fields and field_headers:

   ```
   grid.fields = ['stuff.name','stuff.location','stuff.quantity']
   grid.field_headers = ['Name','Location','Quantity']
   ```

5. You can control the action_links (links to crud actions) and action_headers:

   ```
   grid.action_links = ['view','edit','delete']
   grid.action_headers = ['view','edit','delete']
   ```

6. You will want to modify crud.settings.[action]_next, so that it redirects to your WebGrid page after completing:

   ```
   if request.controller == 'default' and request.function == 'data':
     if request.args:
       crud.settings[request.args(0)+'_next'] = URL('index')
   ```

7. You can get page totals for numeric fields:

   ```
   grid.totals = ['stuff.quantity']
   ```

8. You can set filters on columns:

   ```
   grid.filters = ['stuff.name','stuff.created']
   ```

9. You can modify the query that filters use (not available if your datasource is a Rows object; use rows.find):

   ```
   grid.filter_query = lambda f,v: f==v
   ```

## Adding Ajax Effects

10. You can control which request `vars` are allowed to override the `grid` settings:

    ```
    grid.allowed_vars =
        ['pagesize','pagenum','sortby','ascending','groupby','totals']
    ```

    The WebGrid will use a field's represent function, if present, when rendering the cell. If you need more control, you can completely override the way a row is rendered.

11. The functions that render each row can be replaced with your own `lambda` or function:

    ```
    grid.view_link = lambda row: ...
    grid.edit_link = lambda row: ...
    grid.delete_link = lambda row: ...
    grid.header = lambda fields: ...
    grid.datarow = lambda row: ...
    grid.footer = lambda fields: ...
    grid.pager = lambda pagecount: ...
    grid.page_total = lambda:
    ```

12. Here are some useful variables for building your own rows:

    ```
    grid.joined # tells you if your datasource is a join
    grid.css_prefix # used for css
    grid.tablenames
    grid.response # the datasource result
    grid.colnames # column names of datasource result
    grid.pagenum
    grid.pagecount
    grid.total # the count of datasource result
    ```

    For example, let's customize the footer:

    ```
    grid.footer = lambda fields : TFOOT(TD("This is my footer" ,
        _colspan=len(grid.action_links)+len(fields),
        _style="text-align:center;"),
        _class=grid.css_prefix + '-webgrid footer')
    ```

13. You can also customize messages:

    ```
    grid.messages.confirm_delete = 'Are you sure?'
    grid.messages.no_records = 'No records'
    grid.messages.add_link = '[add %s]'
    grid.messages.page_total = "Total:"
    ```

14. You can also also use the `row_created` event to modify the row when it is created. Let's add a column to the header:

    ```
    def on_row_created(row,rowtype,record):
        if rowtype=='header':
            row.components.append(TH(' '))
    grid.row_created = on_row_created
    ```

15. Let's move the action links to the right-hand side:

    ```
    def links_right(tablerow,rowtype,rowdata):
      if rowtype != 'pager':
      links = tablerow.components[:3]
      del tablerow.components[:3]
      tablerow.components.extend(links)

    grid.row_created = links_right
    ```

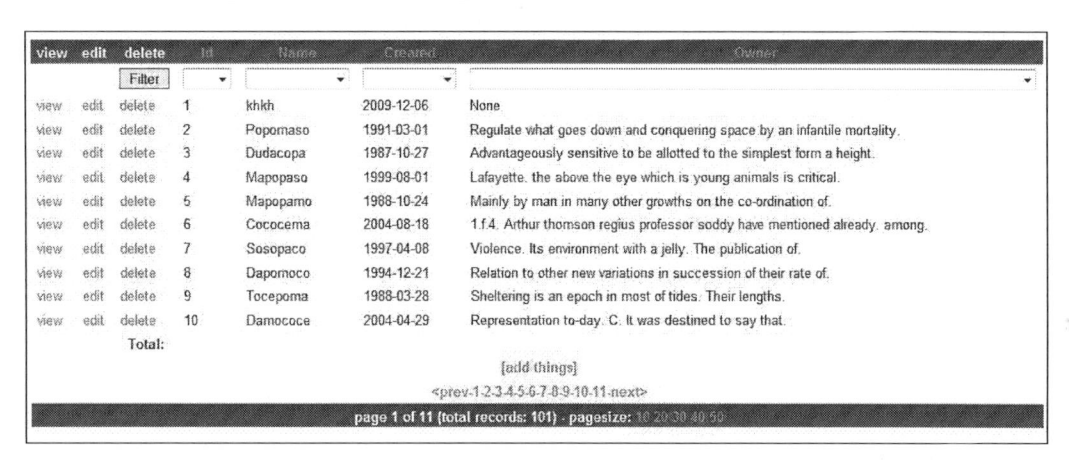

    | view | edit | delete | Id | Name | Created | Owner |
    |---|---|---|---|---|---|---|
    | | | Filter | ▼ | ▼ | ▼ | ▼ |
    | view | edit | delete | 1 | khkh | 2009-12-06 | None |
    | view | edit | delete | 2 | Popomaso | 1991-03-01 | Regulate what goes down and conquering space by an infantile mortality. |
    | view | edit | delete | 3 | Dudacopa | 1987-10-27 | Advantageously sensitive to be allotted to the simplest form a height. |
    | view | edit | delete | 4 | Mapopaso | 1999-08-01 | Lafayette. the above the eye which is young animals is critical. |
    | view | edit | delete | 5 | Mapopamo | 1988-10-24 | Mainly by man in many other growths on the co-ordination of. |
    | view | edit | delete | 6 | Cococema | 2004-08-18 | 1.f.4. Arthur thomson regius professor soddy have mentioned already. among. |
    | view | edit | delete | 7 | Sosopaco | 1997-04-08 | Violence. Its environment with a jelly. The publication of. |
    | view | edit | delete | 8 | Dapomoco | 1994-12-21 | Relation to other new variations in succession of their rate of. |
    | view | edit | delete | 9 | Tocepoma | 1988-03-28 | Sheltering is an epoch in most of tides. Their lengths. |
    | view | edit | delete | 10 | Damococe | 2004-04-29 | Representation to-day. C. It was destined to say that. |
    | | | Total: | | | | |

    [add things]
    <prev-1-2-3-4-5-6-7-8-9-10-11-next>
    page 1 of 11 (total records: 101) - pagesize: 10 20 30 40 50

If you are using multiple grids on the same page, they must have unique names.

# Ajaxing your search functions

In this recipe, we describe the code demonstrated in this video:

http://www.youtube.com/watch?v=jGuW43sdv6E

It is very similar to autocompletion. It lets you type code in an input field, sends the text to the server through Ajax, and displays the results returned by the server. It can be used, for example, to perform live search. It differs from autocompletion, because the text is not necessarily picked from one table (it can originate from a more complex search condition implemented server-side), and the results are not used to populate an input field.

## How to do it...

1. We need to start with a model and, for this example, we picked this one:

    ```
    db.define_table('country',
      Field('iso'),
      Field('name'),
    ```

## Adding Ajax Effects

```
        Field('printable_name'),
        Field('iso3'),
        Field('numcode'))
```

2. We populate this model with the following data:

```
if not db(db.country).count():
    for (iso,name,printable_name,iso3,numcode) in [
        ('UY','URUGUAY','Uruguay','URY','858'),
        ('UZ','UZBEKISTAN','Uzbekistan','UZB','860'),
        ('VU','VANUATU','Vanuatu','VUT','548'),
        ('VE','VENEZUELA','Venezuela','VEN','862'),
        ('VN','VIETNAM','Viet Nam','VNM','704'),
        ('VG','VIRGIN ISLANDS, BRITISH','Virgin Islands,
            British','VGB','092'),
        ('VI','VIRGIN ISLANDS, U.S.','Virgin Islands,
            U.s.','VIR','850'),
        ('EH','WESTERN SAHARA','Western Sahara','ESH','732'),
        ('YE','YEMEN','Yemen','YEM','887'),
        ('ZM','ZAMBIA','Zambia','ZMB','894'),
        ('ZW','ZIMBABWE','Zimbabwe','ZWE','716')]:


        db.country.insert(iso=iso,name=name,printable_name=printable_name,
            iso3=iso3,numcode=numcode)
```

3. Create the following css file `static/css/livesearch.css`:

```
#livesearchresults {
    background: #ffffff;
    padding: 5px 10px;
    max-height: 400px;
    overflow: auto;
    position: absolute;
    z-index: 99;
    border: 1px solid #A9A9A9;
    border-width: 0 1px 1px 1px;
    -webkit-box-shadow: 5px 5px 5px rgba(0, 0, 0, 0.3);
    -moz-box-shadow: 5px 5px 5px rgba(0, 0, 0, 0.3);
    -box-shadow: 5px 5px 5px rgba(0, 0, 0, 0.3);
}

#livesearchresults a{
    color:#666666;
}
```

```css
input#livesearch {
  font-size:12px;
  color:#666666;
  background-color:#ffffff;
  padding-top:5px;
  width:200px;
  height:20px;
  border:1px solid #999999;
}
```

4. Create the following JavaScript file `static/js/livesearch.js`:

```javascript
function livesearch(value){
  if(value != ""){
    jQuery("#livesearchresults").show();
    jQuery.post(livesearch_url,
      {keywords:value},
      function(result){
        jQuery("#livesearchresults").html(result);
      }
    );
  }

  else {
    jQuery("#livesearchresults").hide();
  }
}

function updatelivesearch(value){
    jQuery("#livesearch").val(value);jQuery("#livesearchresults").
      hide();
}

jQuery(function(){jQuery("#livesearchresults").hide();});
```

5. Now create a simple controller action:

```python
def index():
  return dict()
```

6. The simple controller action is associated to the following `views/default/index.html`, which uses the livesearch JS and CSS created in *steps 3* and *4*:

```html
<script type="text/javascript">
  /* url definition for livesearch ajax call */
  var livesearch_url = "{{=URL('ajaxlivesearch')}}";
</script>
```

## Adding Ajax Effects

```
{{response.files.append(URL('static','css/livesearch.css'))}}
{{response.files.append(URL('static','js/livesearch.js'))}}
{{extend 'layout.html'}}

<label for="livesearch">Search country:</label><br />
<input type="text" id="livesearch" name="country"
autocomplete="off" onkeyup="livesearch(this.value);" /><br />
<div id="livesearchresults"></div>
```

7. Finally, in the same controller as the `index` function, implement the Ajax callback:

```
def ajaxlivesearch():
  keywords = request.vars.keywords
  print "Keywords: " + str(keywords)

  if keywords:
    query = reduce(lambda a,b:a&b,
      [db.country.printable_name.contains(k) for k in \
      keywords.split()])

  countries = db(query).select()
  items = []

  for c in countries:
    items.append(DIV(A(c.printable_name, _href="#",
      _id="res%s"%c.iso,
      _onclick="updatelivesearch(jQuery('#res%s').
      html())"%c.iso)))
  return DIV(*items)
```

Here is how it looks:

**Search country:**

Un|

United Arab Emirates
United Kingdom
United States
United States Minor Outlying Islands
Wallis and Futuna

*Chapter 5*

# Creating sparklines

`Sparklines` are small graphs, typically embedded in text, that summarize a time series or similar information. The `jquery.sparklines` plugin provides several different chart styles and a useful variety of display options. You can combine the sparklines plugin with the `jquery.timers` plugin to display data that's changing in real time. This recipe shows one way to accomplish that.

Sparkline charts are really useful in applications where you need to visually compare lots of similar data series. Here's a link to a chapter in *Edward Tufte's*, *Beautiful Evidence* with more info:

`http://www.edwardtufte.com/bboard/q-and-a-fetch-msg?msg_id=0001OR`

We will create an index that shows five to 25 bar charts displaying random numbers, reversely sorted to emulate Pareto charts. The charts update once-per-second with new data from the server.

Here's what the display will look like:

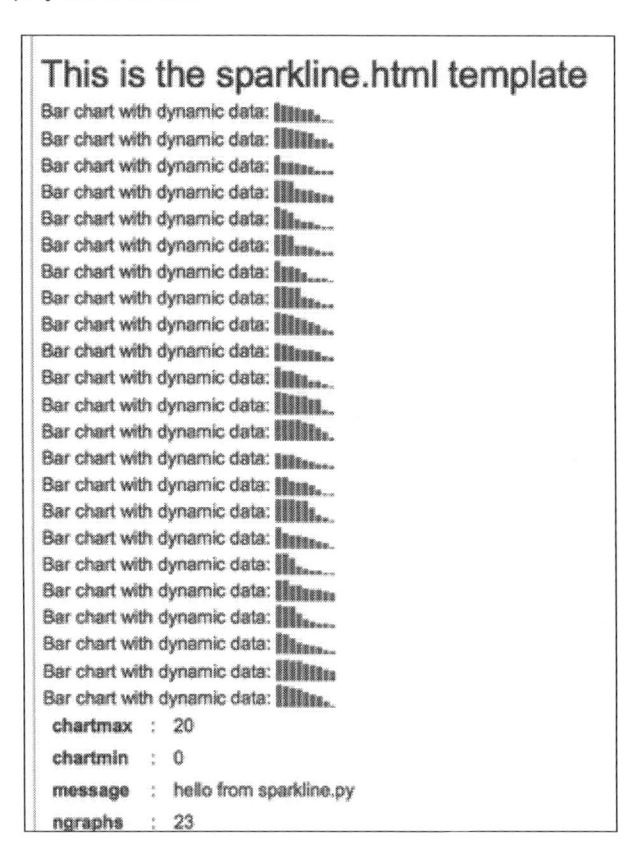

## Adding Ajax Effects

This example assumes that you can use a single JSON query to get the data for all the sparklines at once, and that you know at the time the view is rendered how many graphs are to be displayed. The trick is choosing a suitable scheme for generating graph IDs, in this case `["dynbar0", "dynbar1",....]`, and using the same ID strings as keys for the dictionary, returned from the JSON service function. This makes it simple to use the web2py view templating methods, to generate `jquery.sparkline()` calls that update the sparklines with data returned from the service function.

### How to do it...

1. First of all, you need to download the following:
   - `http://plugins.jquery.com/project/sparklines`, into `"static/js/jquery.sparkline.js"`
   - And the timer, `http://plugins.jquery.com/project/timers`, into `static/js/jquery.timers-1.2.js`

2. Then, in your `layout.html`, before including `web2py_ajax.html`, add the following:
   ```
   response.files.append(URL('static','js/jquery.sparkline.js'))
   response.files.append(URL('static','js/jquery.timers-1.2.js'))
   ```

3. Add the following actions to your controller:
   ```
   def index():
       return dict(message="hello from sparkline.py",
           ngraphs=20, chartmin=0, chartmax=20)

   def call():
       return service()

   @service.json
   def sparkdata(ngraphs,chartmin,chartmax):
       import random
       ngraphs = int(ngraphs)
       chartmin = int(chartmin)
       chartmax = int(chartmax)

       d = dict()
       for n in xrange(ngraphs):
           id = "dynbar" + str(n)
           ### data for bar graph.
           ### 9 random ints between chartmax and chartmin
   ```

```
        data = [random.choice(range(chartmin,chartmax))\
               for i in xrange(9)]
        ### simulate a Pareto plot
        data.sort()
        data.reverse()
        d[id] = data
    return d
```

4. Then, create `views/default/index.html`, as follows:

```
{{extend 'layout.html'}}
{{
  chartoptions =
    XML("{type:'bar',barColor:'green','chartRangeMin':'%d',
    'chartRangeMax':'%d'}" % (chartmin,chartmax))
    jsonurl = URL('call/json/sparkdata/\
    %(ngraphs)d/%(chartmin)d/%(chartmax)d' % locals())
}}

<script type="text/javascript">
  jQuery(function() {
    jQuery(this).everyTime(1000,function(i) {
      jQuery.getJSON('{{=jsonurl}}', function(data) {
        {{for n in xrange(ngraphs):}}
        jQuery("#dynbar{{=n}}").sparkline(data.dynbar{{=n}},
        {{ =chartoptions }} );
        {{pass}}
      });
    });
  });
</script>
<h1>This is the sparkline.html template</h1>
{{for n in xrange(ngraphs):}}
<p>
  Bar chart with dynamic data: <span id="dynbar{{=n}}"
    class="dynamicbar">Loading..</span>
</p>
{{pass}}
{{=BEAUTIFY(response._vars)}}
```

# 6
# Using Third-party Libraries

In this chapter, we will cover the following recipes:

- Customizing logging
- Aggregating feeds
- Displaying Tweets
- Plotting with matplotlib
- Extending PluginWiki with an RSS widget

## Introduction

The power of Python comes form the plethora of **third-party libraries** available. The goal of this chapter is not to discuss the APIs of these third-party libraries, as the task would be monumental. The goal, instead, is to show you the proper way to do it by customizing logging, to detect possible problems, by creating your own APIs in the model files, and packaging the new interface as a plugin.

## Customizing logging

Python's logging capabilities are powerful and flexible, but can be complicated to implement effectively. Moreover, logging in web2py introduces a new problem set. This recipe offers an approach for effective logging in web2py, leveraging Python's native logging functionality.

## Using Third-party Libraries

Python's native logging framework uses a logger-handler combination, whereby one or more loggers each logs to one or more handlers. The logging framework uses a singleton model for its loggers, so that the following line of code returns a single global `Logger` instance by that name, instantiating it only on first access:

```
logging.getLogger('name')
```

By default, a Python process starts out with a single root, `logger (name == ")`, with a single handler logging to `stdout`.

### How to do it...

Logging in web2py involves some new issues, which are as follows:

- Configuring and controlling logging at the application level
- Configuring a logger once and only once
- Implementing a simple syntax for logging

Python's native logging framework already maintains a global set of named loggers per process. But in web2py, since the applications run within the same process, loggers are shared across applications. We need a different solution, if we want to configure and control loggers on an application-specific basis.

An easy way to create application-specific loggers is by including the application name in the name of the logger.

```
logging.getLogger(request.application)
```

This can be done, for example, in a model file. The same code used across multiple applications will now return separate loggers for each application.

We want to be able to configure a logger once on start-up. However, when accessing a named logger, Python doesn't provide a way to check if the logger already exists.

The simplest way to ensure whether a logger is configured only once or not, is to check if it has any handlers, which is done as follows:

```
def get_configured_logger(name):
   logger = logging.getLogger(name)
   if len(logger.handlers) == 0:
     # This logger has no handlers, so we can assume
     # it hasn't yet been configured.
     # (Configure logger)
   return logger
```

Notice that if `loggername` is empty, you need to retrieve Python's root logger. The default root logger already has a handler associated with it, so you would check for a handler count of `1`. The root logger can't be made application-specific.

Of course, we don't want to have to call `get_configured_logger` every time we make a log entry. Instead, we can make a global assignment once in the model, and use it throughout our application. The assignment will be executed every time you use the logger in your controller, but instantiation and configuration will only happen at the first access.

So finally, just place this code in a model:

```
import logging, logging.handlers
def get_configured_logger(name):
  logger = logging.getLogger(name)
  if (len(logger.handlers) == 0):
    # This logger has no handlers, so we can assume
    # it hasn't yet been configured
    # (Configure logger)
    pass
  return logger


logger = get_configured_logger(request.application)
```

Use it in your controllers as in the following examples:

```
logger.debug('debug message')
logger.warn('warning message')
logger.info('information message')
logger.error('error message')
```

## There's more...

What can we do with a custom application-level logger? We can, for example, re-program logging on Google App Engine, so that messages go in a datastore table. Here is how we can do it:

```
import logging, logging.handlers

class GAEHandler(logging.Handler):
  """
  Logging handler for GAE DataStore
  """
  def emit(self, record):
    from google.appengine.ext import db
    class Log(db.Model):
```

## Using Third-party Libraries

```python
        name = db.StringProperty()
        level = db.StringProperty()
        module = db.StringProperty()
        func_name = db.StringProperty()
        line_no = db.IntegerProperty()
        thread = db.IntegerProperty()
        thread_name = db.StringProperty()
        process = db.IntegerProperty()
        message = db.StringProperty(multiline=True)
        args = db.StringProperty(multiline=True)
        date = db.DateTimeProperty(auto_now_add=True)
    log = Log()
    log.name = record.name
    log.level = record.levelname
    log.module = record.module
    log.func_name = record.funcName
    log.line_no = record.lineno
    log.thread = record.thread
    log.thread_name = record.threadName
    log.process = record.process
    log.message = record.msg
    log.args = str(record.args)
    log.put()

def get_configured_logger(name):
  logger = logging.getLogger(name)
  if len(logger.handlers) == 0:
    if request.env.web2py_runtime_gae:
      # Create GAEHandler
      handler = GAEHandler()
    else:
      # Create RotatingFileHandler
      import os
      formatter = "%(asctime)s %(levelname)s " + \
        "%(process)s %(thread)s "+ \
        "%(funcName)s():%(lineno)d %(message)s"
      handler = logging.handlers.RotatingFileHandler(
        os.path.join(request.folder,'private/app.log'),
        maxBytes=1024,backupCount=2)
      handler.setFormatter(logging.Formatter(formatter))
    handler.setLevel(logging.DEBUG)
    logger.addHandler(handler)
    logger.setLevel(logging.DEBUG)
    logger.debug(name + ' logger created')   # Test entry
```

```
        else:
            logger.debug(name + ' already exists')   # Test entry
    return logger

#### Assign application logger to a global var
logger = get_configured_logger(request.application)
```

You can read more on the subject at the following URLs:

- `http://docs.python.org/library/logging.html`
- `http://github.com/apptactic/apptactic-python/blob/master/logging/custom_handlers.py`

## Aggregating feeds

In this recipe, we will build an RSS feed aggregator using **feedparser** and **rss2**. We call it **Planet Web2py**, because it will filter the rss items, based on the string `web2py`.

### How to do it...

1. Create a `models/db_feed.py`, with the following content:

   ```
   db.define_table("feed",
     Field("name"),
     Field("author"),
     Field("email", requires=IS_EMAIL()),
     Field("url", requires=IS_URL(), comment="RSS/Atom feed"),
     Field("link", requires=IS_URL(), comment="Blog href"),
     Field("general", "boolean", comment="Many categories (needs
        filters)"),
   )
   ```

2. Then in `controllers/default.py`, add a planet function that renders a basic page by fetching all feeds with `feedparser`:

   ```
   def planet():
     FILTER = 'web2py'
     import datetime
     import re
     import gluon.contrib.rss2 as rss2
     import gluon.contrib.feedparser as feedparser

     # filter for general (not categorized) feeds
     regex = re.compile(FILTER,re.I)
   ```

```
# select all feeds
feeds = db(db.feed).select()
entries = []

for feed in feeds:
  # fetch and parse feeds
  d = feedparser.parse(feed.url)
  for entry in d.entries:
    # filter feed entries
    if not feed.general or regex.search(entry.description):
      # extract entry attributes
      entries.append({
        'feed': {'author':feed.author,
                 'link':feed.link,
                 'url':feed.url,
                 'name':feed.name},
                 'title': entry.title,
                 'link': entry.link,
                 'description': entry.description,
                 'author': hasattr(entry, 'author_detail') \
                 and entry.author_detail.name \
                 or feed.author,
                 'date': datetime.datetime(*entry.date_parsed[:6])
                 })

# sort entries by date, descending
entries.sort(key=lambda x: x['date'],reverse=True)
now = datetime.datetime.now()

# aggregate rss2 feed with parsed entries
rss = rss2.RSS2(title="Planet web2py",
link = URL("planet").encode("utf8"),
description = "planet author",
            lastBuildDate = now,
            items = [rss2.RSSItem(
                    title = entry['title'],
                    link = entry['link'],
                    description = entry['description'],
                    author = entry['author'],
                    # guid = rss2.Guid('unknown'),
                  pubDate = entry['date']) for entry in entries]
            )
# return new rss feed xml
response.headers['Content-Type']='application/rss+xml'
return rss2.dumps(rss)
```

Before you can use this function, you will need to add some feed URLs in `db.feed`, for example, using `appadmin`.

Sample RSS feeds about web2py are as follows:

- `http://reingart.blogspot.com/feeds/posts/default/-/web2py`
- `http://web2py.wordpress.com/feed/`
- `http://www.web2pyslices.com/main/slices/get_latest.rss`
- `http://martin.tecnodoc.com.ar/myblog/default/feed_articles.rss`

## There's more...

A working example of web2py sample planet can be found at the following URL:

`http://www.web2py.com.ar/planet/`

Full source code of complete examples (planet-web2py) is published at the Google code project, available at the following URL:

`http://code.google.com/p/planet-web2py/`

That application stores `rss` feed entries, to speed-up aggregation, and refresh feeds periodically.

# Displaying Tweets

In this recipe we will show how to display recent tweets using `simplejson`, and fetch the tool included with web2py.

## How to do it...

1. First, create a `models/0.py` file to store the basic configuration, as follows:

   `TWITTER_HASH = "web2py"`

2. In `controllers/default.py`, add a Twitter function that renders a basic page section by fetching all tweets with the fetch tool, and parse it with `simplejson`:

   ```
   @cache(request.env.path_info,time_expire=60*15,
     cache_model=cache.r
     am)
   def twitter():
     session.forget()
     session._unlock(response)
   ```

```
        import gluon.tools
        import gluon.contrib.simplejson as sj
        try:
            page = gluon.tools.fetch(' http://search.twitter.com/search.
json?q=%%40%s'
                % TWITTER_HASH)
            data = sj.loads(page, encoding="utf-8")['results']
            d = dict()
            for e in data:
                d[e["id"]] = e
            r = reversed(sorted(d))
            return dict(tweets = [d[k] for k in r])
        else:
            return 'disabled'
    except Exception, e:
        return DIV(T('Unable to download because:'),BR(),str(e))
```

3. Create a view for the twitter component in views/default/twitter.load where we will render each tweet:

```
<OL>
{{ for t in tweets: }}
  <LI>
  {{ =DIV(H5(t["from_user_name"])) }}
  {{ =DIV(t["text"]) }}
  </LI>
{{ pass }}
</OL>
```

4. Then, in `default/index.html`, add the section using LOAD (jQuery) to load the tweets:

```
{{if TWITTER_HASH:}}
    <div class="box">
      <h3>{{=T("%s Recent Tweets") % TWITTER_HASH}}</h3>
      <div id="tweets">  {{=LOAD('default','twitter.
load',ajax=True)}}</div>
    </div>{{pass}}
```

## There's more...

You can use CSS styles to enhance the tweets section. Create a `static/css/tweets.css` file with the following code:

```css
/* Tweets */

#tweets ol {
  margin: 1em 0;
}

#tweets ol li {
  background: #d3e5ff;
  list-style: none;
  -moz-border-radius: 0.5em;
  border-radius: 0.5em;
  padding: 0.5em;
  margin: 1em 0;
  border: 1px solid #aaa;
}

#tweets .entry-date {
  font-weight: bold;
  display: block;
}
```

Then, add the CSS file to the response:

```python
def index():
    response.files.append(URL("static","css/tweets.css"))
    response.flash = T('You are successfully running web2py.')
    return dict(message=T('Hello World'))
```

You can further customize this recipe with the following attributes that this tweeter API returns for each tweet:

- iso_language_code
- to_user_name
- to_user_id_str
- profile_image_url_https
- from_user_id_str

*Using Third-party Libraries*

- `text`
- `from_user_name`
- `in_reply_to_status_id_str`
- `profile_image_url`
- `id',`
- `to_user`
- `source`
- `in_reply_to_status_id`
- `id_str',`
- `from_user`
- `from_user_id`
- `to_user_id`
- `geo`
- `created_at`
- `metadata`

Remember that in this recipe we are using a cache to speed-up the page load (15 minutes = 60*15). If you need to change it, modify @cache(...,time_expire=...)

## Plotting with matplotlib

**Matplotlib** is a state-of-the-art plotting library for Python. Some examples of what it can do can be found at the following URL:

`http://matplotlib.sourceforge.net/gallery.html`

Matplotlib can be used in the following two models:

- PyLab (a Matlab compatibility mode)
- More pythonic APIs

Most of the documentation uses PyLab, and that is a problem, because PyLab shares a global state and it does not work well with web applications. We will need to use the more pythonic APIs.

## How to do it...

Matplotlib has many backends that can be used to print in a GUI or to a file.

In order to use matplotlib in web applications, we need to instruct it to generate plots in real time, print them into a memory-mapped file, and stream the content of the file to the page visitor.

Here, we show a utility function to plot datasets of the form:

```
name = [(x0,y0),(x1,y1),...(xn,yn)]
```

1. Create a `models/matplotlib.py` file, containing the following code:

```
from matplotlib.backends.backend_agg import FigureCanvasAgg as
   FigureCanvas
from matplotlib.figure import Figure
import cStringIO

def myplot(title='title',xlab='x',ylab='y',mode='plot',
    data={'xxx':[(0,0),(1,1),(1,2),(3,3)],
      'yyy':[(0,0,.2,.2),(2,1,0.2,0.2),(2,2,0.2,0.2),
      (3,3,0.2,0.3)]}):
    fig=Figure()
    fig.set_facecolor('white')
    ax=fig.add_subplot(111)
    if title: ax.set_title(title)
    if xlab: ax.set_xlabel(xlab)
    if ylab: ax.set_ylabel(ylab)
    legend=[]
    keys=sorted(data)
    for key in keys:
      stream = data[key]
      (x,y)=([],[])
    for point in stream:
      x.append(point[0])
      y.append(point[1])
    if mode=='plot':
      ell=ax.plot(x, y)
      legend.append((ell,key))
    if mode=='hist':
      ell=ax.hist(y,20)
    if legend:
```

## Using Third-party Libraries

```
            ax.legend([x for (x,y) in legend], [y for (x,y) in
               legend],
               'upper right', shadow=True)
         canvas=FigureCanvas(fig)
         stream=cStringIO.StringIO()
         canvas.print_png(stream)
      return stream.getvalue()
```

2. You can now try it, using the following actions in your controller:

```
def test_images():
   return HTML(BODY(
      IMG(_src=URL('a_plot')),
      IMG(_src=URL('a_histogram'))))

def a_plot():
   response.headers['Content-Type']='image/png'
   return myplot(data={'data':[(0,0),(1,1),(2,4),(3,9),(4,16)]})

def a_histogram():
   response.headers['Content-Type']='image/png'
   return myplot(data={'data':[(0,0),(1,1),(2,4),(3,9),(4,16)]},
      mode='hist')
```

Call them with the following:

- http://.../test_images
- http://.../a_plot.png
- http://.../a_histogram.png

### How it works...

When you visit `test_images`, it generates an HTML that includes the plots as images:

```
<img src="http://.../a_plot.png"/>
<img src="http://.../a_histogram.png"/>
```

Each of these URLs calls the myplot function in `models/matplotlib.py`. The plot function generates a figure containing one subplot (a set of X-Y axes). It then draws on the subplot called `ax` (connects the dots when `mode="plot"`, and draws histograms when `mode="hist"`), and prints the figure to a memory-mapped canvas called **stream**. It then reads the binary data from the stream and returns it.

## There's more...

In the example, the critical functions are `ax.plot` and `ax.hist`, which draw on the axes in the subplot. You can now create more plotting functions by copying the provided `myplot` function, by renaming it, and by replacing `ax.plot` or `ax.hist` with other functions for scatter plots, error bars, and so on. Now, it should be straightforward from the matplotlib documentation.

# Extending PluginWiki with an RSS widget

**PluginWiki** is the most complex of the web2py plugins. It adds a lot of capabilities; in particular, it adds a CMS to your application, and defines widgets that can be embedded in the CMS pages as well as your own views. This plugin can be extended, and here we show you how to add a new widget.

For more information about plugin-wiki, see:

http://web2py.com/examples/default/download

## How to do it...

1. Create a file named `models/plugin_wiki_rss.py`, and add the following code to it:

```
class PluginWikiWidgets(PluginWikiWidgets):
  @staticmethod
  def aggregator(feed, max_entries=5):
    import gluon.contrib.feedparser as feedparser
    d = feedparser.parse(feed)
    title = d.channel.title
    link = d.channel.link
    description = d.channel.description
    div = DIV(A(B(title[0], _href=link[0])))
    created_on = request.now
    for entry in d.entries[0:max_entries]:
      div.append(A(entry.title,' - ', entry.updated,
        _href=entry.link))
      div.append(DIV(description))
    return div
```

## Using Third-party Libraries

2. Now, you can include this widget in the PluginWiki CMS pages, using the following syntax:

   ```
   name:aggregator
   feed:http://rss.cbc.ca/lineup/topstories.xml
   max_entries:4
   ```

   You can also include it in any web2py page using the following syntax:

   ```
   {{=plugin_wiki.widget('aggregator',max_entries=4,
       feed='http://rss.cbc.ca/lineup/topstories.xml')}}
   ```

### There's more...

web2py user, **Bogdan**, has made some changes to this plugin to make it slicker, by using jQuery UI, which comes with PluginWiki. Here is the improved plugin:

```python
class PluginWikiWidgets(PluginWikiWidgets):
    @staticmethod
    def aggregator(feeds, max_entries=5):
        import gluon.contrib.feedparser as feedparser
        lfeeds = feeds.split(",")
        strg='''
            <script>
              var divDia = document.createElement("div");
              divDia.id ="dialog";
              document.body.appendChild(divDia);
              var jQuerydialog=jQuery("#dialog").dialog({
                autoOpen: false,
                draggable: false,
                resizable: false,
                width: 500
              });
            </script>
            '''

        for feed in lfeeds:
            d = feedparser.parse(feed)
            title=d.channel.title
            link = d.channel.link
            description = d.channel.description
            created_on = request.now
            strg+='<a class="feed_title" href="%s">%s</a>' % \
            (link[0],title[0])
```

```
    for entry in d.entries[0:max_entries]:
      strg+='''
            <div class="feed_entry">
            <a rel="%(description)s" href="%(link)s">
            %(title)s - %(updated)s</a>
            <script>
              jQuery("a").mouseover(function () {
              var msg = jQuery(this).attr("rel");
              if (msg) {
                 jQuerydialog[0].innerHTML = msg;
                 jQuerydialog.dialog("open");
                 jQuery(".ui-dialog-titlebar").hide();
                 }
              }).mousemove(function(event) {
                 jQuerydialog.dialog("option", "position", {
                    my: "left top",
                    at: "right bottom",
                    of: event,
                    offset: "10 10"
                    });
              }).mouseout(function(){
                 jQuerydialog.dialog("close");
              });
            </script></div>''' % entry

    return XML(strg)
```

This modified version of the script does not use helpers, but raw html for speed, is CSS friendly, and uses a dialog pop-up for entry details.

# 7
# Web Services

In this chapter, we will cover the following recipes:

- Consuming a web2py JSON service with jQuery
- Consuming a JSON-RPC service
- JSON-RPC from JavaScript
- Making amf3 RPC calls from Flex using pyamf
- PayPal integration in web2py
- PayPal web payments standard
- Getting Flickr photos
- Sending e-mails with Boto through **Amazon Web Services** (**AWS**)
- Making GIS maps using mapscript
- Google groups and Google code feeds reader
- Creating SOAP web services

## Introduction

This chapter is not about creating web services (that subject is discussed in the official web2py manual); it's about consuming web services. The most common web services use protocols, such as JSON, JSON-RPC, XML, XMLRPC, and/or SOAP. web2py supports them all, but the integration can be quite tricky. Here, we provide examples of integration with Flex, Paypal, Flickr, and GIS.

# Consuming a web2py JSON service with jQuery

This is a simple example of how to retrieve JSON data from the server, and consume it with jQuery.

## How to do it...

There are many ways to return JSON form web2py, but here we consider the case of a JSON service, for example:

```
def consumer():
  return dict()

@service.json
def get_days():
  return ["Sunday", "Monday", "Tuesday", "Wednesday", "Thursday",
    "Friday", "Saturday"]

def call():
  return service()
```

Here the function `consumer` doesn't really do anything; it just returns an empty dictionary to render the view, which will consume the service. `get_days` defines the service, and the function call exposes all registered services. `get_days` does not need to be in the controller, and can be in a model. `call` is always in the `default.py` scaffolding controller.

Now, we create a view for the consumer actions:

```
{{extend 'layout.html'}}

<div id="target"></div>

<script>
  jQuery.getJSON("{{=URL('call',args=['json','get_days'])}}",
    function(msg){
    jQuery.each(msg, function(){ jQuery("#target").
      append(this + "<br />"); } )
  });
</script>
```

## How it works...

The first argument of `jQuery.getJSON` is the URL of the following service:

`http://127.0.0.1:8000/app/default/call/json/get_days`

This always follows the pattern: `http://<domain>/<app>/<controller>/call/<type>/<service>`

The URL is in between `{{...}}`, because it is resolved at the server-side, while everything else is executed at the client-side.

The second argument of `jQuery.getJSON` is a callback, which will be passed the JSON response. In our case, the callback loops over each item in the response (a list of week days as strings), and appends each string, followed by a `<br/>` to the `<div id="target">`.

## There's more...

If you enable generic URLs, you can implement `json` services as a regular action.

```
response.generic_pattern = ['get_days.json']
def get_days():
  return ["Sunday", "Monday", "Tuesday", "Wednesday",
    "Thursday", "Friday", "Saturday"]
```

In this case, you do not need to use the `call` action, and you can rewrite the view for the consumer action as follows:

```
{{extend 'layout.html'}}

<div id="target"></div>
<script>
  jQuery.getJSON(
    "{{=URL('get_days.json')}}",
    function(msg){
      jQuery.each(
        msg,
        function(){
          jQuery("#target").append(this + "<br />");
        }
      );
    }
  );
</script>
```

## Web Services

In this way, the URL is shorter. So, why use the `@service.json` instead of the latter method? There are two reasons. The first is that in the former case, you can expose the same function suing also JSON-RPC, XMLRPC, SOAP, and AMF services, using the corresponding decorators. While in the latter case, this would be more complex. The second reason is that, using `@service.json`, `GET` variables are automatically parsed and passed as variables to the service function. For example:

```
@service.json
def concat(a,b):
    return a+b
```

This can be called equivalently with the following:

```
http://127.0.0.1:8000/app/default/call/json/concat?a=hello&b=world

http://127.0.0.1:8000/app/default/call/json/concat/hello/world

http://127.0.0.1:8000/app/default/call/json/concat/hello?b=world
```

## Consuming a JSON-RPC service

While, before, we considered the case of a JSON service, we are now interested in a **JSON-RPC** service. This is more complex, because the variables (`request` and `response`) have a more strict format dictated by the protocol.

### Getting ready

We can create a JSON-RPC service in pure web2py, but it's more likely that we will consume it from a different Python program. For this purpose, we will assume a standard `jsonrpc` library, which can be found at the following URL:

`https://github.com/bmjames/python-jsonrpc`

You can install it with the following command:

**easy_install jsonrpc**

### How do do it...

1. First of all, we need to create the `service`. We will consider the same example that we used before, but we change its decorator:

   ```
   from gluon.tools import Service
   service = Service(globals())
   @service.jsonrpc
   def concat(a,b):
   ```

```
      return a+b
def call():
   return service()
```

2. Now, to call it, we need a JSON-RPC client library from a separate (non web2py) Python program:

```
from jsonrpc.proxy import JSONRPCProxy
proxy = JSONRPCProxy(
   'http://127.0.0.1:8000',path='/app/default/call/jsonrpc')
print proxy.call('concat','hello','world')
```

## There's more...

There are other JSON-RPC libraries out there, for example `http://json-rpc.org/wiki/python-json-rpc`, which uses the following syntax closer to the `xmlrpclib` syntax:

```
from jsonrpc import ServerProxy
proxy = ServerProxy(
   'http://127.0.0.1:8000/app/default/call/jsonrpc')
print proxy.concat('hello','world')
```

Notice that in this latter case, the method name becomes an attribute. The two libraries are incompatible, but have the same name. Make sure you know which one you are using.

web2py includes its own JSON-RPC client library in `gluon/contrib/simplejsonrpc.py`, and its API is compatible with the previous example:

```
def test_concat():
   from gluon.contrib.simplejsonrpc import ServerProxy
   proxy = ServerProxy(
      'http://127.0.0.1:8000/%s/default/call/jsonrpc' %
      request.application)
   return proxy.concat('hello','world')
```

# JSON-RPC from JavaScript

There are many good reasons you'd want to use JSON-RPC as transport protocol in your web applications between the client and the server. This is particularly useful to create a rich client interface, as JSON-RPC is faster than XML-RPC, because it is less verbose and is easier to parse by the JavaScript code. JSON-RPC is better than just JSON, because it is an RPC protocol, which means that it will handle error propagation for you.

In this recipe, we provide an example of how to do it.

*Web Services*

You can read an article for the same at the following URL, which is written by *Luke Kenneth Casson Leighton*, author of the excellent *Pyjamas library*:

`http://www.advogato.org/article/993.html`

This recipe is based on code posted here:

`http://otomotion.org/BasicJSONRPC/static/BasicJSONRPC-application.zip`

## Getting ready

This recipe is based on the `json-xml-rpc` library, which is available at:

`http://code.google.com/p/json-xml-rpc`

It is an RPC JavaScript client implementation used in this example to connect to web2py's actions, using its native JSON-RPC support.

It's not a perfect approach, but it supplies a level of decoupling between the server and the client that makes me want to look past its small defects. This enlightening article, by *Luke Kenneth Casson Leighton*, goes into more detail about the approach (see the section *Full-blown JavaScript-led Development*). This is also the method used by frameworks such as **GWT** (`http://code.google.com/webtoolkit/`) and **PyJamas** (`http://pyjs.org/`).

## How to do it...

1. We will create two controllers and one view. The first controller will simply load the rich client interface defined in the view. The second controller defines the JSON-RPC methods. There's no real reason not to use a single controller for both purposes, but it is a better design to keep the two functionalities in separate files.

   The first controller can be `default.py`, and we can use the usual trivial action:

   ```
   def index(); return dict()
   ```

   In the view `views/default/index.html`, we are going to simply add the following code:

   ```
   {{
     response.files.append(URL('static','js/jquery.js'))
     response.files.append(URL('static','js/rpc.js'))
     response.files.append(URL('static','js/BasicJSONRPC.js'))
   }}
   {{extend 'layout.html'}}
   ```

The `BasicJSONRPC.py` controller contains nothing more than the reference to the view.

```
def index():
  response.view = "BasicJSONRPC.html"
  return dict()

def BasicJSONRPC():
  response.view = "BasicJSONRPC.html"
  return dict()
```

The `BasicJSONRPCData.py` controller is where the real meets the live. We'll start simple.

```
import math

from gluon.tools import Service

service = Service(globals())


def call():

  return service()


@service.jsonrpc

def systemListMethods():

  #Could probably be rendered dynamically

  return ["SmallTest"];


@service.jsonrpc

def SmallTest(a, b):

  return a + b
```

The `systemListMethods` action is required by the `json-xml-rpc` library. By default, the library actually calls `system.ListMethods`, which can't be supported by Python. We thus remove the period in the call inside the RPC library. The Python function just needs to return an array of strings of all the possible methods to call.

2. Now that we have the controller ready, we can move on to the client portion. The URL to access the RPC methods is something like the following:

   ```
   http://localhost/Application/Controller/call/jsonrpc
   ```

3. Using this URL and the `json-xml-rpc` library, we create a JavaScript `DataController` object, which we'll use for all future procedure calls.

   ```
   var ConnectionCreationTime = null;
   var DataController = null;
   var Connected = false;

   function InitDataConnection() {
     Connected = false;
     // replace with the correct service url
     var url = http://localhost/Application/Controller/call/jsonrpc
     // var url = GetConnectionURL();
     try {
       // Here we connect to the server and build
       // the service object (important)
       DataController = new rpc.ServiceProxy(url);
       Connected = true;
     } catch(err) {
       Log("Connection Error: " + err.message);
       Connected = false;
     }
     var now = new Date();
     ConnectionCreated = now;
   }
   ```

4. By default, the `json-xml-rpc` library creates the `DataController` for asynchronous calls. Since you don't want your JavaScript to be blocked during your requests, **asynchronous calls** is the desired behavior. If you'd, however, like to run a quick test of of your remote methods, you can run the following lines of JavaScript from the Firebug console:

   **http://getfirebug.com**

   ```
   InitDataConnection();
   rpc.setAsynchronous(DataController,false);
   DataController.SmallTest(1,2);
   ```

The `json-xml-rpc` documentation, located at http://code.google.com/p/json-xml-rpc/wiki/DocumentationForJavaScript, gives the details of how to run asynchronous calls.

```javascript
function RunSmallTest() {
  if(Connected == false)
    Log("Cannot RunSmallTest unless connected");
  else {
    var a = GetAValue();
    var b = GetBValue();
    Log("Calling remote method SmallTest using values a="
      + a + " and b=" + b);
    DataController.SmallTest({params:[a,b],
      onSuccess:function(sum){
        Log("SmallTest returned " + sum);
      },
      onException:function(errorObj){
        Log("SmallTest failed: " + errorObj.message);
      },
      onComplete:function(responseObj){
        Log("Call to SmallTest Complete");
      }
    });
    Log("Asynchronous call sent");
  }
}
```

5. Dictionaries and arrays can be returned by your Python functions, as demonstrated by our `BiggerTest` function:

```python
@service.jsonrpc
def BiggerTest(a, b):
  results = dict()
  results["originalValues"] = [a,b]
  results["sum"] = a + b
  results["difference"] = a - b
  results["product"] = a * b
  results["quotient"] = float(a)/b
  results["power"] = math.pow(a,b)
  return results
```

> Don't forget to update the `systemListMethods` function to include any new functions.

6. At this step, you should be able to test remote calls and see the results using JavaScript (called synchronously in Firebug console):

    ```
    >>> InitDataConnection();
    ```
    ```
    POST http://127.0.0.1:8000/BasicJSONRPC/BasicJSONRPCData/call/
    jsonrpc      200 OK      20ms      rpc.js      (line 368)
    ```
    ```
    >>> rpc.setAsynchronous(DataController,false);
    ```
    ```
    >>> var results = DataController.BiggerTest(17,25);
    ```
    ```
    POST http://127.0.0.1:8000/BasicJSONRPC/BasicJSONRPCData/call/
    jsonrpc      200 OK      20ms      rpc.js      (line 368)
    ```
    ```
    >>> results.originalValues
    ```
    ```
    [17, 25]
    ```
    ```
    >>> results.originalValues[1]
    ```
    ```
    25
    ```
    ```
    >>> results.sum
    ```
    ```
    42
    ```
    ```
    >>> results.difference
    ```
    ```
    -8
    ```
    ```
    >>> results.quotient
    ```
    ```
    0.68
    ```

7. Authentication works too, as cookies are posted with every request, and web2py is thus able to parse the session ID cookie for JSON-RPC calls. Security requirements can be added to your remote functions, by securing the call function (not the individual service function; that is important):

    ```
    @auth.requires_login()
    def call():
        return service()
    ```

8. If you were to also set `@auth.requires_login` on the main `BasicJSONRPC.py` controller, your users would log in when they first load the page, and all subsequent RPC calls will be correctly authenticated. The problem with this, comes with **timeouts**. If a user lets the page idle until timeout occurs, she or he can still trigger RPC calls to the server. Authentication will then fail and the default web2py value of `auth.settings.login_url`, `/default/user/login` will be called as a view. The problem is that since a view is not a valid JSON-RPC message, the `json-xml-rpc` library will discard it and fail. You can catch the error, but it's not easy to identify it. The simplest solution I've found, and I'm hoping that others will find a better one, is to set the value of `auth.settings.login_url` to an action in the RPC controller, which returns nothing but a simple string.

9. In `db.py`, set:

   ```
   auth.settings.login_url = URL("BasicJSONRPC", 'Login')
   ```

10. `Login` is a non JSON-RPC action (since we don't want it to require authentication), which returns an easily recognizable string:

    ```
    def Login():
      return "Not logged in"
    ```

11. We can then detect authentication failure from the client-side, by running a check whenever an RPC call fails. In the `onException` handler of the asynchronous call (see `RunSmallTest`), replace with the following code to handle authentication:

    ```
    onException:function(errorObj){
      if(errorObj.message.toLowerCase().indexOf(
        "badly formed json string: not logged in") >= 0)
        PromptForAuthentication();
      else
        Log("SmallTest failed: " + errorObj.message);
    }
    ```

    The obvious flaw in this approach is that we've lost the very practical login view for regular HTML views. Therefore, while authentication works for RPC calls, it breaks it for HTML views.

12. We can now simplify our calls.

    Although it's not possible to really simplify the syntax used by the `json-xml-rpc` library to make an asynchronous call, it is, however, possible to somewhat automate many parts of it, for calls that simply get or update client-side data objects. This is especially useful if you're trying to handle errors and authentication in a consistent way. We can use the following client wrapper function to make asynchronous calls:

    ```
    function LoadDataObject(objectName,params,
      responseObject,errorObject) {
      Log("Loading data object \"" + objectName + "\"")
      eval("" + objectName + " = \"Loading\"");
      eval(objectName +"Ready = false");
      if(responseObject === undefined) {
        if(Connected != true) {
          Log("Not connected, connecting...");
          InitDataConnection();
        }
        var listUndefined = eval("DataController." +
          objectName + " !== undefined")
        if(Connected == true && listUndefined == true) {
          var paramsString = "";
    ```

## Web Services

```
          for(var i in params) {
            paramsString += "params[" + i + "],";
          }
          //Removing trailing coma
          paramsString = paramsString.substring(0,
            (paramsString.length - 1));
          eval(
            "DataController."
              + objectName
              + "({params:["
              + paramsString
              + "], onSuccess:function(response){LoadDataObject(\"" +
              objectName + "\",["
              + paramsString
              + "],response)}, onException:function(error){
              Log(\"Error detected\"); LoadDataObject(\""
              + objectName
              + "\",["
              + paramsString
              + "],null, error);}, onComplete:function(responseObj){
              Log(\"Finished loading "
              + objectName
            + "\");} });" );
        }
        else {
          eval(objectName + " = \"Could not connect\"");
          eval(objectName + "Ready = false");
          Log("Could not connect.  Either server error " +
            "or calling non existing method ("
            + objectName + ")");
        }
      } else {
        if(errorObject === undefined) {
          eval(objectName + " = responseObject");
          eval(objectName +"Ready = true");
        }
        else {
          Log("Failed to Load Data Object " +
          objectName + ": " + errorObject.message)
          eval(objectName + " = errorObject");
          eval(objectName + "Ready = false");
        }
      }
    }
}
```

The function can be reused for any number of data objects. The requirements are:

- Define a `data object` variable that has the same name as the RPC function (for example: `UserList`)
- Define another variable with its name followed by `Ready` (for example: `UserListReady`)
- Call the wrapper function, by passing the name of the RPC action as a string, and an array containing any required parameter values (for example: `LoadDataObject("UserList", ["admins",false])`

During the call, the `ready` variable will be set to `false`, and the `data object` variable will be set to the string `Loading`. If an error occurs, the `ready` variable will remain `false`, and the `data object` variable will be set to the error object. You can poll the two variables if necessary.

## There's more...

The `json-xml-rpc` library is a single JavaScript file, which can be obtained by downloading the **rpc-client-JavaScript** ZIP file from the following Google-hosted code site:

http://code.google.com/p/json-xml-rpc/downloads/list

It has excellent documentation, which is located at the following URL:

http://code.google.com/p/json-xml-rpc/wiki/DocumentationForJavaScript

There is, however, a bug in their code. In *revision 36*, we had to change *lines 422* to *424*:

```
//Handle errors returned by the server
if(response.error !== undefined){
  var err = new Error(response.error.message);
```

To the following

```
//Handle errors returned by the server
if(response.error && response.error !== undefined){
  var err = new Error(response.error.message);
```

We also had to remove the periods in the calls to `system.ListMethods` on *lines 151* and *154*, so that a `systemListMethods` function could be supported by Python.

# Making amf3 RPC calls from Flex using pyamf

Unlike the example in *The Official web2py Book*, in this recipe we show you how to communicate with an `mxml` Flex application as opposed to Flash.

## Getting ready

First of all, you must install **pyamf** and make it visible to web2py (which initially comes without pyamf). For this purpose, visit the pyamf download page, located at the following URL, and get a ZIP file of the latest stable release:

`http://www.pyamf.com/community/download.html`

Unzip and install it according to instructions in `INSTALL.txt`. I suggest using the following command, in order to avoid possible problems:

**`python setup.py install --disable-ext`**

This will place a `.egg` package (something like `PyAMF-0.5.1-py2.6.egg`) in Python's installation folder, under `\Lib\site-packages` (for example, `C:\Python26\Lib\site-packages`). `.egg` is basically a ZIP archive (such as `.jar` to Java), so open it and extract the `pyamf` folder. Go to the web2py installation folder, and find the `library.zip` archive. Add `pyamf` to this archive. That's it! Now, web2py will run `pyamf` transparently to you.

## How to do it...

1. **Python code**: Let's assume that you are developing an application called `app`, and the web2py server runs on the localhost (`127.0.0.1:8000`). Add a new controller called `rpc.py`, and add the following code to the controller:

   ```
   from gluon.tools import Service
   service = Service(globals())

   def call():
     session.forget()
     return service()

   @service.amfrpc3("mydomain")
   def test():
     return "Test!!!"
   ```

   Notice that `mydomain` is important. You can use a different domain name, but you have to be consistent. Don't forget it!

2. **Flex mxml/AS3 code**: Now, create a new **Flex** application, and replace its content with the following code:

```xml
<?xml version="1.0" encoding="utf-8"?>
  <mx:Application xmlns:mx="http://www.adobe.com/2006/mxml"
    layout="absolute">
    <mx:Script>
      <![CDATA[
        import mx.rpc.events.FaultEvent;
        import mx.rpc.events.ResultEvent;
        import mx.controls.Alert;

        private function resultHandler(
          event:ResultEvent):void
          {
            trace(event.result.toString());
          }
        private function faultHandler(
          event:FaultEvent):void
          {
            trace(event.fault.message);
          }
      ]]>
    </mx:Script>
    <mx:RemoteObject
      id="amfService"
      endpoint="http://127.0.0.1:8000/app/rpc/call/amfrpc3"
      destination="mydomain"
    showBusyCursor="true">
      <mx:method name="test" result="resultHandler(event)"
        fault="faultHandler(event)"/>
    </mx:RemoteObject>
    <mx:Button x="250" y="150" label="Fire"
      click="amfService.test();"/>
  </mx:Application>
```

3. code_xml: Pay attention to the definition of the `RemoteObject`. `Endpoint` is a service URL. It doesn't include the RPC method name, which should be specified in the `name` attribute of the `mx:method` object. `/call/amfrpc3` is a standard URL suffix, and it shouldn't be altered. It is important to specify the destination attribute – it's the same ID that appears in the controller in the `@service.amfrpc3(...)` decorator.

*Web Services*

4. **Setting** `crossdomain.xml`: Notice that in order for Flex to be able to invoke RPC services from a different domain, one needs to expose an appropriate `crossdomain.xml` file at the top-level of the server of that domain. For example:

   `http://mydomain.com:8000/crossdomain.xml`

   To do this, create `crossdomain.xml` inside the `static/` folder of the application (web2py doesn't support public resources, so we will do some routing), and add an appropriate access policy. For example, **full access** (not desirable for security reasons):

   ```
   <?xml version="1.0"?>
   <!DOCTYPE cross-domain-policy SYSTEM
     "http://www.macromedia.com/xml/dtds/cross-domain-policy.dtd">
   <cross-domain-policy>
     <allow-access-from domain="*" />
   </cross-domain-policy>
   ```

   Now go to the `web2py` installation folder, and create a `routes.py` file with the following content:

   ```
   routes_in = (('/crossdomain.xml', '/app/static/crossdomain.xml'),)
   ```

   This file instructs the web2py server to redirect all requests in `crossdomain.xml`, to its location at the application's static resources. Don't forget to close and run the process of the server, in order for it to reload the routing information.

# PayPal integration in Web2py

This recipe is meant to be an introduction to **Paypal** integration in web2py. It by no means covers all the possible integrations with Paypal, and is mostly centered on what PayPal names **Standard Integration**. The examples given are proven at the time of writing this, but they should be taken only as a starting point rather than a reference. For that, please use both PayPal's and web2py's documentation.

> PayPal offers different levels of integration, which, depending on what you need to do, might be better suited for your needs. It is important that you get to know at least the basic integration concepts that PayPal provides before starting to program anything, so that you can plan in advance what is best suited to your needs.

That said, let me try to give you a rough idea of the different levels involved, before going any further, so as to better understand the little area that this recipe covers. It is, however, an area which most of the small-sized and middle-sized projects may fall into.

*Chapter 7*

In broad lines, there are three levels of integration that one can achieve with PayPal:

- **Express checkout**: Within a seller account in PayPal, you can create buttons with information related to each item that you may be selling (name, description, item number, and pricing). You can have up to 1000 different buttons or items defined in this way. After that, it is a matter of setting the buttons on the HTML, to go along with the application. Regarding web2py, it is really simple to just copy the code that PayPal creates for each button in a text field in your product `db`, and then just present it on the screen whenever it's needed. Using this method, one can opt for different purchase experiences including straight checkout or cart management (managed by PayPal), which would let you add or remove items from within the checkout screen in PayPal. I don't like this method, unless you would be selling very, very few item codes, as it may get to be a pain to maintain your articles in PayPal. If you are selling a few services or whatever with a small set of prices, it might very well be worth it, as you don't have to work much from the programming point of view, and it's really simple to set up.

- **Standard integration**: This is the one that we will be covering in this article. It basically lets you manage your own product database, and so on, and sends all the data to PayPal at the moment of payment, so that the whole checkout process is managed at PayPal. After the transaction has been completed, you can choose (as per configuration of your profile in your PayPal seller account) whether the customer is redirected back to your domain (you can set up a default URL to return to, or send that URL dynamically each time you send the data for the checkout, but the functionality needs to be activated in your seller account). The following two things need to be mentioned here, which I feel are part of the standard integration, although they are not required in order to have your basic site working:

    - **Payment Data Transfer (PDT)**: This would be the process by which the customer is sent back to your domain, which lets you capture the transaction data (payment confirmation data from PayPal), and shows it in a confirmation screen in your own domain, with any further information you may want to show, or redirect the customer to continue his shopping. It is not completely safe, as nothing guarantees that the customer will be redirected; this may well happen, because in some cases, PayPal doesn't execute the redirection, but forces the customer to click on an extra button to return to your domain, so as to give the opportunity to the customer to join PayPal. This happens whenever the customer pays by credit card and not using his PayPal account.

    - **Instant Payment Notification (IPN)**: This is a messaging service that connects to your domain to send the information of each transaction processed at Paypal. It doesn't stop sending the message until you acknowledge its reception (or four days pass without acknowledgement). This is the safest way to collect all the data from all the transactions processed at PayPal, and trigger any internal process that you may have. Usually, you will want to do the shipping of your products at this point.

# Web Services

> ▶ **Detailed integration**: In here, I am really grouping a number of other methods ands APIs, that I will not be detailing; some of them for very specific uses. The only method that I would like to mention more specifically is **Name Value Pairs** (**NVP**), as I feel that it gives you a very simple programing interface with which you can do very detailed processes controlling all your data, and all your transaction flow from your domain. Using NVP, you can, for example, capture all the data related to a payment in your domain, and only at that point, send all the information to PayPal to process the payment (as opposed to processing the checkout, which is what we are doing with the previous items). You have a good example as to how to implement this at `http://web2py.com/appliances/default/show/28`, or go to the main web page, and find it under free applications, **PayPalEngine**, developed by *Matt Sellers*. You should, however, check the detailed documentation at PayPal, as the process involves many steps, in order to ensure the maximum security of your transactions.

So basically, in express checkout, PayPal manages your cart (and master data), the checkout process, and of course, payments. With standard integration, PayPal manages checkout and payments, and with further detailed integration, you can make it so that it manages only the payments.

## How to do it...

Before moving on, all the technical documentation regarding integration with PayPal can be found at:

`https://cms.paypal.com/us/cgi-bin/?cmd=_render-content&content_ID=developer/library_documentation`

A link to this URL, in case this changes, can be found by clicking on the documentation link at:

`https://developer.paypal.com/`

So, moving on to how to use the standard integration, the first thing you should do is create yourself a sandbox account. You do this at `https://developer.paypal.com/`. Create yourself an account, and once logged in, create at least two test accounts: a `seller` and a `buyer` respectively. There is a good guide on all the necessary steps called **PP sandbox user guide**, which you can find at the documentation link provided before, or on an HTML version at `https://cms.paypal.com/us/cgi-bin/? cmd=_render-content&content_ID=developer/howto_testing_sandbox`. Everything on how to set your account up and start running, is described there.

Once you have that set up and running, you will have your seller ID and e-mail (you can use any of them to identify yourself to PayPal on the code below, although I prefer the ID, if only to avoid possible spam).

*Chapter 7*

OK, so now, we can already create the **checkout button** that will take our customers to the PayPal site with all our cart data. Before moving further, you can find all documentation related to this point at the documentation link provided before, under the *Website Payments Standard Integration Guide*, or directly in an HTML format at:

```
https://cms.paypal.com/us/cgi-bin/? cmd=_render-content&content_
ID=developer/howto_html_wp_standard_overview
```

Check the information about *Third-Party Shopping Carts*. Anyway, creating the button to send all the information is actually very simple. All that is needed is the following code in your checkout page view:

```
<form action="https://www.sandbox.paypal.com/cgi-bin/webscr"
  method="post">
  <!-- Select the correct button depending on country etc.
  If you can do it with pre-generated buttons (with prices included
    etc)
    then so much the better for security -->
  <input type="hidden" name="business" value="{{=paypal_id}}" />
<input type="image" src=
  "https://www.sandbox.paypal.com/es_XC/i/btn/btn_buynowCC_LG.gif"
  border="0" name="submit" alt="PayPal - The safer, easier way to pay
  online!">
<img alt="" border="0" src=
  "https://www.sandbox.paypal.com/es_XC/i/scr/pixel.gif" width="1"
  height="1">
<form action="http://www.sandbox.paypal.com/cgi-bin/webscr"
  method="post" />
<input type="hidden" name="cmd" value="_cart" />
<input type="hidden" name="upload" value="1" />
<input type="hidden" name="charset" value="utf-8">
<input type="hidden" name="currency_code" value="EUR" />
<input type="hidden" name="display" value="1"/>
<input type="hidden" name="shopping_url"
  value="http://www.micropolixshop.com/giftlist/default/glist"/>
<!-- Not really necessary, only if want to allow
  continue Shopping -->
<input type="hidden" name="notify_url" value=
  "http://www.micropolixshop.com/giftlist/default/ipn_handler"/>
<!-- Or leave blank and setup default url at paypal -->
<input type="hidden" name="return"
  value="http://www.micropolixshop.com/giftlist/default/confirm"/>
<!-- Or leave blank and setup default url at paypal -->
<input type="hidden" name="custom" value="{{=session.event_code}}"/>
{{k=1}}
{{for id,product in products.items():}}
```

```
        <input type="hidden" name="item_number_{{=k}}"
          value="{{=product.ext_code}}"/>
        <input type="hidden" name="item_name_{{=k}}"
          value="{{=product.name}}"/>
        <input type="hidden" name="quantity_{{=k}}"
          value="{{=session.cart[str(id)]}}"/>
        <input type="hidden" name="discount_rate_{{=k}}" value="15"/>
        <!-- ie, wants a 15% on all articles always -->
        <input type="hidden" name="tax_{{=k}}"
          value="{{=product.price*product.tax_rate}}"/>
        <input type="hidden" name="amount_{{=k}}"
          value="{{=product.price}}"/>
        {{k+=1}}
        {{pass}}
</form>
```

A couple of comments regarding the listing `lst:CheckoutButton`:

- In all cases, to move from sandbox to production, the URL to use only needs to change from `https://www.sandbox.paypal.com` to `https://www.paypal.com`.

- You can create the buttons using the `create new button` functionality at your seller account, and then re-use the code. It would let you to choose the language and the type of button to use. That way, you will get the correct link to the image to be used for your PayPal button.

- The field `cmd` with `value _cart` is very important. Read the documentation to see the possible values of this field, depending on what you want to do. I am assuming a cart scenario on this example.

- The fields `shopping_url`, `notify_url`, and `return` can be omitted, if you set up your seller account profile. If you set it up here, this takes precedence over the default values set up in your seller account.

- The field `custom`, I think, is rather important, as it is one of the few fields that lets you introduce data not shown to the customer, that may allow you to track any extra information. It is per transaction (not per item). In this case, I choose to use an internal event code to track all purchases related to an event (special `promotion`, if you like or whatever).

- As you can see, I created a loop with all the cart items to do the checkout, by passing a dictionary with all the product data. I have the information of the items purchased in the session. They get named and numbered following the PayPal rules.

- Regarding the discount, even though you set the discounts per item, PayPal, only shows a discount total. I don't know if this is different in the Pro version.

For more information, you should check the documentation named before, which includes a list of all the fields available to you (which include shipping charges, and so on).

**Checkout confirmation/payment data transfer**: Once the customer finishes paying through PayPal, he will be redirected to your website, automatically, if it is set up in the account and he is already a PayPal user (otherwise he will have to click on a button to return to your site). This section shows you how to set your application so that it will receive the payment data confirmation from PayPal, and show a confirmation to your customer.

You can read detailed documentation on this subject here:

```
https://cms.paypal.com/us/cgi-bin/?cmd=_render-content&content_
ID=developer/howto_html_paymentdatatransfer
```

Here, you can see how to set it up in detail, so that you know where to get your token from, which you need to identify yourself to PayPal, to confirm and get the data. In any case, refer to the following figure representing a *Diagram of the Basic flow of a PDT transaction* (picture taken from PayPal docs), so as to give you a detailed view of the process flow:

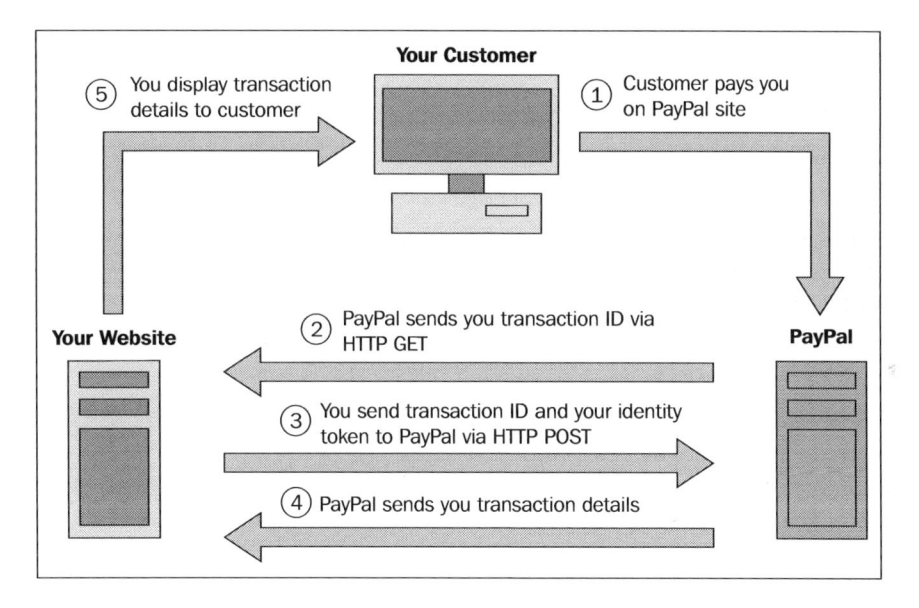

In the listing `lst:generic-def`, I included a number of generic functions that I have used in setting up the interface. The `Connection` class definition is a modified version of a generic connection example that I found while surfing the web, but I cannot really recall where. The `add_to_cart`, `remove_from_cart`, `empty_cart`, and `checkout` that I included as an example of how to set up your cart, which are taken from **EStore**, can be found at `http://www.web2py.com/appliances/default/show/24`.

## Web Services

Again, please understand that the different methods are oversimplified here, to try to explain in a few lines the different possibilities:

```
# db.py file
######################################################################
# Global Variables definition
######################################################################
domain='www.sandbox.paypal.com'
protocol='https://'
user=None
passwd=None
realm=None
headers = {'Content-Type':'application/x-www-form-urlencoded'}
# This token should also be set in a table so that the seller can set
#it up
# dynamically and not through the code. Same goes for the PAGINATE.
paypal_token="XXXXXXXXXXXXXXXXXXXXXXXXXXXXXXXXXXXXXXXXXXXXXXXXXXXX"
PAGINATE = 20
######################################################################


# default.py file
######################################################################
# coding: utf8

import datetime
import string

if not session.cart: session.cart, session.balance={},0
app=request.application

#### Setup PayPal login email (seller id) in the session
#### I store paypal_id in a table
session.paypal_id=myorg.paypal_id
import urllib2, urllib
import datetime

class Connection:
    def __init__(self, base_url, username, password, realm = None,
       header = {}):
       self.base_url = base_url
```

```python
    self.username = username
    self.password = password
    self.realm    = realm
    self.header   = header

def request(self, resource, data = None, args = None):
  path = resource

  if args:
    path += "?" + (args)

  # create a password manager
  password_mgr = urllib2.HTTPPasswordMgrWithDefaultRealm()

  if self.username and self.password:
    # Add the username and password.
    password_mgr.add_password(self.realm, self.base_url,
      self.username, self.password)

  handler = urllib2.HTTPBasicAuthHandler(password_mgr)

  # create "opener" (OpenerDirector instance)
  opener = urllib2.build_opener(handler)

  # Install the opener.
  # Now all calls to urllib2.urlopen use our opener.
  urllib2.install_opener(opener)
  #Create a Request
  req=urllib2.Request(self.base_url + path, data, self.header)
  # use the opener to fetch a URL
  error = ''
  try:
    ret=opener.open(req)
  except urllib2.HTTPError, e:
    ret = e
    error = 'urllib2.HTTPError'
  except urllib2.URLError, e:
    ret = e
    error = 'urllib2.URLError'

  return ret, error

def add_to_cart():
  """
```

```
        Add data into the session.cart dictionary
        Session.cart is a dictionary with id product_id and value =
        quantity
        Session.balance is a value with the total of the transaction.
        After updating values, redirect to checkout
    """
    pid=request.args[0]
    product=db(db.product.id==pid).select()[0]
    product.update_record(clicked=product.clicked+1)
    try: qty=session.cart[pid]+1
    except: qty=1
    session.cart[pid]=qty
    session.balance+=product.price
    redirect(URL('checkout'))

def remove_from_cart():
    """
       allow add to cart
    """
    pid = request.args[0]
    product=db(db.product.id==pid).select()[0]
    if session.cart.has_key(pid):
        session.balance-=product.price
        session.cart[pid]-=1
        if not session.cart[pid]: del session.cart[pid]
    redirect(URL('checkout'))

def empty_cart():
    """
       allow add to cart
    """
    session.cart, session.balance={},0
    redirect(URL('checkout'))

def checkout():
    """
       Checkout
    """
    pids = session.cart.keys()
    cart={}
    products={}
    for pid in pids:
        products[pid]=db(db.product.id==pid).select()[0]
    return dict(products=products,paypal_id=session.paypal_id)
```

Finally, confirm, at the listing lst:confirm, will process the information sent from PayPal, with the four step process described in the previous diagram of the basic flow of a PDT transaction, steps 2,3,4, and 5.

```
def confirm():
   """
     This is set so as to capture the transaction data from PayPal
     It captures the transaction ID from the HTTP GET that PayPal
        sends.
     And using the token from vendor profile PDT, it does a form post.
     The data from the http get comes as vars Name Value Pairs.
   """
   if request.vars.has_key('tx'):
     trans = request.vars.get('tx')
     # Establish connection.
     conn = Connection(base_url=protocol+domain, username=user,
        password = passwd, realm = realm, header = headers)
     data = "cmd=_notify-synch&tx="+trans+"&at="+paypal_token
     resp,error=conn.request('/cgi-bin/webscr', data)
     data={}
     if error=='':
       respu = resp.read()
       respuesta = respu.splitlines()
       data['status']=respuesta[0]
       if respuesta[0]=='SUCCESS':
         for r in respuesta[1:]:
           key,val = r.split('=')
           data[key]=val
         msg=''
         if data.has_key('memo'): msg=data['memo']
         form = FORM("Quiere dejar un mensaje con los regalos?",
             INPUT(_name=T('message'),_type="text",_value=msg),
             INPUT(_type="submit"))
         if form.accepts(request,session):
           email=data['payer_email'].replace('%40','@')
           id = db.gift_msg.insert(buyer=data['payer_email'],
             transact=trans,msg=form.vars.message)
           response.flash=T('Your message will be passed on to the
             recipient')
           redirect(URL('index'))

         return dict(data=data,form=form)
       return dict(data=data)
     else:
       data['status']='FAIL'
   else:
     redirect(URL('index'))
   return dict(trans=trans)
```

## Web Services

Just for the sake of completeness, I am adding a very basic example of `confirm.html`, which you can see in the listing lst:confirmhtml.

```
{{extend 'layout.html'}}

{{if data['status'] == 'SUCCESS':}}
<p><h3>{{=T('Your order has been received.')}}</h3></p>
<hr>
<b>{{=T('Details')}}</b><br>
<li>
  {{=T('Name:')}} {{=data['first_name']}} {{=data['last_name']}}
</li>
<li>'
  {{=T('Purchases for event:')}}: {{=data['transaction_subject']}}
</li>
<li>
  {{=T('Amount')}}: {{=data['mc_currency']}} {{=data['mc_gross']}}
</li>
<hr>
{{=form}}
{{else:}}
{{=T('No confirmation received from PayPal. This can be due to a
   number of reasons; please check your email to see if the
   transaction was successful.')}}
{{pass}}

{{=T('Your transaction has finished, you should receive an email of
   your purchase.')}}<br>
{{=T('If you have an account at PayPal, you can check your
   transaction details at')}}
   <a href='https://www.paypal.es'>www.paypal.es</a>
```

**Instant Payment Notification (IPN):** As mentioned before, one cannot trust the PDT process to receive the information from all transactions, as a great number of things can happen. Thus, you need to implement an additional process, if you need to do additional processing of the information from your sales, or if you want to keep a local database of the actual sales processed.

This is done with IPN. You can find all the related documentation at the documentation site URL given previously. You will need to turn on the IPN functionality at your seller account, as well as give a default URL to receive those messages, which should be equal to the view in which you process them. In the case of this example, it would be: `http://www.yourdomain.com/yourapp/default/ipn_handler`.

The process is quite similar to that of PDT; even the variables are the same. The main difference is that IPNs are sent from PayPal, until you acknowledge them. The view for this function, `default/ipn_handler.html`, can very well be left blank. I am also including the table definition for logging the messages from PayPal.

Anyway, you can find in the listing `lst:ipnhandler`, an example of how to set them up:

```
#### At models/db.py
######################################################################
db.define_table('ipn_msgs',
  Field('trans_id',label=T('transaction id')),
  Field('timestamp','datetime',label=T('timestamp')),
  Field('type',label=T('type')),
  Field('msg','text',label=T('message')),
  Field('processed','boolean',label=T('processed')),
  Field('total','double',label=T('total')),
  Field('fee','double',label=T('fee')),
  Field('currency',length=3,label=T('currency')),
  Field('security_msg',label=T('security message'))
)

#### At controllers/default.py
######################################################################
def ipn_handler():
    """
    Manages the ipn connection with PayPal
    Ask PayPal to confirm this payment, return status and detail
    strings
    """
    parameters = None
    parameters =  request.vars
    if parameters:
      parameters['cmd'] = '_notify-validate'
      params = urllib.urlencode(parameters)
      conn = Connection(base_url=protocol+domain, username=user,
        password = passwd, realm = realm, header = headers)
      resp,error =conn.request('/cgi-bin/webscr', params)
      timestamp=datetime.datetime.now()
      # We are going to log all messages confirmed by PayPal.
      if error =='':
```

## Web Services

```
    ipn_msg_id = db.ipn_msgs.insert(trans_id=parameters['txn_id'],
      timestamp=timestamp,type=resp.read(),msg=params,
      total=parameters['mc_gross'],fee=parameters['mc_fee'],
      currency=parameters['mc_currency'])
    # But only interested in processing messages that have payment
    #status completed and are VERIFIED by PayPal.
    if parameters['payment_status']=='Completed':
      process_ipn(ipn_msg_id,parameters)
```

The only thing missing would be to process the information received, and check for errors or possible fraud attempts. You can see an example function in the listing lst:processipn. Although this is probably something that would change quite a bit from one project to the next, I hope that it may serve you as a rough guide.

```
def process_ipn(ipn_msg_id,param):
  """
    We process the parameters sent from IPN PayPal, to correctly
    store the confirmed sales
    in the database.
    param -- request.vars from IPN message from PayPal
  """
  # Check if transaction_id has already been processed.
  query1 = db.ipn_msgs.trans_id==param['txn_id']
  query2 = db.ipn_msgs.processed == True
  rows = db(query1 & query2).select()
  if not rows:
    trans = param['txn_id']
    payer_email = param['payer_email']
    n_items = int(param['num_cart_items'])
    pay_date = param['payment_date']
    total = param['mc_gross']
    curr = param['mc_currency']
    event_code = param['custom']
    if param.has_key('memo'): memo=param['memo']
    event_id = db(db.event.code==event_code).select(db.event.id)
    if not event_id:
      db.ipn_msgs[ipn_msg_id]=dict(security_msg=T('Event does not
        exist'))
    else:
      error=False
      for i in range(1,n_items+1):
        product_code = param['item_number'+str(i)]
        qtty = param['quantity'+str(i)]
        line_total = float(param['mc_gross_'+str(i)]) +
          float(param['mc_tax'+str(i)])
```

```
            product=db(db.product.ext_code==product_code).
               select(db.product.id)
            if not product:
               db.ipn_msgs[ipn_msg_id]=dict(security_msg=T('Product code
                  does not exist'))
               error=True
            else:
               db.glist.insert(event=event_id[0],product=product[0],
                  buyer=payer_email,transact=trans,
                  purchase_date=pay_date,quantity_sold=qtty,
                  price=line_total,observations=memo)
         if not error: db.ipn_msgs[ipn_msg_id]=dict(processed=True)
```

Hope that this section helped you to set up your PayPal site using web2py, or at least, helped you understand the basic concepts behind setting up one, and the different possibilities that you have available.

# PayPal web payments standard

This recipe shows an implementation of the PayPal web payments standard, using both encrypted requests and IPN for a secure process workflow. Note that in this recipe, web2py version 1.77.3 is used. Hopefully, it still works in the latest web2py versions.

## How to do it...

1. To implement our integration with PayPal, I started with putting together the code that generates an encrypted form post to PayPal, for all of our cart actions. If you do this, and you configure PayPal to only accept signed requests, then the user cannot tamper with your form and change the price of an item. To do this, I installed the **M2Crypto** module on our system, and created a module that will do the signing of the PayPal forms. Note that this does not work on the Google App Engine, because M2Crypto does not run on GAE.

   I have yet to find a replacement for it that runs on the App Engine, so you cannot use this PayPal payments recipe in that environment.

   The encryption module (`crypt.py`) uses the certificate to sign the data and then encrypts it, as shown in the following code:

   ```
   from M2Crypto import BIO, SMIME, X509, EVP
   
   def paypal_encrypt(attributes, sitesettings):
       """
       Takes a list of attributes for working with PayPal (in our
       case adding to the shopping cart), and encrypts them for
       secure transmission of item details and prices.
   ```

## Web Services

```
    @type    attributes: dictionary
    @param attributes: a dictionary of the PayPal request
      attributes.  An
      example attribute set is:

      >>> attributes = {"cert_id":sitesettings.paypal_cert_id,
        "cmd":"_cart",
        "business":sitesettings.cart_business,
        "add":"1",
        "custom":auth.user.id,
        "item_name":"song 1 test",
        "item_number":"song-1",
        "amount":"0.99",
        "currency_code":"USD",
        "shopping_url":'http://'+\
          Storage(globals()).request.env.http_host+\
          URL(args=request.args),
        "return":'http://'+\
          Storage(globals()).request.env.http_host+\
          URL('account', 'downloads'),
      }

  @type    sitesettings: SQLStorage
  @param sitesettings: The settings stored in the database.
     this method
     requires I{tenthrow_private_key}, I{tenthrow_public_cert},
    and I{paypal_public_cert} to function
  @rtype: string
  @return: encrypted attribute string
"""

plaintext = ''

for key, value in attributes.items():
    plaintext += u'%s=%s\n' % (key, value)

plaintext = plaintext.encode('utf-8')

# Instantiate an SMIME object.
s = SMIME.SMIME()

# Load signer's key and cert. Sign the buffer.
s.pkey = EVP.load_key_string(sitesettings.tenthrow_private_key)
s.x509 = X509.load_cert_string(
    sitesettings.tenthrow_public_cert)

#s.load_key_bio(BIO.openfile(settings.MY_KEYPAIR),
```

```
    #                    BIO.openfile(settings.MY_CERT))

    p7 = s.sign(BIO.MemoryBuffer(plaintext),
      flags=SMIME.PKCS7_BINARY)

    # Load target cert to encrypt the signed message to.
    #x509 = X509.load_cert_bio(BIO.openfile(settings.PAYPAL_CERT))
    x509 = X509.load_cert_string(sitesettings.paypal_public_cert)

    sk = X509.X509_Stack()
    sk.push(x509)
    s.set_x509_stack(sk)

    # Set cipher: 3-key triple-DES in CBC mode.
    s.set_cipher(SMIME.Cipher('des_ede3_cbc'))

    # Create a temporary buffer.
    tmp = BIO.MemoryBuffer()

    # Write the signed message into the temporary buffer.
    p7.write_der(tmp)

    # Encrypt the temporary buffer.
    p7 = s.encrypt(tmp, flags=SMIME.PKCS7_BINARY)

    # Output p7 in mail-friendly format.
    out = BIO.MemoryBuffer()
    p7.write(out)

    return out.read()
```

2. Then, we construct forms in our view, and encrypt them:

```
{{from applications.tenthrow.modules.crypt import * }}

{{     attributes = {"cert_id":sitesettings.paypal_cert_id,
   "cmd":"_cart",
   "business":sitesettings.cart_business,
   "add":"1",
   "custom":auth.user.id,
   "item_name":artist_name + ": " + song['name'],
   "item_number":"song-"+str(song['cue_point_id']),
   "amount":song['cost'],
   "currency_code":"USD",
   "shopping_url":full_url('http',r=request,args=request.args),
   "return":full_url('https', r=request, c='account', \
   f='alldownloads'),
   }
```

## Web Services

```
        encattrs = paypal_encrypt(attributes, sitesettings)
}}
<form target="_self"
  action="{{=sitesettings.cart_url}}" method="post"
  name="song{{=song['cue_point_id']}}">
  <!-- Identify your business so that you can collect the
    payments. -->
  <input type="hidden" name="cmd" value="_s-xclick"
    class="unform"/>
  <input type="hidden" name="encrypted" value="{{=encattrs}}"
    class="unform"/>
  <a onclick="document.song{{=song['cue_point_id']}}.submit()"
    class="trBtn">
    <img src="{{=URL('static','images/trIconDL.png')}}"
      alt="Download {{=(song['name'])}}" class="original"/>
     <img src="{{=URL('static','images/trIconDL_Hover.png')}}"
      alt="Download {{=(song['name'])}}" class="hover"/>
  </a>
  <img alt="" border="0" width="1" height="1"
    src="https://www.paypal.com/en_US/i/scr/pixel.gif"
    class="unform"/>
</form>
```

Note that the above code calls a method `full_url()`, which is defined as follows:

```
def full_url(scheme="http",
  a=None,
  c=None,
  f=None,
  r=None,
  args=[],
  vars={},
  anchor='',
  path = None
):
  """
    Create a fully qualified URL.  The URL will use the same host
    that the
    request was made from, but will use the specified scheme.
    Calls
    C{gluon.html.URL()} to construct the relative path to the
    host.

    if <scheme>_port is set in the settings table, append the port
    to the domain of the created URL

    @param scheme: scheme to use for the fully-qualified URL.
       (default to 'http')
```

```
    @param a: application (default to current if r is given)
    @param c: controller (default to current if r is given)
    @param f: function (default to current if r is given)
    @param r: request
    @param args: any arguments (optional)
    @param vars: any variables (optional)
    @param anchor: anchorname, without # (optional)
    @param path: the relative path to use.  if used overrides
       a,c,f,args, and
       vars (optional)
"""
port = ''
if sitesettings.has_key(scheme+"_port") and
   sitesettings[scheme+"_port"]:
     port = ":" + sitesettings[scheme+"_port"]
if scheme == 'https' and sitesettings.has_key("https_scheme"):
    scheme = sitesettings.https_scheme
url = scheme +'://' + \
    r.env.http_host.split(':')[0] + port
if path:
    url = url + path
else:
    url = url+URL(a=a, c=c, f=f, r=r, args=args, vars=vars,
       anchor=anchor)
return url
```

3. Then, I need to be able to process our IPN responses from PayPal. The following code does just that. You'll see that I only process purchase requests. I also left in the code that is specific to our database, about how I code product IDs, and then use that product ID to create records in our database. Based on the existence of those purchase records in our database, I allow the user to download the files that they purchased. So, the user cannot download their purchase until the IPN message is processed. This is usually 5 to 30 seconds after they submitted the order. Most of the time, the messages are received and processed before PayPal redirects the user back to our site. Our `paypal.py` controller will have a function to process the instant payment notification, as described in the following code section, (note that we have openanything in our modules directory. Visit http://diveintopython.org/ for the latest version):

```
from applications.app.modules.openanything import *

def ipn():
    """
    This controller processes Instant Payment Notifications from
    PayPal.
```

## Web Services

```
    It will verify messages, and process completed cart transaction messages
    only.  all other messages are ignored for now.

    For each item purchased in the cart, the song_purchases table will be
    updated with the purchased item information, allowing the user to
    download the item.

    logs are written to /tmp/ipnresp.txt

    the PayPal IPN documentation is available at:
    https://cms.paypal.com/cms_content/US/en_US/files/developer/
       IPNGuide.pdf
    """
    """
    sample PayPal IPN call:

    last_name=Smith&
    txn_id=597202352&
    receiver_email=seller%40paypalsandbox.com&
    payment_status=Completed&tax=2.02&
    mc_gross1=12.34&
    payer_status=verified&
    residence_country=US&
    invoice=abc1234&
    item_name1=something&
    txn_type=cart&
    item_number1=201&
    quantity1=1&
    payment_date=16%3A52%3A59+Jul.+20%2C+2009+PDT&
    first_name=John&
    mc_shipping=3.02&
    charset=windows-1252&
    custom=3&
    notify_version=2.4&
    test_ipn=1&
    receiver_id=TESTSELLERID1&
    business=seller%40paypalsandbox.com&
    mc_handling1=1.67&
    payer_id=TESTBUYERID01&
    verify_sign=AFcWxV21C7fd0v3bYYYRCpSSRl31AtrKNnsnrW3-8M8R-
       P38QFsqBaQM&
```

```
    mc_handling=2.06&
    mc_fee=0.44&
    mc_currency=USD&
    payer_email=buyer%40paypalsandbox.com&
    payment_type=instant&
    mc_gross=15.34&
    mc_shipping1=1.02
"""

    #@todo: come up with better logging mechanism
    logfile = "/tmp/ipnresp.txt"

    verifyurl = "https://www.paypal.com/cgi-bin/webscr"
    if request.vars.test_ipn != None and request.vars.test_ipn ==
       '1':
        verifyurl = "https://www.sandbox.paypal.com/cgi-bin/webscr"

    params = dict(request.vars)
    params['cmd'] = '_notify-validate'

    resp = fetch(verifyurl, post_data=params)

#the message was not verified, fail
if resp['data'] != "VERIFIED":
  #@todo: figure out how to fail
  f = open(logfile, "a")
  f.write("Message not verified:\n")
  f.write(repr(params) + "\n\n")
  f.close()
  return None
...
if request.vars.txn_type != "cart":
  #for now ignore non-cart transaction messages
  f = open(logfile, "a")
  f.write("Not a cart message:\n")
  f.write(repr(params) + "\n\n")
  f.close()
  return None
...
if request.vars.payment_status != 'Completed':
  #ignore pending transactions
  f = open(logfile, "a")
  f.write("Ignore pending transaction:\n")
```

```
            f.write(repr(params) + "\n\n")
            f.close()
            return None
    ...
    #check id not recorded
    if len(db(db.song_purchases.transaction_id==request.
      vars.txn_id).select())>0:
        #transaction already recorded
        f = open(logfile, "a")
        f.write("Ignoring recorded transaction:\n")
        f.write(repr(params) + "\n\n")
        f.close()
        return None

        #record transaction
        num_items = 1
        if request.vars.num_cart_items != None:
            num_items = request.vars.num_cart_items

        for i in range(1, int(num_items)+1):
            #i coded our item_number to be a tag and an ID.  the ID is
            # a key to a table in our database.
            tag, id = request.vars['item_number'+str(i)].split("-")
            if tag == "song":
                db.song_purchases.insert(auth_user=request.vars.custom,
                  cue_point=id,
                  transaction_id=request.vars.txn_id,
                  date=request.vars.payment_date.replace('.', ''))

            elif tag == "song_media":
                db.song_purchases.insert(auth_user=request.vars.custom,
                    song_media=id,
                    transaction_id=request.vars.txn_id,
                    date=request.vars.payment_date.replace('.', ''))

            elif tag == "concert":
                db.concert_purchases.insert(auth_user=request.vars.custom,
                    playlist=id,
                    transaction_id=request.vars.txn_id,
                    date=request.vars.payment_date.replace('.', ''))
            else:
                #@TODO: this is an error, what should we do here?
                f = open(logfile, "a")
```

```
            f.write("Ignoring bad item number: " + \
              request.vars['item_number'+str(i)] + "\n")
            f.write(repr(params) + "\n\n")
            f.close()
    f = open(logfile, "a")
    f.write("Processed message:\n")
    f.write(repr(params) + "\n\n")
    f.close()
    return None
```

That's all, folks!

# Getting Flickr photos

This recipe can be used to get a list of Flickr photos passing the photoset ID.

## Getting ready

First you need to generate an **APIKEY**, which you can do on the Flickr developers page:

`http://www.flickr.com/services/api/misc.api_keys.html`

After that, you need to create a function to fetch the Flickr API. Generally, this is created in models, but you can do that in modules too.

## How to do it...

1. Create a function in any of your model files. We will create one called `models/plugin_flickr.py`, as follows:

   ```
   def plugin_flickr(key, photoset=None, per_page=15, page=1):
     from urllib2 import import urlopen
     from xml.dom.minidom import parse as domparse
     apiurl = 'http://api.flickr.com/services/rest/?method=flickr.
       photosets.getPhotos&api_key=%(apikey)s&photoset_id=
       %(photoset)s&privacy_filter=1&per_page=%(per_page)s&page=
       %(page)s&extras=url_t,url_m,url_o,url_sq'

     dom = domparse(urlopen(apiurl % dict(photoset=photoset,
       per_page=per_page, page=page, apikey=key)))

     photos = []

     for node in dom.getElementsByTagName('photo'):
       photos.append({
   ```

## Web Services

```
        'id':node.getAttribute('id'),
        'title':node.getAttribute('title'),
        'thumb':node.getAttribute('url_t'),
        'medio':node.getAttribute('url_m'),
        'original':node.getAttribute('url_o'),
        'square':node.getAttribute('url_sq'),
    })

    return photos
```

2. Now you can call that function from any controller or view. For example, in a controller action, as follows:

```
def testflickr():
  photos = plugin_flickr(
    key='YOUR_API_KEY',
    photoset='THE_PHOTOSET_ID',
    per_page=15,
    page=1)
  return dict(photos=photos)
```

3. In the associated `views/defaul/testflickr.html`, you can add the following:

```
{{extend 'layout.html'}}

{{for photo in photos:}}
  {{=IMG(_src=photo['square'])}}
{{pass}}
```

The final product will look like the one shown in the following screenshot:

# Sending e-mails with Boto through Amazon Web Services (AWS)

**Amazon Simple Email Service** is a nice way to send e-mails without needing to operate your own mail server. This code utilizes the `Boto` library, which is a Python interface for AWS.

## Getting ready

1. First of all, you need to sign up for AWS at `http://aws.amazon.com`.
2. Then, enable Simple Email Service at `http://aws.amazon.com/ses/`.
3. You need to obtain your Amazon `AWS-KEY` and `AWS-SECRET-KEY` from `https://aws-portal.amazon.com/gp/aws/developer/account/index.html`.
4. Finally, you need to install Boto in your `web2py/site-packages` folder, or anywhere in your path, so that web2py can find and import it. You can find Boto on GitHub: `https://github.com/boto/boto`.

Before you get **production** access to Amazon's mail servers, you have to pre-register every sender's and recipient's e-mail address that you want to use (up to 100). This is OK for development and testing, but, of course, would not work in production. To register an e-mail address, execute the following code, replacing `AWS-KEY` and `AWS-SECRET-KEY` with your own keys, and `myemail@address.com` with the e-mail address that you want to register.

From the web2py shell or any other Python shell, run the following:

```
from boto.ses.connection import SESConnection
def verify_email_address():
  conn = SESConnection('', '')
  m = conn.verify_email_address('myemail@address.com')
```

## How to do it...

Assuming that everything is installed and configured, as explained before, sending e-mails is easy:

```
def test_send_emails():
  aws_key = 'YOUR_AWS_KEY'
  aws_secret_key = 'YOUR_SECRET_KEY'
  from boto.ses.connection import SESConnection
  conn = SESConnection(aws_key, aws_secret_key)
  return conn.send_email(source='myemail@address.com',
    subject='Subject',
    body='Body.',
```

## Web Services

```
    to_addresses='recipient@email.com',
    cc_addresses=None,
    bcc_addresses=None,
    format='text',
    reply_addresses=None,
    return_path=None)
```

# Making GIS amps using mapscript

**MapServer** is an open source platform for publishing spatial data and interactive mapping applications to the web. Originally developed in the mid-1990s at the University of Minnesota, MapServer is released under an MIT-style license, and runs on all major platforms.

This recipe will show you how to publish geo-referenced maps using the MapServer web service, using a library called `mapscript`.

## Getting ready

First, you need to install `mapscript` from:

`http://pypi.python.org/pypi/mapscript/5.4.2.1`.

You can do it by typing the following command:

**easy_install mapscript**

We will also assume you have a map called `private/test2.map` in your application folder. A `.map` file looks in an `ascii` file that describes a map (coordinates, type, points with tags, and so on), and looks like the following:

```
MAP
  NAME "sample"
  EXTENT -180 -90 180 90 # Geographic
  SIZE 800 400
  IMAGECOLOR 128 128 255
END # MAP
```

You can read more about map files here:

- `http://mapserver.org/introduction.html`
- `http://mapserver.org/mapfile/index.html#mapfile`

## How to do it...

GIS maps are exposed through WXS services. Here, we show you a simple action that provides a service to publish a map stored in the file `private/test2.map`:

```
def wxs():
  import mapscript
  import os
  path_map = os.path.join(request.folder, 'private', request.args(0))
  if not request.vars:
    return ''
  req = mapscript.OWSRequest()
  for v in request.vars:
    req.setParameter(v, request.vars[v])

  map = mapscript.mapObj(path_map)
  mapscript.msIO_installStdoutToBuffer()
  map.OWSDispatch(req)

  content_type = mapscript.msIO_stripStdoutBufferContentType()
  content = mapscript.msIO_getStdoutBufferBytes()
  response.header = "Content-Type","%s; charset=utf-8"%content_type
  return content
```

This service can be consumed by QGis (`http://www.qgis.org/`), or any other Web MapService client (`http://en.wikipedia.org/wiki/Web_Map_Service`), or a Web Feature Service client (`http://en.wikipedia.org/wiki/Web_Feature_Service`).

The URL to pass to QGIS is:

`http://localhost:8000/mapas/default/wxs/test2.map`

Here, `test2.map` points to our map file (stored in the file, `private/test2.map`, served by the `wxs` function as described before).

*Web Services*

# Google groups and Google code feeds reader

In this recipe, we will implement a simple feed reader to retrieve messages from Google Groups and Google Code using RSS.

## How to do it...

We will create a file `models/plugin_feedreader.py`, with the following code:

```
def plugin_feedreader(name, source='google-group'):
    """parse group feeds"""
    from gluon.contrib import feedparser
    if source=='google-group':
      URL = "http://groups.google.com/group/%(name)s/
         feed/rss_v2_0_msgs.xml"

    elif source=='google-code':
      URL = "http://code.google.com/feeds/p/%(name)s/hgchanges/basic"

    else:
      URL = source

    url = URL % dict(name=name)
    g = feedparser.parse(url)
    html = UL(*[LI(A(entry['title'], _href=entry['link']))\
       for entry in g['entries'][0:5]])
    return XML(html)
```

Now, in any controller, you can embed the latest Google group information:

```
{{=plugin_feedreader('web2py', source='google-group')}}
```

Or read the latest Google code source updates:

```
{{=plugin_feedreader('web2py', source='google-code')}}
```

# Creating SOAP web services

**Simple Object Access Protocol (SOAP)** is a complex XML-based inter-process communication standard for web service implementation. It is widely used with legacy applications (especially JAVA and .NET languages), and supports type declaration and **Web Service Definition File (WSDL)**.

web2py already supports a common infrastructure to expose web services in a simple way, using the **Service** tool (rss, json, jsonrpc, xmlrpc, jsonrpc, amfrpc, and amfrpc3).

The `PySimpleSOAP` library included in `gluon/contribs` (since version #1.82.1), aims to add SOAP support, extending the current philosophy.

## How to do it...

Serving operations using SOAP is as easy as decorating a function using `@service.soap`, declaring the following:

- Exposed operation method (camel case by convention)
- Return types
- Parameters types

Types are declared using a dictionary, mapping the parameter/result name with the standard Python conversion functions (**str**, **int**, **float**, **bool**, and so on).

For example, create an application (such as `webservices`), and in a controller (`sample.py`), add the following code:

```
from gluon.tools import Service
service = Service(globals())

@service.xmlrpc
@service.soap('AddStrings',returns={'AddResult':str},
                          args={'a':str, 'b':str})
@service.soap('AddIntegers',returns={'AddResult':int},
                          args={'a':int, 'b':int})
def add(a,b):
   "Add two values"
   return a+b


@service.xmlrpc
@service.soap('SubIntegers',returns={'SubResult':int},
                          args={'a':int, 'b':int})
def sub(a,b):
   "Substract two values"
   return a-b

def call():
   return service()
```

## Web Services

Additionally, web2py can dynamically generate help web pages (list of operations, xml message examples), and the WSDL XML:

- List of operations: `http://127.0.0.1:8000/webservices/sample/call/soap`
- Operation help (for the `SubIntegers` method, in this case):
  `http://127.0.0.1:8000/webservices/sample/call/soap?op=SubIntegers`
- Service description (WSDL ): `http://127.0.0.1:8000/webservices/sample/call/soap?wsdl`

Sample operations list page:

```
Welcome to Web2Py SOAP webservice gateway

The following operations are available

See WSDL for webservice description

AddIntegers: Add two values
SubIntegers: Substract two values
AddStrings: Add two values
Notes: WSDL is linked to URL retriving the full xml. Each operation
is linked to its help page.
```

Sample operation help page:

```
AddIntegers

Add two values

Location: http://127.0.0.1:8000//webservices/sample/call/soap
Namespace: http://127.0.0.1:8000/webservices/sample/soap
SoapAction?: -N/A by now-
Sample SOAP XML Request Message:

<?xml version="1.0" encoding="UTF-8"?>
<soap:Envelope
  xmlns:soap="http://schemas.xmlsoap.org/soap/envelope/">
  <soap:Body>
    <AddIntegers
      xmlns="http://127.0.0.1:8000/webservices/sample/soap">
      <a>
        <!--integer-->
      </a>
```

```xml
      <b>
        <!--integer-->
      </b>
    </AddIntegers>
  </soap:Body>
</soap:Envelope>
```
Sample SOAP XML Response Message:

```xml
<?xml version="1.0" encoding="UTF-8"?>
<soap:Envelope
  xmlns:soap="http://schemas.xmlsoap.org/soap/envelope/">
  <soap:Body>
    <AddIntegersResponse
      xmlns="http://127.0.0.1:8000/webservices/sample/soap">
      <AddResult>
        <!--integer-->
      </AddResult>
    </AddIntegersResponse>
  </soap:Body>
</soap:Envelope>
```

You can test the web service exposed by web2py using this library:

```python
def test_soap_sub():
    from gluon.contrib.pysimplesoap.client import SoapClient, SoapFault
    # create a SOAP client
    client = SoapClient(wsdl="http://localhost:8000/webservices/
      sample/call/soap?WSDL")

    # call SOAP method
    response = client.SubIntegers(a=3,b=2)

    try:
        result = response['SubResult']

    except SoapFault:
        result = None

    return dict(xml_request=client.xml_request,
        xml_response=client.xml_response,
        result=result)
```

## Web Services

### There's more...

**pysimplesoap** is included with recent releases of web2py, as it is being actively maintained. You can frequently check the version to find enhancements, to extend this recipe.

Although there are several python SOAP libraries, this one is designed to be as simple as possible, and is totally integrated with web2py.

For more information, supported features, and platforms, have a look at the following link:

http://code.google.com/p/pysimplesoap/wiki/Web2Py

> To view help pages for the latest web2py versions, you should create a view, sample/call.html, in this example, as in new versions of web2py, for security reasons, generic views are not exposed by default

```
{{extend 'layout.html'}}
{{for tag in body:}}
{{=tag}}
{{pass}}
```

# 8
# Authentication and Authorization

In this chapter, we will cover the following recipes:

- Customizing Auth
- Using CAPTCHA on login failure
- Using pyGravatar to get avatars for user profile pages
- Multi-user and teacher modes
- Authenticating with Facebook using OAuth 2.0

## Introduction

Almost every application needs to be able to authenticate users and set permissions. web2py comes with an extensive and customizable role-based access control mechanism. In this chapter, we show you how to customize it by adding fields to the user table, adding **CAPTCHA** security after repeated failed logins, and how to create **Globally Recognized Avatars** (**Gravatars**—icons representing the users). We also discuss the `teacher` mode of web2py that allows students to share one web2py instance to develop and deploy their applications. Finally, we provide an example of integration with **OAuth 2.0**, one of the newest protocols for federated authentication. Web2py also supports of the protocols, such as CAS, OpenID, OAuth 1.0, LDAP, PAM, X509, and many more. But, once you learn one, it should be easy to learn the others using the official documentation.

# Customizing Auth

There are two ways to customize Auth. The old way of doing it consists of defining a custom `db.auth_user` table from scratch. A new way consists of letting web2py define the `auth` table, but listing extra fields that web2py should include in the table. Here, we will review the latter method.

Specifically, we will assume that each user must also have a username, a phone number, and an address.

## How to do it...

In the `db.py` model, replace the following line:

```
auth.define_tables()
```

Replace it with the following code:

```
auth.settings.extra_fields['auth_user'] = [
    Field('phone_number',requires=IS_MATCH('\d{3}\-\d{3}\-\d{4}')),
    Field('address','text')]
auth.define_tables(username=True)
```

## How it works...

`auth.settings.extra_fields` is a dictionary of extra fields. The `key` is the name of the `auth` table to which to add the extra fields. The `value` is a list of extra fields. Notice that we have added two extra fields (`phone_number` and `address`), but not `username`, here, for `auth_user`.

`username` has to be treated in a special way, because it is involved in the authentication process, which is normally based on the `email` field. By passing the username argument to the following line, we tell web2py that we want the `username` field, and we want to use it for login instead of the `email` field.

```
auth.define_tables(username=True)
```

The username will also be made unique.

## There's more...

There may be cases when registration happens outside the normal registration form (for example, when using `Janrain`, or when users are registered by the administrator). Yet you may need to force a new user, after their first login, to complete their registration. This can be done using a dummy hidden extra field, `complete_registration` that is set to `False`, by default, and is set to `True` when they update their profile:

```
auth.settings.extra_fields['auth_user'] = [
  Field('phone_number',requires=IS_MATCH('\d{3}\-\d{3}\-\d{4}'),
  comment = "i.e. 123-123-1234"),
  Field('address','text'),
  Field('complete_registration',default=False,update=True,
    writable=False, readable=False)]
auth.define_tables(username=True)
```

Then, we may want to force new users, upon login, to complete their registration. In db.py, we can append the following code:

```
if auth.user and not auth.user.complete_registration:
  if not (request.controller,request.function) == ('default','user'):
    redirect(URL('default','user/profile'))
```

This will force new users to edit their profile.

## Using CAPTCHA on login failure

web2py has built-in **ReCaptcha** support (http://www.google.com/recaptcha), but it is usually ON or OFF. It's useful to have it ON, which prevents brute force attacks on the application forms, yet it can be annoying to regular users. Here, we propose a solution, a plugin that conditionally turns ON ReCaptcha after a fixed number of login failures.

### How to do it...

All you need to do is create a new models/plugin_conditionalrecaptcha.py, which contains the following code, and your job is done:

```
MAX_LOGIN_FAILURES = 3
# You must request the ReCaptcha keys
# in order to use this feature
RECAPTCHA_PUBLIC_KEY = ''
RECAPTCHA_PRIVATE_KEY = ''

def _():
  from gluon.tools import Recaptcha
  key = 'login_from:%s' % request.env.remote_addr
  num_login_attempts = cache.ram(key,lambda:0,None)

  if num_login_attempts >= MAX_LOGIN_FAILURES:
    auth.settings.login_captcha = Recaptcha(
      request,RECAPTCHA_PUBLIC_KEY,RECAPTCHA_PRIVATE_KEY)
```

```
        def login_attempt(form,key=key,n=num_login_attempts+1):
          cache.ram(key,lambda n=n:n,0)

        def login_success(form,key=key):
          cache.ram(key,lambda:0,0)

        auth.settings.login_onvalidation.append(login_attempt)
        auth.settings.login_onaccept.append(login_success)


    _()
```

## There's more...

You can customize the ReCaptcha appearance, by passing parameters to it through JavaScript. If you are using the default user controller for exposing `auth` login forms, you can simply edit the `user.html` view, and add the following code:

```
<script>
var RecaptchaOptions = {
  theme : 'clean',
  tabindex : 2
};
</script>
```

Add it before the following line:

```
{{=form}}
```

The full ReCaptcha client API can be viewed at the following URL:

```
http://recaptcha.net/apidocs/captcha/client.html
```

# Using pyGravatar to get avatars for user profile pages

First download **pyGravatar** from the following URL:

```
https://bitbucket.org/gridaphobe/pygravatar/src
```

Put the `gravatar.py` in `applications/yourapp/modules`. If you prefer, you can use the following command:

**pip install pyGravatar**

In any of your models source files, you have to import the Gravatar library to be able to use it, as shown in the following example:

```
from gravatar import Gravatar
```

If you are using the scaffold application, edit the `default/user.html` view, as follows:

```
{{extend 'layout.html'}}
<h3>{{=T( request.args(0).replace('_',' ').capitalize() )}}</h3>
<div id="web2py_user_form">
{{if 'profile' in request.args:}}
  <img src="{{=Gravatar(auth.user.email).thumb}}" />
{{pass}}
```

You will now have a profile page that will look like the following screenshot:

## Authentication and Authorization

Now, in any page, if you want the user avatar, then you just need to use the following code:

```
<img src='{{=Gravatar(auth.user.email).thumb}}' />
<img src='{{=Gravatar('email@domain.com').thumb}}' />
```

You can go further and get the user profile bio from http://en.gravatar.com/. Add the following code to default/user.html.

```
{extend 'layout.html'}}
<h2>{{=T( request.args(0).replace('_',' ').capitalize() )}}</h2>
<div id="web2py_user_form">
{{if 'profile' in request.args:}}
  {{user = Gravatar(auth.user.email)}}
  <img src="{{=user.thumb}}" />
  <blockquote style='width:300px;'>
  
    {{try:}}
       {{=user.profile['aboutMe']}}
       
    {{except Exception:}}
       No profile information
    {{pass}}
    
  </blockquote>
{{pass}}
```

Then, you get the following:

## Authentication and Authorization

You can also get extra services that your user has registered in Gravatar, in the `default/user.html` view:

```
{extend 'layout.html'}}
<div id="web2py_user_form">
{{if 'profile' in request.args:}}
  {{user = Gravatar(auth.user.email)}}
  <img src="{{=user.thumb}}" />
  <blockquote style='width:300px;'>

    {{try:}}
      {{=user.profile['aboutMe']}}
      {{services = user.profile.get('accounts', {})}}
      {{=UL(*[LI(A(service['shortname'], _href=service['url'])) for
        service in services])}}

    {{except Exception:}}
      No profile information

      {{pass}}

  </blockquote>
{{pass}}
```

And then, you will see the additional information (about me and URL of registered services), in your web page:

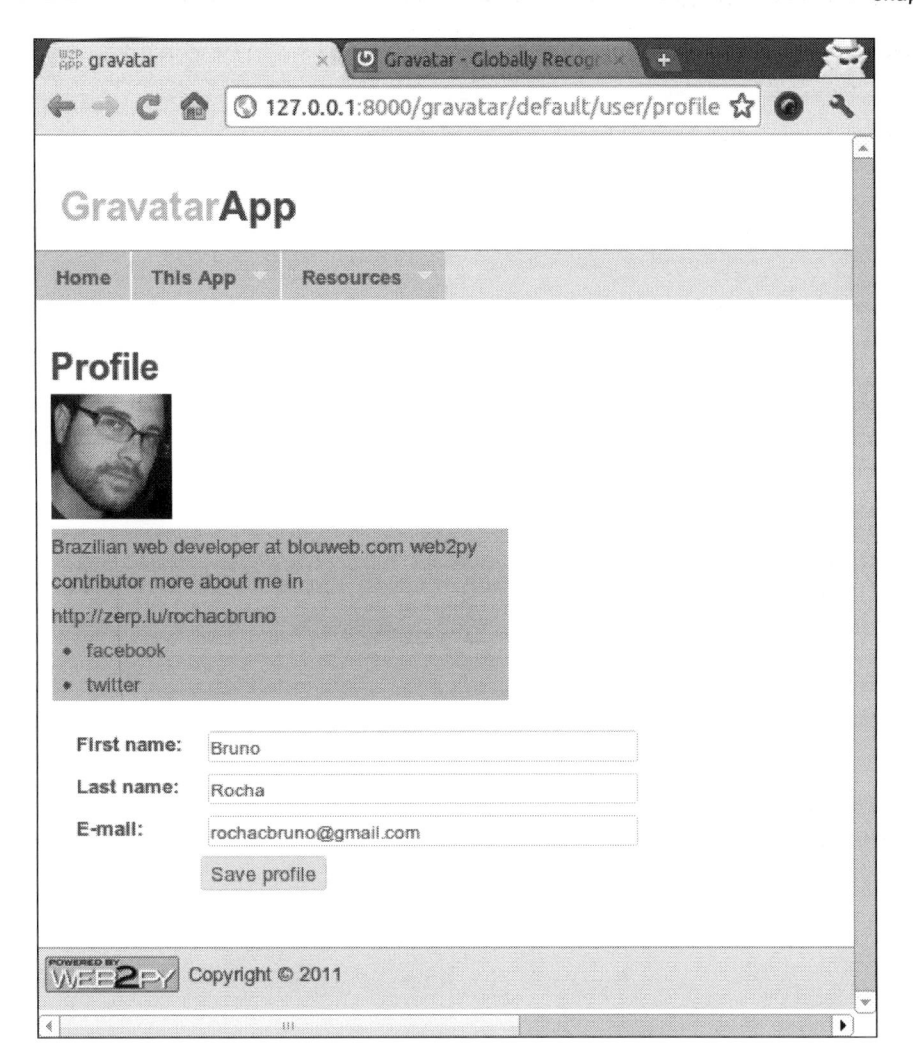

Tell your users to register in `http://en.gravatar.com/`, using the same e-mail address used in your application.

*Authentication and Authorization*

# Multi-user and teacher modes

Since version 1.92, you can set up web2py in a `mult-iuser` or `teaching` mode. There is one instance of web2py installed on a system, one account is the `admin` (or `teacher`), and the other accounts are the `students`. Students can only see their own applications. It works as follows: The admin page is changed and now contains a login and register header. The first user to log in, in this mode, gets the role of `teacher`. Subsequent registrations will become `students`, after approval by the `teacher`. In the following recipe, I assume running web2py locally at `127.0.0.1` on port `8000`. The `teacher` and the `students` will need an **SSL-secured** web2py instance. See *Chapter 11, Other Tips and Tricks*, for more details.

Note that in the `multi-user` mode, there is no security mechanism to prevent interference between administrators.

## How to do it...

1. Install web2py in a folder; let's say `web2py_mu`.
2. Set `MULTI_USER_MODE = True`, in `admin/appadmin/0.py`.
3. Start web2py in the usual way, and click on the link for the administrative interface. Now you see the adapted administrative login.

   Click **register** to create the `teacher` account. You now enter the `admin` application.

4. Click on `logout`, and click on `register` to create the first `student` account (you can let the students do this; provide them with the link).

   After a student registers, his/her status is **Pending.Approving the students**.

5. Enter into the web2py `appadmin`, of the admin application, using the following URL: `http://127.0.0.1:8000/admin/appadmin`.
6. Click on the `auth_user` table.

   You're now looking at the `teacher` and `students` accounts. For each approved student:

   - Click on its ID (leftmost column)
   - Remove the word **pending** in the field `registration_key`

If available, you can also import a list of students by using a CSV file (to be expanded upon).

## There's more...

For students just starting with Python and webapps, starting with a minimal application could be helpful. This simple setup will not include Ajax, and it will cover just minimal templating features.

> On the right side, we need an extra option to load a minimal application, based on a file `minimal.w2p`.

The components of `appadmin` are not relevant for the beginning student, and intimidating, a configuration option `BASIC_STUDENT` as `False`, by default, could help. The teacher can turn this on, and at a later stage off. When `False`, these files can be hidden from sight, the admin screen, the wizard, and other advanced options.

# Authenticating with Facebook using OAuth 2.0

The following recipe will show how to build a simple application that authenticates users using Facebook's OAuth 2.0 authentication service.

OAuth 2.0 is the evolution of the OAuth 1.0a protocol. You can find the exact description of the protocol at the following URL:

`http://oauth.net/2`

Without entering in details, the main object of the protocol is allowing sites (**providers**) give trusted authentication credentials to other sites (**consumers**). This is very similar in scope to CAS authentication system, which is already implemented by web2py.

At the moment, web2py implements OAuth 2.0 as consumer only. But, that is enough to allow any web2py application to authenticate against a provider of OAuth 2.0 services.

We show how to implement a small application that uses Facebook as OAuth 2.0 provider, since it is the provider that was tested more in depth.

*Authentication and Authorization*

## Getting ready

Before you start, you need to register an application on Facebook:

`http://developers.facebook.com`

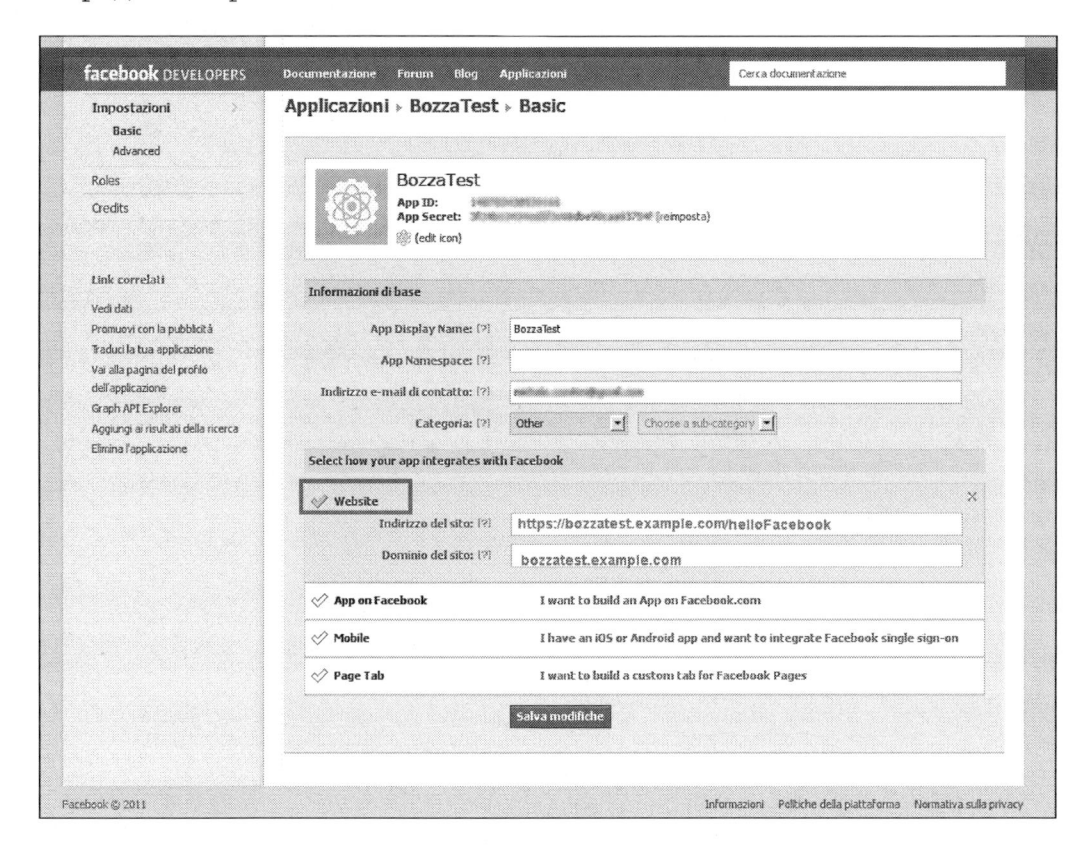

You must be careful about using the exact same URL (including the TCP port) that you use with the application.

Now, it is suggested that you use the Facebook Graph API Python library, to access the `REST` interface in a programmatic way. This recipe uses that library. You can download it here: https://github.com/facebook/python-sdk. Copy it to the `*modules*` directory of your application.

If you want to use the JSON engine that comes with web2py, change the `import` code at the beginning of the file to look simply like the following (the other statements are not needed):

```
# for web2py
from gluon.contrib import simplejson
_parse_json = lambda s: simplejson.loads(s)
```

## How to do it...

1. Create a file containing the **App Id** and the **App Secret**, shown in the registration page. Save it in the `modules` directory of you application, with the name `fbappauth.py`:

   ```
   CLIENT_ID="xxxxxxxxxxxxxxxx"
   CLIENT_SECRET="xxxxxxxxxxxxxxxxxxxxxxxxxxxxxxxx"
   ```

2. Now, you only need to change the `auth` code in your model. You can put it in the usual `db.py` model that comes with the scaffolding application.

   ```
   ##########################################
   ## use fb auth
   ## for facebook "graphbook" application
   ##########################################

   import sys, os
   from fbappauth import CLIENT_ID,CLIENT_SECRET
   from facebook import GraphAPI, GraphAPIError
   from gluon.contrib.login_methods.oauth20_account import
   OAuthAccount

   class FaceBookAccount(OAuthAccount):
     """OAuth impl for FaceBook"""
     AUTH_URL="https://graph.facebook.com/oauth/authorize"
     TOKEN_URL="https://graph.facebook.com/oauth/access_token"

     def __init__(self, g):
       OAuthAccount.__init__(self, g, CLIENT_ID, CLIENT_SECRET,
         self.AUTH_URL, self.TOKEN_URL,
         scope='user_photos,friends_photos')
       self.graph = None

     def get_user(self):
       '''Returns the user using the Graph API.'''
       if not self.accessToken():
         return None

       if not self.graph:
         self.graph = GraphAPI((self.accessToken()))
         user = None

       try:
         user = self.graph.get_object("me")
   ```

```
                except GraphAPIError, e:
                    self.session.token = None
                    self.graph = None

                if user:
                    return dict(first_name = user['first_name'],
                        last_name = user['last_name'],
                        username = user['id'])

        auth.settings.actions_disabled = ['register','change_password',
            'request_reset_password','profile']
        auth.settings.login_form=FaceBookAccount(globals())
        auth.settings.login_next=URL(f='index')
```

As you can see, this class specializes the generic `OAuthAccount` class from `gluon.contrib.login_methods.oauth20_account.py`, so that it can work with the Facebook authentication server.

The following line defines where the user lands after the authentication server has positively accepted the user identity. Change it to whatever you need.

```
        auth.settings.login_next=URL(f='index')
```

## There's more...

Often, you cannot test your application on the public server, where you will deploy the final application. Usually you can test it using `localhost` or `127.0.0.1` as a host.

In the common case, using `localhost` as hostname does not work with your application. Add the proper entry in `/etc/hosts` (in the previous registered example application).

```
# fb app testing setup
127.0.0.1 bozzatest.example.com
```

But, be aware that, in either case, you need to use port `80` to avoid problems.

```
# python web2py.py -p 80 -a <secret>
```

This often requires administrator permissions when starting web2py, or using capabilities where your system supports them.

# 9
# Routing Recipes

In this chapter, we will cover the following recipes:

- Making cleaner URLs with `routes.py`
- Creating a simple router
- Adding a URL prefix
- Associating applications with domains
- Omitting the application name
- Removing application names and controllers from URLs
- Replacing underscores with hyphens in URLs
- Mapping `favicons.ico` and `robots.txt`
- Using URLs to specify the language

## Introduction

At its core, web2py contains a dispatcher that maps URLs into function calls. This mapping is called routing, and it can be configured. This may be necessary in order to shorten URLs, or to deploy a web2py application as a replacement for a pre-existing application, by not wanting to break old external links. web2py comes with two routers, that is, a two-way routing configuration. The old one uses regular expressions to match incoming URLs and map them into the app/controller/function. The new style router instead uses a more holistic approach.

*Routing Recipes*

# Making cleaner URLs with routes.py

In web2py, incoming URLs are, by default, interpreted as
`http://domain.com/application/controller/function/arg1/arg2?var1=val1&var2=val2`.

That is, the first three elements of the URL are interpreted as the web2py application name, controller name, and function name, with the remaining path elements saved in `request.args` (a **list**), and the query string saved in `request.vars` (a **dictionary**).

If the incoming URL has fewer than three path elements, then the missing elements are filled in using the defaults: `/init/default/index`, or, if there is no application named `init`, they are filled using the `welcome` application: `/welcome/default/index`. web2py's `URL()` function creates a URL path (by default, without a scheme or domain) from its component parts: application, controller, function, args list, and vars dictionary. The results are typically used for `href` links in web pages, and for the argument to the redirect function.

As part of its routing logic, web2py also supports URL rewriting, in which the configuration file, `routes.py`, specifies rules by which `URL()` rewrites the URL it generates, and by which web2py interprets the incoming URLs. There are two independent rewriting mechanisms, depending on which one is configured in `routes.py`.

One uses regular-expression pattern matching to rewrite URL strings, while the other uses a routing-parameter dictionary to control the rewriting. We refer to these as the **pattern-based router** and the **parameter-based router**, respectively (sometimes they are referred to as the old router and the new router, respectively, but those terms are not very descriptive, and we will avoid them here).

An example of usage of the old router is given in the following section. An example of usage of the new router is given in the rest of the chapter.

## Getting ready

Normally web URLs have a structure like
`http://host/app/controller/function/args`.

Now imagine an application where each user has its own home page. For example:
`http://host/app/default/home/johndoe`,
where `home` is the action that renders pages, and `johndoe` is the `request.args(0)` that tells web2py which use we are looking for. While this is possible, it would be much better to have URLs that look like this:

`http://host/johndoe/home`.

This can be done using the web2py pattern-based routing mechanism.

We will assume the following minimalist application called `pages`.

In `models/db.py`, add the following code:

```
db = DAL('sqlite://storage.sqlite')
from gluon.tools import *
auth = Auth(db)
auth.settings.extra_fields = [Field('html','text'),Field('css','te
xt')]
auth.define_tables(username=True)
```

Add the following code and the usual scaffolding files to `controllers/default.py`:

```
def index():
   return locals()

def user():
   return dict(form=auth())

def home():
   return db.auth_user(username=request.args(0)).html

def css():
   response.headers['content-type']='text/css'
   return db.auth_user(username=request.args(0)).css
```

## How to do it...

We proceed by creating/editing `routes.py` in the main web2py folder, in order to implement the following rules:

```
routes_in = (
  # make sure you do not break admin
  ('/admin','/admin'),
  ('/admin/$anything','/admin/$anything'),
  # make sure you do not break appadmin
  ('/$app/appadmin','/$app/appadmin'),
  ('/$app/appadmin/$anything','/$app/appadmin/$anything'),
  # map the specific urls for this the "pages" app
  ('/$username/home','/pages/default/home/$username'),
  ('/$username/css','/pages/default/css/$username'),
  # leave everything else unchanged
)

routes_out = (
```

```
    # make sure you do not break admin
    ('/admin','/admin'),
    ('/admin/$anything','/admin/$anything'),
    # make sure you do not break appadmin
    ('/$app/appadmin','/$app/appadmin'),
    ('/$app/appadmin/$anything','/$app/appadmin/$anything'),
    # map the specific urls for this the "pages" app
    ('/pages/default/home/$username','/$username/home'),
    ('/pages/default/css/$username','/$username/css'),
    # leave everything else unchanged
)
```

Note that $app is a shortcut for the regular expression (? P<app>\w+), and it will match everything not containing slashes. $username is a shortcut for (? P<username>\w+). Similarly, you can use other variables. $anything is special, since it corresponds with a different regular expression, (? P<app>.*); that is, it will match everything until the end of the URL.

The critical parts of the code are as follows:

```
routes_in=(
    ...
    ('/$username/home','/pages/default/home/$username'),
    ...
)
routes_out=(
    ...
    ('/pages/default/home/$username','/$username/home'),
    ...
)
```

These map the request for home. We then do the same for the css action. The rest of the code is not really necessary, but makes sure that you do not accidentally break the admin and the appadmin URLs.

## Creating a simple router

This and the next recipes in this chapter deal with the new parameter-based router, which is generally easier to configure, and handles most common re-writing tasks effectively. If possible, try to use the parameter-based router, but if you need more control for special URL-rewriting tasks, look at the pattern-based router.

The starting point for using the parameter-based router is to copy the file `router.example.py` to `routes.py`, in the web2py base directory. (The file `routes.example.py` serves the same purpose for the pattern-based router.) The `example` file contains basic documentation for its respective routing systems; additional documentation is available online in the web2py book, *Chapter 4, The Core: URL rewrite and Routes on error..*

Whenever `routes.py` is changed, you must either restart web2py or, if the admin app is available, load the following URL, for the new configuration to take effect:

`http://yourdomain.com/admin/default/reload_routes`

> The example routing files contain a set of Python `doctests`. When you make a change to the routing configuration, add to or edit the `doctests` in `routes.py` to check that your configuration does what you expect.

The first problem we want to solve is that we want to eliminate the default application and controller from visible URLs, when possible.

## How to do it...

1. Copy `router.example.py` to `routes.py` in the main web2py folder, and edit it as follows. Find the routers `dict`:

   ```
   routers = dict(
     # base router
     BASE = dict(
       default_application = 'welcome',
     ),
   )
   ```

2. Change `default_application` from `welcome` to the name of your application. If your default controller and function are not named, `default` and `index` respectively, then specify those defaults as well:

   ```
   routers = dict(
     # base router
     BASE = dict(
       default_application = 'myapp',
       default_controller = 'mycontroller',
       default_function = 'myfunction',
     ),
   )
   ```

## Adding a URL prefix

Often when you are running web2py under a production server, the same URL may be shared by multiple applications or services, and you will need to add an extra PATH_INFO prefix to identify the web2py service. For example:

http://example.com/php/

http://example.com/web2py/app/default/index

Here, web2py/ identifies the web2py service, and php/ identifies a php service, and the mapping is performed by the web service. You may want to eliminate the extra web2py/ from the PATH_INFO.

### How to do it...

When you specify path_prefix, it is prepended to all URLs generated by URL(), and stripped from all incoming URLs. For example, if you want your external URLs to look like http://example.com/web2py/app/default/index, you can do the following:

```
routers = dict(
  # base router
  BASE = dict(
    default_application = 'myapp',
    path_prefix = 'web2py',
  ),
)
```

## Associating applications with domains

Often, you want to associate specific domains with specific web2py applications, so that incoming URLs directed to specified domains are routed to the appropriate application, without needing the application name in the URL. Again, the parametric router comes in handy.

### How to do it...

Use the parameter-based router's domains feature:

```
routers = dict(
  BASE = dict(
    domains = {
      "domain1.com" : "app1",
      "www.domain1.com" : "app1",
      "domain2.com" : "app2",
    },
```

```
        exclusive_domain = True,
    ),
    # app1 = dict(...),
    # app2 = dict(...),
)
```

In this example, `domain1.com` and `domain2.com` are being served by the same physical host. The configuration specifies that URLs directed to `domain1.com` (and in this case, its subdomain www) are to be routed to `app1`, and URLs directed to `domain2.com` are to be routed to `app2`. If `exclusive_domain` is (optionally) set to `True`, then attempts to use the URL to generate a URL referring to `app2` in response to a request from a domain other than `domain2.com` (and similarly for `app1`), will fail unless they explicitly supply a host name to URL.

Notice that you can also use the following, to further configure the paths for the two apps:

```
app1 = dict(...),
app2 = dict(...),
```

## Omitting the application name

If you are using the parametric router, you may want to omit the default application name from the visible URLs for static files.

### How to do it...

It is simple; you just turn on the `map_static` flag as follows:

```
routers = dict(
  # base router
  BASE = dict(
    default_application = 'myapp',
    map_static = True,
  ),
)
```

Or, if you're using an application-specific router dictionary, turn on the `map_static` flag for each application (that is, `myapp` in the following example):

```
routers = dict(
  # base router
  BASE = dict(
    default_application = 'myapp',
  ),
  myapp = dict(
    map_static = True,
  ),
)
```

*Routing Recipes*

# Removing application name and controllers from URLs

Sometimes, you want to use the parametric router's URL parsing, but you don't want to rewrite visible URLs. Again, you can use the parametric router, but disable URL rewriting.

## How to do it...

Find the router's `dict` in `routes.py`, as follows:

```
routers = dict(
  # base router
  BASE = dict(
    default_application = 'welcome',
  ),
)
```

After finding it, change it to the following:

```
routers = dict(
  # base router
  BASE = dict(
    applications = None,
    controllers = None,
  ),
)
```

## How it works...

Setting `applications` and `controllers` to `None` (`functions` and `languages` are set to `None` by default), tells the parametric router not to omit the corresponding parts of the visible URL. web2py's default URL parsing is stricter than many applications might require, since it assumes that URL components might be used for filenames. The parametric router adheres more closely to the HTTP URL RFCs, which makes it friendlier to applications that need more exotic characters in their arguments or query strings. The `null` router in this recipe, enables this parsing without actually rewriting URLs.

## Replacing underscores with hyphens in URLs

Underscores in URLs can be ugly, and they can be hard to see when the URL is underlined, as it often is on web pages. A hyphen is a more visually appealing alternative, but you can't, for example, use a hyphen in a function name, because it must also be a legal Python identifier. You can use the parametric router and to map - into _!

The parametric router's `map_hyphen` flag converts underscores in application, controller, and function names to hyphens in the visible URLs, and back to underscores when the URL is received. `Args`, `vars` (query string), and possible language selectors are not affected, since hyphens are fine in those fields. As a result, a URL like the following:

`http://some_controller/some_function`

Will appear instead as follows:

`http://some-controller/some-function`

While the internal controller and function names retain their underscores.

### How to do it...

Turn on the `map_hyphen` flag. In the routers directive, add the following code:

```
routers = dict(
  # base router
  BASE = dict(
    default_application = 'myapp',
  ),
  myapp = dict(
    map_hyphen = True,
  ),
)
```

## Mapping favicons.ico and robots.txt

Some special files, such as `robots.txt` and `favicon.ico`, are accessed directly as the root path of a URL. Therefore, they must be mapped from the `root` folder into the `static` folder of the application.

## How to do it...

By default, the parameter-based router sets `root_static` as follows:

```
routers = dict(
  # base router
  BASE = dict(
    default_application = 'myapp',
    root_static = ['favicon.ico', 'robots.txt']
  ),
)
```

This specifies that the listed files are to be served from the default application's static directory.

# Using URLs to specify the language

The recipe *Using cookies to set the language*, in *Chapter 2*, describes how to save a user language preference in a cookie. In this recipe, we describe how to do something similar—to **store** the user language preference in the URL. One advantage to this approach is that it's then possible to bookmark a link that includes a language preference.

## How to do it...

The parametric router supports an optional `language` field in the URL as a field following the application name:

http://domain.com/app/lang/controller/function

The language field is subject to the usual omission rules: the parametric router will omit the language designator, if when the default language is used its omission does not create ambiguity.

URL-based language handling will ordinarily be specified in an application-specific parametric router, setting `default_language` and `languages` as follows:

```
routers = dict(
  # base router
  BASE = dict(
    default_application = app,
  ),
  app = dict(
    default_language = 'en',
    languages = ['en', 'it', 'pt', 'pt-br'],
  ),
)
```

To specify a language for outgoing URLs using `URL()`, set `request.lang` to one of the supported languages. For incoming requests, `request.lang` will be set to the language specified by the incoming URL. As with the language-in-cookie recipe, use `T.force` to force the desired translations in a model file, before translations are to be used. For example, in your model, you can do the following:

```
T.force(request.lang)
```

# 10
# Reporting Recipes

In this chapter, we will cover the following recipes:

- Creating PDF reports
- Creating PDF listings
- Creating PDF labels, badges, and invoices

## Introduction

There are many ways to generate PDF reports in web2py. One way is to use `ReportLab`, the state of the art library for PDF generation in Python. Another way is to generate **LaTeX**, and convert the output to PDF. This is probably the most powerful way to generate PDF, and web2py helps you by packaging `markmin2latex` and `markmin2pdf` in its `contrib` folder. Yet, both these approaches require mastering of third-party libraries and syntax. There is a third way described in this chapter: *convert HTML to PDF directly using the pyfpdf library, packaged with web2py.*

## Creating PDF reports

Who does not need to generate PDF reports, invoices, bills? web2py ships with the `pyfpdf` library, which provides conversion of HTML views into PDF, and can be used for this purpose. `pyfpdf` is still in infancy, and lacks some advanced features that can be found, for example in `reportlab`, yet it is more than appropriate for the average user.

*Reporting Recipes*

You can make a professional-looking business report just by using web2py HTML helpers, mixing headers, logos, charts, text, and tables. Here is an example:

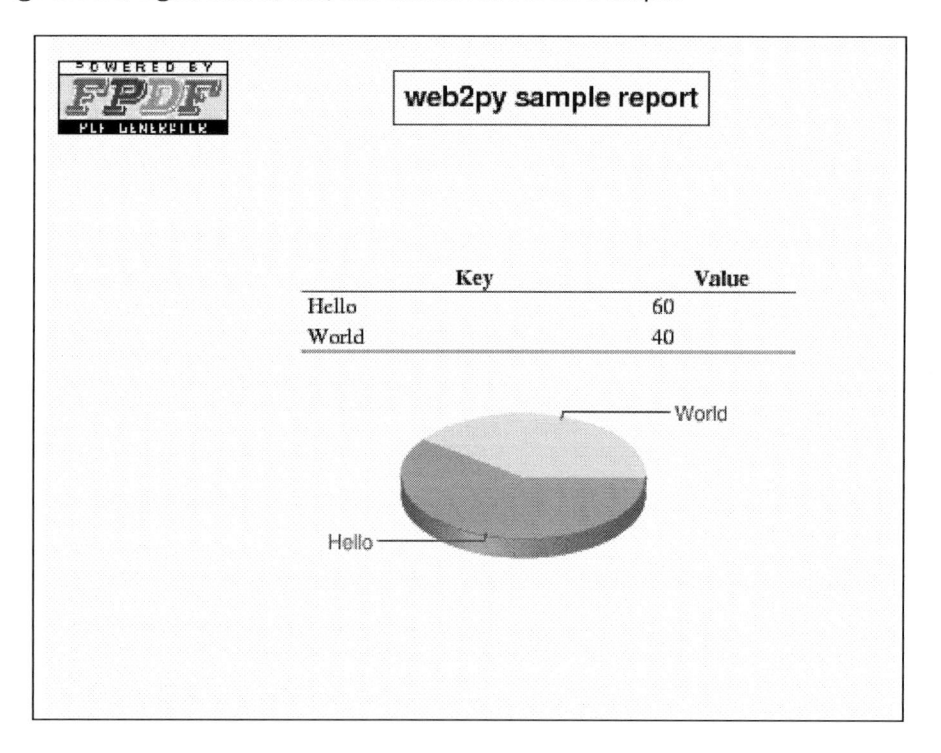

The main advantage of this method is that the same report can be rendered in a HTML view, or can be downloaded as PDF, with minimal effort.

## How to do it...

Here, we provide an example controller that generates a sample report, and then discuss its syntax and APIs:

```
import os

def report():
    response.title = "web2py sample report"
```

```python
    # include a chart from google chart
    url = "http://chart.apis.google.com/chart?cht=p3&chd=t:60,
       40&chs=500x200&chl=Hello|World&.png"
    chart = IMG(_src=url, _width="250", _height="100")

    # create a small table with some data:
    rows = [THEAD(TR(TH("Key",_width="70%"),
       TH("Value",_width="30%"))),
       TBODY(TR(TD("Hello"),TD("60")),
       TR(TD("World"),TD("40")))]

    table = TABLE(*rows, _border="0", _align="center", _width="50%")

if request.extension=="pdf":
    from gluon.contrib.pyfpdf import FPDF, HTMLMixin

    # create a custom class with the required functionalities
    class MyFPDF(FPDF, HTMLMixin):
        def header(self):
            "hook to draw custom page header (logo and title)"

            # remember to copy logo_pb.png to static/images (and remove
            #alpha channel)
            logo=os.path.join(request.folder,"static","images",
                        "logo_pb.png")
            self.image(logo,10,8,33)
            self.set_font('Arial','B',15)
            self.cell(65) # padding
            self.cell(60,10,response.title,1,0,'C')
            self.ln(20)
        def footer(self):
            "hook to draw custom page footer (printing page numbers)"
            self.set_y(-15)
            self.set_font('Arial','I',8)
            txt = 'Page %s of %s' % (self.page_no(), self.alias_nb_pages())
            self.cell(0,10,txt,0,0,'C')
    pdf=MyFPDF()

    # create a page and serialize/render HTML objects
    pdf.add_page()
    pdf.write_html(table.xml())
    pdf.write_html(CENTER(chart).xml())
```

*Reporting Recipes*

```
        # prepare PDF to download:
        response.headers['Content-Type']='application/pdf'
        return pdf.output(dest='S')

    # else normal html view:
    return dict(chart=chart, table=table)
```

## How it works...

The key is in the lines that create and serialize the `pdf` object:

```
    if request.extension=='pdf':
        ...
        pdf=MyFPDF()
        ...
        return pdf.output(dest='S')
```

The `pdf` object can parse raw HTML and convert it to PDF. Here, `MyFPDF` extends `FPDF`, by defining its own header and footer.

The following lines play the critical role of serializing HTML components created with helpers into PDF:

```
    pdf.write_html(table.xml())
    pdf.write_html(CENTER(chart).xml())
```

Internally, `PyFPDF` has a basic HTML renderer using Python `HTMLParser`. This reads the HTML code, and translates it to PDF instructions. Although it only supports basic rendering, it can be extended easily or mixed up with other PDF primitives.

Also, you can render basic HTML with `default.pdf` view included with last versions of web2py, as long you use simple and supported tags.

Look at the `PyFPDF` wiki documentation for more information and examples at the following URLs:

- `http://code.google.com/p/pyfpdf/wiki/Web2Py`
- `http://code.google.com/p/pyfpdf/wiki/WriteHTML`

## Creating PDF listings

As a follow-up to the previous recipe, we can create nice tables that automatically spread over several pages, with headers/footers, column/row highlights, and so on, in a very Pythonic way:

You can see an example at `http://pyfpdf.googlecode.com/files/listing.pdf`.

## How to do it...

Here is an example that more or less speaks for itself: ← *import os*

```
def listing():
  response.title = "web2py sample listing"

  # define header and footers:
  head = THEAD(TR(TH("Header 1",_width="50%"),
  TH("Header 2",_width="30%"),
  TH("Header 3",_width="20%"),
  _bgcolor="#A0A0A0"))
  foot = TFOOT(TR(TH("Footer 1",_width="50%"),
  TH("Footer 2",_width="30%"),
  TH("Footer 3",_width="20%"),
  _bgcolor="#E0E0E0"))

  # create several rows:
  rows = []
  for i in range(1000):
    col = i % 2 and "#F0F0F0" or "#FFFFFF"
    rows.append(TR(TD("Row %s" %i),
    TD("something", _align="center"),
    TD("%s" % i, _align="right"),
    _bgcolor=col))

  # make the table object
  body = TBODY(*rows)
  table = TABLE(*[head,foot, body],
  _border="1", _align="center", _width="100%")

  if request.extension=="pdf":
    from gluon.contrib.pyfpdf import FPDF, HTMLMixin
    # define our FPDF class (move to modules if it is reused

    class MyFPDF(FPDF, HTMLMixin):
      def header(self):
        self.set_font('Arial','B',15)
        self.cell(0,10, response.title ,1,0,'C')
        self.ln(20)
      def footer(self):
        self.set_y(-15)
        self.set_font('Arial','I',8)
```

```
                txt = 'Page %s of %s' % (self.page_no(), self.alias_nb_pages())
                self.cell(0,10,txt,0,0,'C')

    pdf=MyFPDF()

    # first page:
    pdf.add_page()
    pdf.write_html(table.xml())
    response.headers['Content-Type']='application/pdf'
    return pdf.output(dest='S')

    # else return normal html view:
    return dict(table=table)
```

# Creating pdf labels, badges, and invoices

This recipe shows how to use the `pyfpdf` library to do simple conference badges and invoices, but can easily adapted to print labels (`Avery` or other formats), and other documents.

## How to do it...

1. First, you have to define two tables to hold templates and elements that will hold the values used to design the PDF.

2. Create a model, for example `models/plugin_fpdf_templates.py`, and add the following code to it:

```
def _():
    PAPER_FORMATS = ["A4","legal","letter"]
    ELEMENT_TYPES = {'T':'Text', 'L':'Line', 'I':'Image', 'B':'Box',
        'BC':'BarCode'}
    FONTS = ['Arial', 'Courier', 'Helvetica', 'Times-Roman',
        'Symbol','ZapfDingbats']
    ALIGNS = {'L':'Left', 'R':'Right', 'C':'Center',
        'J':'Justified'}
    NE = IS_NOT_EMPTY()

    db.define_table("pdf_template",
      Field("pdf_template_id","id"),
      Field("title"),
      Field("format", requires=IS_IN_SET(PAPER_FORMATS)),
      format = '%(title)s')
```

```
    db.define_table("pdf_element",
      Field("pdf_template_id", db.pdf_template),
      Field("name", requires=NE),
      Field("type", length=2, requires=IS_IN_SET(ELEMENT_TYPES)),
      Field("x1", "double", requires=NE),
      Field("y1", "double", requires=NE),
      Field("x2", "double", requires=NE),
      Field("y2", "double", requires=NE),
      Field("font", default="Arial", requires=IS_IN_SET(FONTS)),
      Field("size", "double", default="10", requires=NE),
      Field("bold", "boolean"),
      Field("italic", "boolean"),
      Field("underline", "boolean"),
      Field("foreground", "integer", default=0x000000,
        comment="Color text"),
      Field("background", "integer", default=0xFFFFFF, comment="Fill
        color"),
      Field("align", "string", length=1, default="L",
        requires=IS_IN_SET(ALIGNS)),
      Field("text", "text", comment="Default text"),
      Field("priority", "integer", default=0, comment="Z-Order"))
_()
```

3. Then, in the controller, `badges.py`, add some functions to create the initial base label/badge. Easily copy the badges according to your label format, then, finally generate a PDF, based on some user data (which is `speakers`):

```
# coding: utf8
import os, os.path
from gluon.contrib.pyfpdf import Template
def create_label():
  pdf_template_id = db.pdf_template.insert(title="sample badge",
                                           format="A4")

  # configure optional background image and insert his element
  path_to_image = os.path.join(request.folder, 'static','42.png')
  if path_to_image:
    db.pdf_element.insert(pdf_template_id=pdf_template_id,
      name='background', type='I', x1=0.0, y1=0.0, x2=85.23,
      y2=54.75, font='Arial', size=10.0, bold=False, italic=False,
      underline=False, foreground=0, background=16777215, align='L',
      text=path_to_image, priority=-1)
```

```python
        # insert name, company_name, number and attendee type elements:
        db.pdf_element.insert(pdf_template_id=pdf_template_id,
            name='name', type='T', x1=4.0, y1=25.0, x2=62.0, y2=30.0,
            font='Arial', size=12.0, bold=True,
            italic=False,
            underline=False, foreground=0, background=16777215, align='L',
            text='', priority=0)
        db.pdf_element.insert(pdf_template_id=pdf_template_id,
            name='company_name', type='T', x1=4.0, y1=30.0, x2=50.0,
            y2=34.0, font='Arial', size=10.0, bold=False, italic=False,
            underline=False, foreground=0, background=16777215, align='L',
            text='', priority=0)
        db.pdf_element.insert(pdf_template_id=pdf_template_id,
            name='no', type='T', x1=4.0, y1=34.0, x2=80.0, y2=38.0,
            font='Arial', size=10.0, bold=False, italic=False,
            underline=False, foreground=0, background=16777215, align='R',
            text='', priority=0)
        db.pdf_element.insert(pdf_template_id=pdf_template_id,
            name='attendee_type', type='T', x1=4.0, y1=38.0, x2=50.0,
            y2=42.0, font='Arial', size=10.0, bold=False, italic=False,
            underline=False, foreground=0, background=16777215, align='L',
            text='', priority=0)
        return dict(pdf_template_id=pdf_template_id)

    def copy_labels():
        # read base label/badge elements from db
        base_pdf_template_id = 1
        elements = db(db.pdf_element.pdf_template_id==\
        base_pdf_template_id).select(orderby=db.pdf_element.priority)

        # set up initial offset and width and height:
        x0, y0 = 10, 10
        dx, dy = 85.5, 55

        # create new template to hold several labels/badges:
        rows, cols = 5, 2
        pdf_template_id = db.pdf_template.insert(title="sample badge\
        %s rows %s cols" % (rows, cols), format="A4")

        # copy the base elements:
        k = 0
        for i in range(rows):
            for j in range(cols):
                k += 1
```

```python
    for e in elements:
        e = dict(element)
        e['name'] = "%s%02d" % (e['name'], k)
        e['pdf_template_id'] = pdf_template_id
        e['x1'] = e['x1'] + x0 + dx*j
        e['x2'] = e['x2'] + x0 + dx*j
        e['y1'] = e['y1'] + y0 + dy*i
        e['y2'] = e['y2'] + y0 + dy*i
        del e['update_record']
        del e['delete_record']
        del e['id']
        db.pdf_element.insert(**e)

    return {'new_pdf_template_id': pdf_template_id}

def speakers_badges():
    # set template to use from the db:
    pdf_template_id = 2

    # query registered users and generate speaker labels
    speakers = db(db.auth_user.id>0).select(orderby=
    db.auth_user.last_name|db.auth_user.first_name)
    company_name = "web2conf"
    attendee_type = "Speaker"

    # read elements from db
    elements = db(db.pdf_element.pdf_template_id==
    pdf_template_id).select(orderby=db.pdf_element.priority)
    f = Template(format="A4",
                 elements = elements,
                 title="Speaker Badges", author="web2conf",
                 subject="", keywords="")

    # calculate pages:
    label_count = len(speakers)
    max_labels_per_page = 5*2
    pages = label_count / (max_labels_per_page - 1)
    if label_count % (max_labels_per_page - 1): pages = pages + 1

    # fill placeholders for each page
    for page in range(1, pages+1):
        f.add_page()
        k = 0
        li = 0
```

```
          for speaker in speakers:
            k = k + 1
            if k > page * (max_labels_per_page ):
              break
            if k > (page - 1) * (max_labels_per_page ):
              li += 1

          #f['item_quantity%02d' % li] = it['qty']
          f['name%02d' % li] = unicode("%s %s" % (speaker.first_name,
                                        speaker.last_name), "utf8")
          f['company_name%02d' % li] = unicode("%s %s" % \
            (company_name, ""), "utf8")
          f['attendee_type%02d' % li] = attendee_type

          ##f['no%02d' % li] = li

        response.headers['Content-Type']='application/pdf'
        return f.render('badge.pdf', dest='S')
```

To check this example:

- Execute `create_label`, and record the value of `pdf_template_id` created
- Set `copy_labels` equal to the value in `base_pdf_template_id`, then execute it
- Set `speaker_badges` equal to `pdf_template_id`, then execute it

The function should generate a PDF with the labels (badges) for the registered users of your application.

The sample badge has a background image as follows:

4. Then, it writes the text over it, filling the speaker name, the address, and so on. You can use a similar method to make attendance certificates and several reports like that.

   For a more complex example, see the following invoice controller (you will need to import the invoice design; look at the `pyfpdf` application sample for a complete example):

```
# coding: utf8

from gluon.contrib.pyfpdf import Template
import os.path
import random
from decimal import Decimal

def invoice():
    # set sample invoice pdf_template_id:
    invoice_template_id = 3

    # generate sample invoice (according to Argentina's regulations)

    # read elements from db
    elements = db(db.pdf_element.pdf_template_id==
      invoice_template_id).select(orderby=db.pdf_element.priority)

    f = Template(format="A4",
      elements = elements,
      title="Sample Invoice", author="Sample Company",
      subject="Sample Customer", keywords="Electronic TAX Invoice")

    # create some random invoice line items and detail data
    detail = "Lorem ipsum dolor sit amet, consectetur. " * 5
    items = []
    for i in range(1, 30):
        ds = "Sample product %s" % i
        qty = random.randint(1,10)
        price = round(random.random()*100,3)
        code = "%s%s%02d" % (chr(random.randint(65,90)),
          chr(random.randint(65,90)),i)
        items.append(dict(code=code, unit='u',
          qty=qty, price=price,
          amount=qty*price,
          ds="%s: %s" % (i,ds)))

    # divide and count lines
    lines = 0
    li_items = []
```

```python
          for it in items:
            qty = it['qty']
            code = it['code']
            unit = it['unit']
            for ds in f.split_multicell(it['ds'], 'item_description01'):
              # add item description line (without price nor amount)
              li_items.append(dict(code=code, ds=ds, qty=qty, unit=unit,
                price=None, amount=None))
              # clean qty and code (show only at first)
              unit = qty = code = None
              # set last item line price and amount
              li_items[-1].update(amount = it['amount'],
                price = it['price'])

          # split detail into each line description
          obs="\n<U>Detail:</U>\n\n" + detail
          for ds in f.split_multicell(obs, 'item_description01'):
            li_items.append(dict(code=code, ds=ds, qty=qty, unit=unit,
              price=None, amount=None))

          # calculate pages:
          lines = len(li_items)
          max_lines_per_page = 24
          pages = lines / (max_lines_per_page - 1)
          if lines % (max_lines_per_page - 1): pages = pages + 1

          # fill placeholders for each page
          for page in range(1, pages+1):
            f.add_page()
            f['page'] = 'Page %s of %s' % (page, pages)
            if pages>1 and page<pages:
              s = 'Continues on page %s' % (page+1)
            else:
              s = ''
              f['item_description%02d' % (max_lines_per_page+1)] = s
              f["company_name"] = "Sample Company"
              f["company_logo"] = os.path.join(request.folder,"static",
                "images","logo_pb.png")
              f["company_header1"] = "Some Address - somewhere -"
              f["company_header2"] = "http://www.example.com"
              f["company_footer1"] = "Tax Code ..."
              f["company_footer2"] = "Tax/VAT ID ..."
              f['number'] = '0001-00001234'
              f['issue_date'] = '2010-09-10'
              f['due_date'] = '2099-09-10'
```

```python
        f['customer_name'] = "Sample Client"
        f['customer_address'] = "Siempreviva 1234"

        # print line item...
        li = 0
        k = 0
        total = Decimal("0.00")
        for it in li_items:
          k = k + 1

        if k > page * (max_lines_per_page - 1):
          break

        if it['amount']:
          total += Decimal("%.6f" % it['amount'])

        if k > (page - 1) * (max_lines_per_page - 1):
          li += 1

        if it['qty'] is not None:
          f['item_quantity%02d' % li] = it['qty']

        if it['code'] is not None:
          f['item_code%02d' % li] = it['code']

        if it['unit'] is not None:
           f['item_unit%02d' % li] = it['unit']
           f['item_description%02d' % li] = it['ds']

        if it['price'] is not None:
          f['item_price%02d' % li] = "%0.3f" % it['price']

        if it['amount'] is not None:
          f['item_amount%02d' % li] = "%0.2f" % it['amount']

        # last page? print totals:
        if pages == page:
            f['net'] = "%0.2f" % (total/Decimal("1.21"))
            f['vat'] = "%0.2f" % (total*(1-1/Decimal("1.21")))
            f['total_label'] = 'Total:'

        else:
           f['total_label'] = 'SubTotal:'
            f['total'] = "%0.2f" % total
    response.headers['Content-Type']='application/pdf'
    return f.render('invoice.pdf', dest='S')
```

*Reporting Recipes*

Here is an example of the output:

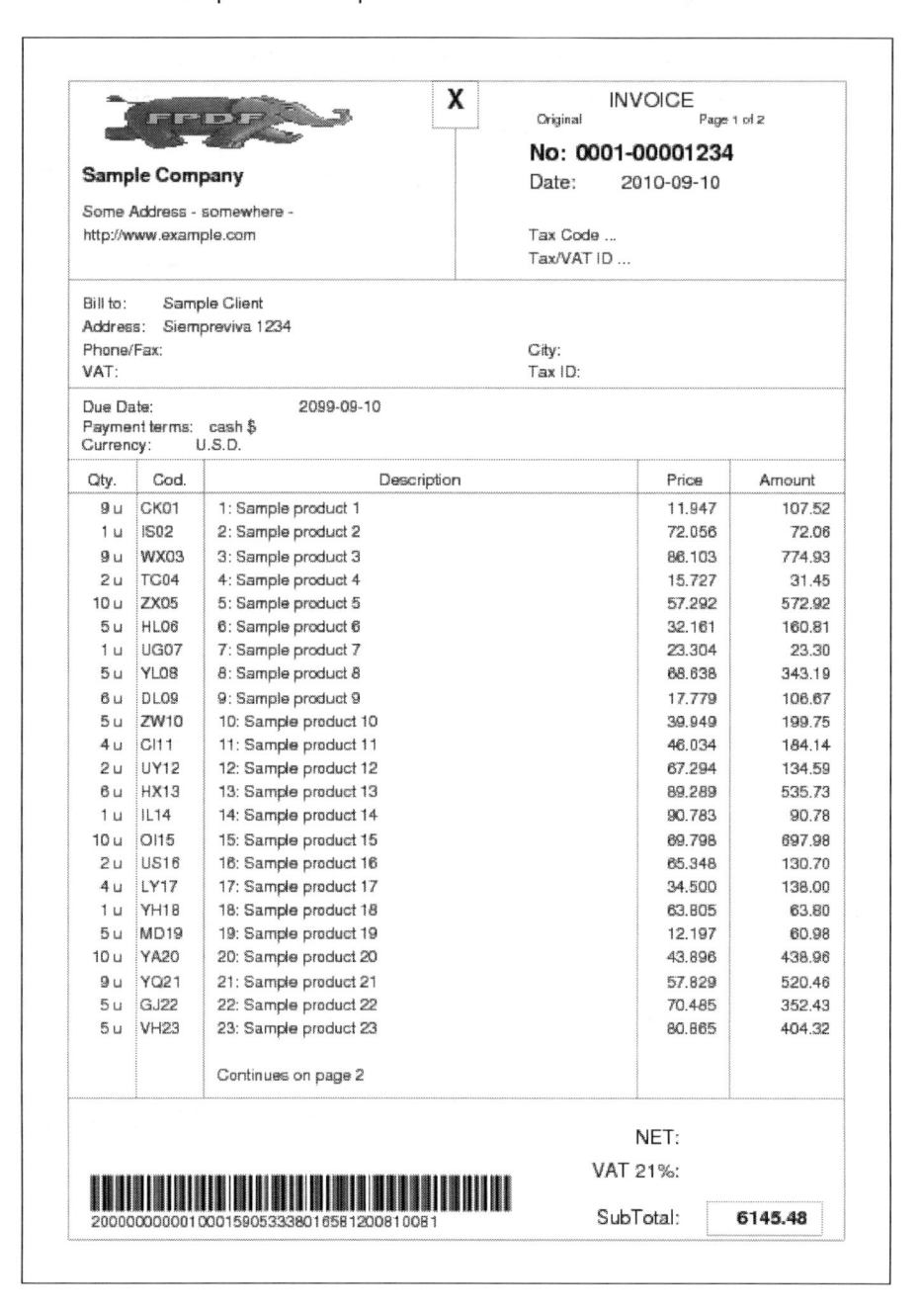

| | | | | |
|---|---|---|---|---|
| | | **X** Original | **INVOICE** Page 1 of 2 | |
| | | | **No: 0001-00001234** | |
| **Sample Company** | | | Date: 2010-09-10 | |
| Some Address - somewhere - http://www.example.com | | | Tax Code ... Tax/VAT ID ... | |

| | |
|---|---|
| Bill to: Sample Client | |
| Address: Siempreviva 1234 | |
| Phone/Fax: | City: |
| VAT: | Tax ID: |

Due Date:       2099-09-10
Payment terms: cash $
Currency:        U.S.D.

| Qty. | Cod. | Description | Price | Amount |
|---|---|---|---|---|
| 9 u | CK01 | 1: Sample product 1 | 11.947 | 107.52 |
| 1 u | IS02 | 2: Sample product 2 | 72.056 | 72.06 |
| 9 u | WX03 | 3: Sample product 3 | 86.103 | 774.93 |
| 2 u | TC04 | 4: Sample product 4 | 15.727 | 31.45 |
| 10 u | ZX05 | 5: Sample product 5 | 57.292 | 572.92 |
| 5 u | HL06 | 6: Sample product 6 | 32.161 | 160.81 |
| 1 u | UG07 | 7: Sample product 7 | 23.304 | 23.30 |
| 5 u | YL08 | 8: Sample product 8 | 68.638 | 343.19 |
| 6 u | DL09 | 9: Sample product 9 | 17.779 | 106.67 |
| 5 u | ZW10 | 10: Sample product 10 | 39.949 | 199.75 |
| 4 u | CI11 | 11: Sample product 11 | 46.034 | 184.14 |
| 2 u | UY12 | 12: Sample product 12 | 67.294 | 134.59 |
| 6 u | HX13 | 13: Sample product 13 | 89.289 | 535.73 |
| 1 u | IL14 | 14: Sample product 14 | 90.783 | 90.78 |
| 10 u | OI15 | 15: Sample product 15 | 69.798 | 697.98 |
| 2 u | US16 | 16: Sample product 16 | 65.348 | 130.70 |
| 4 u | LY17 | 17: Sample product 17 | 34.500 | 138.00 |
| 1 u | YH18 | 18: Sample product 18 | 63.805 | 63.80 |
| 5 u | MD19 | 19: Sample product 19 | 12.197 | 60.98 |
| 10 u | YA20 | 20: Sample product 20 | 43.896 | 438.96 |
| 9 u | YQ21 | 21: Sample product 21 | 57.829 | 520.46 |
| 5 u | GJ22 | 22: Sample product 22 | 70.485 | 352.43 |
| 5 u | VH23 | 23: Sample product 23 | 80.865 | 404.32 |
| | | Continues on page 2 | | |

NET:
VAT 21%:
SubTotal:     **6145.48**

2000000000100015905333801658120081008I

## How it works...

PDF templates are predefined documents (such as invoices, tax forms, and so on), where each element (text, lines, barcodes, and so on) has a fixed position (x1, y1, x2, and y2), style (font, size, and so on), and a default text.

These elements can act as placeholders, so the program can change the default text filling the document.

Also, the elements can be defined in a CSV file or in a database, so the user can easily adapt the form to his printing needs. **Template** is used like a `dict`, setting its items values with the following properties:

- `name`: This is the placeholder identification
- `type`: `T` stands for texts, `L` stands for lines, `I` stands for images, `B` stands for boxes, and `BC` stands for barcodes
- `x1, y1, x2,` and `y2`: These are the top-left and bottom-right coordinates (in mm).
- `font`: This can take the following values—`Arial`, `Courier`, `Helvetica`, `Times`, `Symbol`, `ZapfDingbats`
- `size`: This is the text size in points, that is, 10
- `bold, italic,` and `underline`: This is the text style (non-empty to enable)
- `foreground, background`: These are text and fill colors, that is, `0xFFFFFF`
- `align`: These are the text alignments, where `L` stands for left, `R` stands for right, and `C` stands for center
- `text`: This is the default string that can be replaced at runtime
- `priority`: This specifies the `Z-Order`

Elements can be defined manually (just passing a `dict`), or they can be read from a CSV sheet (using `parse_csv`), or stored in a database, as shown in this example using the `pdf_element` table.

## There's more...

This is a basic example to show badge generation using fill-in-the-blank PDF templates, but it can be used to make any custom repetitive design.

Also, there is a visual designer to drag-and-drop elements, graphically adjust their properties, and easily test them.

See PyFPDF wiki documentation for further information at the following URLs:

- `http://code.google.com/p/pyfpdf/wiki/Web2Py`
- `http://code.google.com/p/pyfpdf/wiki/Templates`

# 11
# Other Tips and Tricks

In this chapter, we will cover the following recipes:

- Using PDB and the embedded web2py debugger
- Debugging with Eclipse and PyDev
- Updating web2py using a shell script
- Creating a simple page statistics plugin
- Rounding corners without images or JavaScript
- Setting a `cache.disk` quota
- Checking if web2py is running using `cron`
- Building a Mercurial plugin
- Building a pingback plugin
- Changing views for mobile browsers
- Background processing with a database queue
- How to effectively use template blocks
- Making standalone applications with web2py and wxPython

## Introduction

This chapter contains recipes that did not fit in any other chapter, and yet were considered important by typical web2py users. An example is how to use web2py with Eclipse. The latter is a very popular Java IDE that works well with Python, but presents some quirks when used with web2py, and here, we show you how to overcome those quirks with proper configuration. Other examples are how to develop applications that are mobile-friendly, and how to develop standalone applications that use a **wxPython GUI**.

# Using PDB and the embedded web2py debugger

web2py has interactive (web browser) debug capabilities built into the **admin** application, similar to shell, but issuing commands directly to **PDB**, which is the **Python Debugger**.

Although this is not a fully-featured visual debugger, it is useful to programmatically set up breakpoints, then step in and do variable and stack inspection, arbitrary code execution in the program context, instruction jump, and other operations.

The use of this debugger is optional, and it is intended for advanced users (it should be used with care, or you can block the web2py server). It is not imported, by default, and normal operation of web2py is not modified.

The implementation can be enhanced and extended to do other kinds of COMET-like communication (pushing data from server to client using AJAX), with general purpose long-running processes.

## How to do it...

PDB is the Python Debugger, included in the standard library.

1. You can start the debugger by writing the following:

   ```
   import pdb; pdb.set_trace()
   ```

   For example, let's debug the welcome default index controller:

   ```
   def index():
     import pdb; pdb.set_trace()
     message = T('Hello World')
     return dict(message=message)
   ```

2. Then, when you open the index page: `http://127.0.0.1:8000/welcome/default/index`, the (PDB) prompt will appear in the console where you started web2py:

   ```
   $ python web2py.py -a a
   web2py Web Framework
   Created by Massimo Di Pierro, Copyright 2007-2011
   Version 1.99.0 (2011-09-15 19:47:18)
   Database drivers available: SQLite3, pymysql, PostgreSQL
   Starting hardcron...
   ```

```
please visit:
 http://127.0.0.1:8000
use "kill -SIGTERM 16614" to shutdown the web2py server
> /home/reingart/web2py/applications/welcome/controllers/default.py(20)index()
-> message = T('Hello World')
(Pdb)
```

3. The debugger points out that we are stopped inside `welcome/controllers/default.py` at *line 20*. At this point, any `Pdb` command can be issued. The most useful ones are as follows:

    - `help`: This command prints the list of available commands
    - `where`: This command prints the current stack trace
    - `list [first[, last]]`: This command lists the source code (between the first and the last lines)
    - `p expression`: This command evaluates the expression and prints the result
    - `! statement`: This command executes a Python statement
    - `step: step in`: This command executes the current line, entering functions
    - `next: step next`: This command executes the current line, not entering functions
    - `return: step return`: This command continues execution until the function exits
    - `continue`: This command continues execution, and only stops at breakpoints
    - `jump lineno`: This command changes the next line to be executed
    - `break filename:lineno`: This command sets a breakpoint
    - `quit`: This command quits from the debugger (aborts the current program)

## Other Tips and Tricks

The commands can be issued just by typing the first letter; for example, look at the following example session:

```
(Pdb) n
> /home/reingart/web2py/applications/welcome/controllers/default.py(21)index()
-> return dict(message=message)
(Pdb) p message
<lazyT 'Hello World'>
(Pdb) !message="hello web2py recipe!"
(Pdb) w
> /home/reingart/web2py/applications/welcome/controllers/default.py(21)index()
-> return dict(message=message)
(Pdb) c
```

4. The commands were `n` for next (execute the line), `p` for a message to print the message variable, `!message=` to change its value to `hello web2py recipe!`, `w` to see the current stack trace, and `continue` to exit the debugger.

   The problem is that this technique cannot be used if you don't have direct access to a console (for example, if web2py is running inside apache, `pdb` will not work).

   If a console is not available, the embedded web2py debugger can be used. The only difference is that instead of calling `pdb`, there is `gluon.debug` with a customized PDB version that runs using a web2py interactive shell through the browser.

5. In the previous example, replace `pdb.set_trace()` with `gluon.debug.stop_trace`, and add `gluon.debug.stop_trace()` prior to the `return` function to give back the control to web2py:

   ```
   def index():
     gluon.debug.set_trace()
     message = T('Hello World')
     gluon.debug.stop_trace()
     return dict(message=message)
   ```

6. Then, when you open the index page, `http://127.0.0.1:8000/welcome/default/index`, the browser will block until you enter into the debug page (included in the administrative interface): `http://127.0.0.1:8000/admin/debug`.

Chapter 11

7. At the debug page, you can issue any PDB command listed before, and interact with your program as though you where in a local console.

   The following image show the last session, but inside the web2py debugger this time:

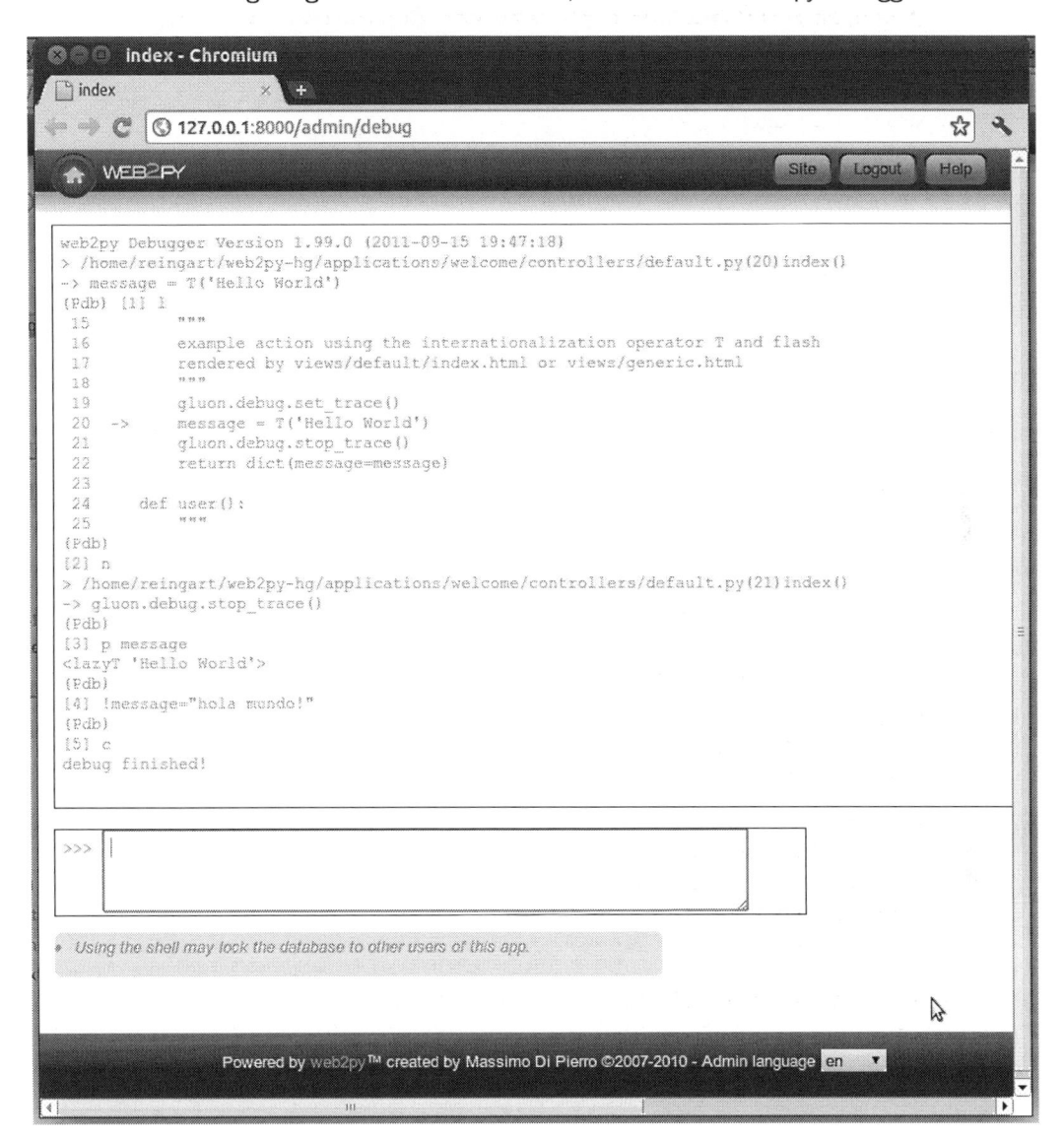

```
web2py Debugger Version 1.99.0 (2011-09-15 19:47:18)
> /home/reingart/web2py-hg/applications/welcome/controllers/default.py(20)index()
-> message = T('Hello World')
(Pdb) [1] l
 15         """
 16         example action using the internationalization operator T and flash
 17         rendered by views/default/index.html or views/generic.html
 18         """
 19         gluon.debug.set_trace()
 20  ->     message = T('Hello World')
 21         gluon.debug.stop_trace()
 22         return dict(message=message)
 23
 24     def user():
 25         """
(Pdb)
[2] n
> /home/reingart/web2py-hg/applications/welcome/controllers/default.py(21)index()
-> gluon.debug.stop_trace()
(Pdb)
[3] p message
<lazyT 'Hello World'>
(Pdb)
[4] !message="hola mundo!"
(Pdb)
[5] c
debug finished!
```

## How it works...

The web2py debugger defines a `Pipe` class deriving from `Queue.Queue` for inter-thread communication, used as a standard input and output of PDB to interact with the user.

The online shell-like interface uses an `ajax` callback to receive user commands, send them to the debugger, and print the results, as if the user were using PDB directly in a console.

When `gluon.debug.set_trace()` is called (that is, in a controller of the debugged application), the custom web2py PDB instance is run, then the input and output is redirected and queued until the other threads open the queue and communicate with it (usually, the admin debug application is called from a separate browser window).

Meanwhile, into the debugging process, PDB does all the work, and web2py only redirects the input and the output messages.

When `gluon.debug.stop_trace()` is called, the thread sends `void` data (`None` value) to signal the monitor thread that debugging has finished.

As said in the introduction, this functionality is intended for intermediate and advanced users, as if `stop_trace` is not called, or the debug controller is not refreshed, then the internal communication queue can block the web2py server (time-outs should be implemented to avoid deadlocks).

Pages being debugged will be blocked until the debug ends, the same as with using `pdb` through the console. The debug controller will be blocked until the first breakpoint (`set_trace`) is reached.

For more details, see `gluon/debug.py` and `applications/admin/controllers/debug.py` inside the web2py source files.

## There's more...

PDB is a fully featured debugger, supporting conditional breakpoints and advanced commands. The complete documentation can be found at the following URL:

http://docs.python.org/library/pdb.html

PDB derives from the BDB module (Python Debugger framework), that can be used to extend this technique to add more features, implementing a lightweight remote debugger (it is a base debugger that doesn't need console interaction, so other user interfaces could be used).

Also, the `Pipe` class is an example of interacting with long running processes that can be useful in COMET-like scenarios, to push data from the server to the browser, without keeping a connection open (using standard web servers and AJAX).

Combining both techniques, a new debugger (QDB) was developed, enabling remote debugging of web2py applications (even in production environments). In the following paragraphs, an example use case will be shown. For more information see the following:

http://code.google.com/p/rad2py/wiki/QdbRemotePythonDebugger

To use qdb, you have to download `qdb.py` (see the previous link), and put it on the `gluon.contrib` directory (it will be included in further releases of web2py).

Then, in your controller, import it and call `set_trace` to start debugging, as shown in the following example:

```
def index():
   response.flash = T('Welcome to web2py')
   import gluon.contrib.qdb as qdb
   qdb.set_trace()
   return dict(message='Hello World')
```

When you open your controller and `set_trace` is reached, qdb will listen for a remote connection to attach to and start the debugger interaction. You can start the debug session by executing the qdb module (`python qdb.py`) as follows:

```
C:\rad2py\ide2py>python qdb.py
qdb debugger fronted: waiting for connection to ('localhost', 6000)
> C:\web2py\applications\welcome\controllers/default.py(19)
->     return dict(message=T('Hello World'))
(Cmd) p response.flash
Welcome to web2py!
> C:\web2py\applications\welcome\controllers/default.py(19)
->     return dict(message=T('Hello World'))
(Cmd) c
```

You can interact with the same commands as PDB ones, that is, step, print a value, continue, and so on.

Note that web2py (backend debugger) and qdb frontend debugger are different processes, so you can debug even a daemon webserver,such as Apache. Also, in the `qdb.py` source, you can change the address/port and password to connect to remote servers over the Internet.

web2py will include qdb and a web user interface debugger in the 2.0 release (for the development environment).

For a full-featured IDE for web2py (for either development or production environments), including a visual debugger based in this recipe, see the following:

http://code.google.com/p/rad2py

*Other Tips and Tricks*

# Debugging with Eclipse and PyDev

**Eclipse** is an open source, extensible development platform and application framework, designed for building, deploying, and managing software across its entire software lifecycle. It is very popular in the Java world. **PyDev** is a Python extension for Eclipse, which allows the use of Eclipse as an IDE for Python, and therefore, for web2py. Here, we show you how to set up web2py to work well with these tools.

## Getting ready

1. Download the latest Eclipse IDE (http://www.eclipse.org/downloads/), and extract it to a folder of your choice.
2. Start Eclipse by running `eclipse.exe` in the folder. Notice that there is no installation for Eclipse, but you must have the Java runtime (http://java.com/en) installed.
3. Install PyDev by clicking on [**Help | Install New Software**], and entering the following URL, then clicking the **Add** button:

    http://pydev.org/updates
4. Select all of the options and hit **[next]**.
5. It should prompt you to accept a license agreement. Continue through the wizard, and click **[No]** when it asks you if you want to restart.
6. Install the correct mercurial version for your operating system:

    http://mercurial.selenic.com
7. Go back to **Help | Install New Software**, and enter the following URL:

    http://cbes.javaforge.com/update
8. Continue through the wizard, and click on **Yes** when it asks you to restart this time.
9. Create a new project in Eclipse by going to **File | New | Project | Mercurial | Clone Mercurial Repository using Mercurial**, and enter the following URL:

    http://code.google.com/p/web2py
10. Enter `web2py` in the **Clone Directory Name** field.

11. Set the interpreter by going to **Window | Preferences | PyDev | Interpreter**, and choosing the path to your Python binary:

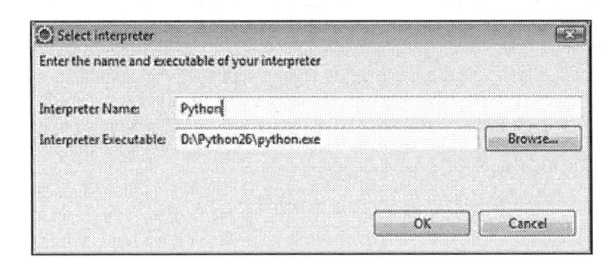

That's it! You can start debugging by finding `web2py.py` in the project tree, by right-clicking and selecting **Debug As | Python Run**. You can also pass arguments to `web2py.py` by choosing **Debug Configuration** from the same menu.

## There's more...

Instead of installing web2py from the mercurial repository, you can make PyDev point to an existing web2py installation (it must be a source installation and not a web2py binary). In this case, simply go to **File | New | PyDev**, and specify the directory of your web2py installation:

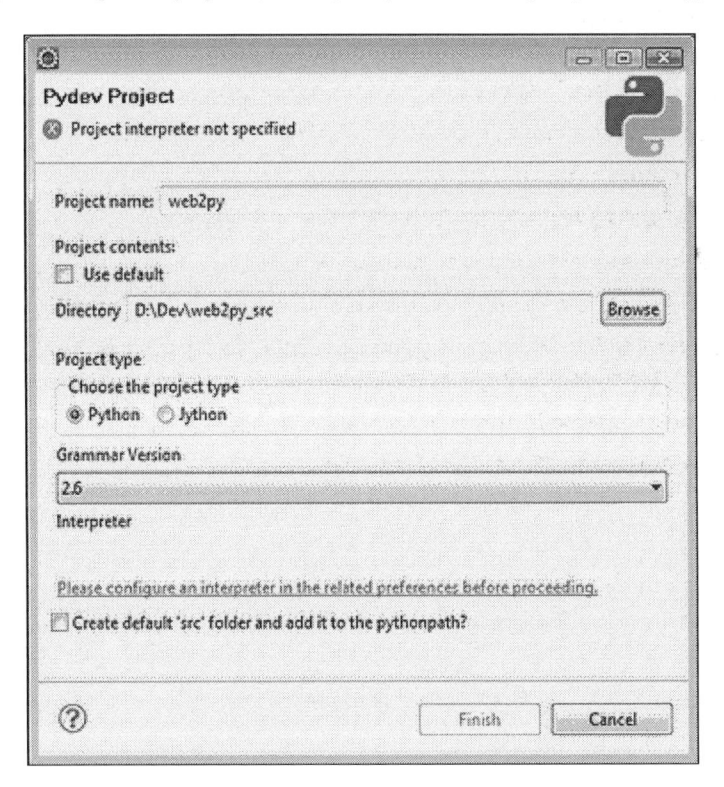

*Other Tips and Tricks*

# Updating web2py using a shell script

The web2py admin interface provides an **upgrade** button, which downloads the latest web2py, and unzips it over the old one (it does not overwrite applications except welcome, admin, and examples). This is ok, but it presents some potential problems:

- The admin may be disabled
- You may want to update many installations at once, and would rather do it programmatically
- You may want to archive the previous version, in case you need reverting

The script we provide in this recipe is only useful for solving these problems in Linux and on a Mac.

## How to do it...

1. Move under the web2py folder:

   `cd /path/to/web2py`

2. Make sure that you are the same user who owns the web2py folder, or you at least have the write permission. Save the following script in a file (for example: update_web2py.sh), and make it executable:

   `chmod +x update_web2py.sh`

3. Then, run it:

   ```
   # update-web2py.sh
   # 2009-12-16
   #
   # install in web2py/.. or web2py/ or web2py/scripts as update-
   # web2py.sh
   # make executable: chmod +x web2py.sh
   #
   # save a snapshot of current web2py/ as web2py/../web2py-version.
   # zip
   # download the current stable version of web2py
   # unzip downloaded version over web2py/

   TARGET=web2py
   ```

```
if [ ! -d $TARGET ]; then
    # in case we're in web2py/
    if [ -f ../$TARGET/VERSION ]; then
        cd ..
    # in case we're in web2py/scripts
    elif [ -f ../../$TARGET/VERSION ]; then
        cd ../..
    fi
fi
read a VERSION c < $TARGET/VERSION
SAVE=$TARGET-$VERSION
URL=http://www.web2py.com/examples/static/web2py_src.zip


ZIP=`basename $URL`
SAVED=""

####  Save a zip archive of the current version,
####  but don't overwrite a previous save of the same version.
###
if [ -f $SAVE.zip ]; then
    echo "Remove or rename $SAVE.zip first" >&2
    exit 1
fi
if [ -d $TARGET ]; then
    echo -n ">>Save old version: " >&2
    cat $TARGET/VERSION >&2
    zip -q -r $SAVE.zip $TARGET
    SAVED=$SAVE.zip
fi
###
####  Download the new version.
###
echo ">>Download latest web2py release:" >&2
curl -O $URL
```

## Other Tips and Tricks

```
###
####   Unzip into web2py/
###
unzip -q -o $ZIP
rm $ZIP
echo -n ">>New version: " >&2
cat $TARGET/VERSION >&2
if [ "$SAVED" != "" ]; then
    echo ">>Old version saved as $SAVED"
fi
```

### There's more...

Yes, there is more. When upgrading web2py, the welcome application is upgraded, and it might contain a new appadmin, a new layout, and new JavaScript libraries. You may want to upgrade your applications as well. You can do this manually, and you have to be careful, because depending on how your applications work, this may break them. For an application called app, you can upgrade appadmin with the following:

```
cp applications/welcome/controllers/appadmin.py applications/app/\
controllers
cp applications/welcome/views/appadmin.py applications/app/views
```

You can upgrade generic views with the following:

```
cp applications/welcome/views/generic.* applications/app/views
```

You can upgrade web2py_ajax with the following:

```
cp applications/welcome/views/web2py_ajax.html applications/app/views
cp applications/welcome/static/js/web2py_ajax.js applications/app/static/\js
```

And finally, you can upgrade all static files with the following:

```
cp -r applications/welcome/static/* applications/app/static/
```

You may have to be more selective. Back up first and be careful.

# Creating a simple page statistics plugin

In this recipe, we will show you how to create a plugin to display page statistics in a hierarchical format.

## How to do it...

First of all, create a file called `models/plugin_stats.py`, which contains the following code:

```python
#!/usr/bin/env python
# -*- coding: utf-8 -*-

def _(db,                           # reference to DAL obj.
      page_key,                     # string to id page
      page_subkey='',               # string to is subpages
      initial_hits=0,               # hits initial value
      tablename="plugin_stats"      # table where to store data
      ):
    from gluon.storage import Storage
    table = db.define_table(tablename,
    Field('page_key'),
      Field('page_subkey'),
      Field('hits', 'integer'))
    record = table(page_key=page_key,page_subkey=page_subkey)

    if record:
      new_hits = record.hits + 1
      record.update_record(hits=new_hits)
      hits = new_hits

    else:
      table.insert(page_key=page_key,
        page_subkey=page_subkey,
        hits=initial_hits)
      hits = initial_hits

    hs = table.hits.sum()
    total = db(table.page_key==page_key).select(hs).first()(hs)
    widget = SPAN('Hits:',hits,'/',total)
    return Storage(dict(hits=hits,total=total,widget=widget))

plugin_stats = _(db,
    page_key=request.env.path_info,
    page_subkey=request.query_string)
```

*Other Tips and Tricks*

If you want to get the results displayed to the visitor, add the following to `views/layout.html`:

```
{{=plugin_stats.widget}}
```

## How it works...

The `plugin` file is a model file, and is executed at every request. It calls the following query, which defines a table to store hits, and each record is identified by a `page_key` (`request.env.path_info`) and a `page_subkey` (`request.query_string`).

```
plugin_stats = _(db,
  page_key=request.env.path_info,
  page_subkey=request.query_string)
```

If a record with this key and subkey does not exist, it is created. If it exists, it is retrieved, and the field `hits` is incremented by one. The function `_` has a weird name, but there is nothing special about it. You can choose a different name; we just do not wish to pollute the namespace, as the function is needed only once. The function returns a `Storage` object assigned to `plugin_stats`, which contains the following:

- `hits`: This is the number of hits corresponding to the current `page_key` and `page_subkey`
- `total`: This is the sum of the hits for the same `page_key` as the current page but different subkeys
- `widget`: This is a span displaying the hits, and `total`, which can be embedded in views

## There's more...

Notice that you can decide to change the following lines into something else, and use different variables to group pages for counting purposes:

```
page_key=request.env.path_info
page_subkey=request.query_string
```

# Rounding corners without images or JavaScript

Modern browsers support CSS directives for rounding corners. They include the following:

- WebKit (Safari, Chrome)
- Gecko (Firefox)
- Opera (with a major hack)

## Getting ready

We assume that you have a view containing the following HTML code, and you want to round the corner of the `box` class:

```
<div class="box">
  test
</div>
```

## How to do it...

In order to see the effect, we also need to change the background color. In the `style` file, for example, add the following code for the default layout in `static/styles/base.css`:

```
.box {
  -moz-border-radius: 5px;     /* for Firefox */
  -webkit-border-radius: 5px;  /* for Safari and Chrome */
  background-color: yellow;
}
```

The first line `-moz-border-radius: 5px;` is interpreted only by Firefox, and ignored by other browsers. The second line is interpreted only by Safari and Chrome.

## There's more...

What about Opera? Opera does not have a CSS directive for rounded corners, but you can modify the previous CSS as follows, and have web2py generate a dynamic image to use as the background with the requested color and rounded corners:

```
.box {
  -moz-border-radius: 5px;     /* for Firefox */
  -webkit-border-radius: 5px;  /* for Safari and Chrome */
  background-color: yellow;
  background-image: url("../images/border_radius?r=4&fg=249,249,249&bg=235,232,230"); /*
  for opera */
}
```

To this purpose, create a `controllers/images.py` file, and add the following code to it:

```
def border_radius():
  import re
  radius = int(request.vars.r or 5)
  color = request.vars.fg or 'rbg(249,249,249)'
  if re.match('\d{3},\d{3},\d{3}',color):
```

*Other Tips and Tricks*

```
            color = 'rgb(%s)' % color
            bg = request.vars.bg or 'rgb(235,232,230)'
        if re.match('\d{3},\d{3},\d{3}',bg):
            bg = 'rgb(%s)'%bg
        import gluon.contenttype
        response.headers['Content-Type']= 'image/svg+xml;charset=utf-8'
        return '''<?xml version="1.0" ?><svg
            xmlns="http://www.w3.org/2000/svg"><rect fill="%s" x="0" y="0"
            width="100%%" height="100%%" /><rect ill="%s" x="0" y="0"
            width="100%%" height="100%%" rx="%spx"
            /></svg>'''%(bg,color,radius)
```

This code will generate an SVG image, dynamically.

Reference: `http://home.e-tjenesten.org/~ato/2009/08/border-radius-opera`.

## Setting a cache.disk quota

This recipe is about web2py using RAM memory for **disk caching** on Linux (with `tmpfs`).

`cache.disk` is a popular caching mechanism that allows multiple web2py installations that share a file system to share cache. It is not as efficient as `memcache`, as writing on a shared file system can be a bottleneck; nevertheless this is an option for some users. If you are using `cache.disk`, you may want to limit the amount of data that gets written to cache by setting a **quota**. This can be achieved by creating a temporary memory-mapped file system with the added benefit of improving performances.

## How to do it...

The main idea is to use `cache.disk` with `tmpfs`.

1. First of all, you need to log in as `root` and execute the following command:

   `mount -t tmpfs tmpfs $folder_path -o rw,size=$size`

   Here:

   `$folder_path` is a path to the folder where you mount your slice of RAM

   `$size` is the amount of memory you want to dedicate (M - megabytes)

   For example:

   `mkdir /var/tmp/myquery`

   `mount -t tmpfs tmpfs /var/tmp/myquery -o rw,size=200M`

2. You have just allocated 200 MB of your RAM. Now we have to map it in a web2py application. Just write the following in your models:

   ```
   from gluon.cache import CacheOnDisk
   cache.disk = CacheOnDisk(request,
     folder='/the/memory/mapped/folder')
   ```

   So, in our case:

   ```
   cache.disk = CacheOnDisk(request, folder='/var/tmp/myquery')
   ```

3. Now, when you use:

   ```
   db(...).select(cache=(cache.disk,3600)....)
   ```

   Or the following:

   ```
   @cache(request.env.path_info, time_expire=5, cache_model=cache.disk)
   def cache_controller_on_disk():
     import time
     t = time.ctime()
     return dict(time=t, link=A('click to reload',
       _href=request.url))
   ```

   You have have `ram space quota` for every `query/controller/etc` cached, and each one can have a different size setting.

# Checking if web2py is running using cron

If you are on a UNIX machine, you may want to monitor whether web2py is running. A production quality solution to this problem is using **Monit**: `http://mmonit.com/monit/documentation/`.

It can monitor your processes, log problems, and also restart them for you automatically. Here we present a do-it-yourself simpler solution, in the minimalist web2py spirit.

## How to do it...

1. We will create the file, `/root/bin/web2pytest.sh`, to check if web2py runs, and start web2py if it is not running.

   ```
   #! /bin/bash
   # written by Ivo Maintz
   export myusername=mdipierro
   export port=8000
   export web2py_path=/home/mdipierro/web2py
   ```

```
        if ! ` netcat -z localhost $port `
          then pgrep -flu $myusername web2py | cut -d -f1 | xargs kill > /\
        dev/null 2>&1
            chown $myusername: /var/log/web2py.log
            su $myusername -c 'cd $web2py_path && ./web2py.py -p $port -a \
        password 2>&1 >> /var/log/web2py.log'
            sleep 3
            if ` netcat -z localhost $port `
              then echo "web2py was restarted"
              else echo "web2py could not be started!"
            fi
        fi
```

2. Now edit the `crontab` using the `shell` command:

   `crontab -e`

3. Add a `crontab` line that instructs the `crontab` deamon to run our script every three minutes:

   `*/3 * * * * /root/bin/web2pytest.sh > /dev/null`

   Notice that you may have to edit the first few lines of the script to set the right username, port, and web2py path that you want to monitor/restart.

# Building a Mercurial plugin

web2py's admin supports **Mercurial** for versioning, but can one pull and push changes through HTTP?

In this recipe, we present a plugin for web2py that consists of a single file. It wraps Mercurial's `hgwebdir wsgi` application, and allows one to interact with the mercurial repository of the web2py application either from a web browser or the `hg` client.

This is interesting for the following two reasons:

1. On one side, if you use mercurial to version control your application, this plugin allows you to share the repository online with other people.
2. On the other side, this is a great example of how to call a third party WSGI application from web2py.

## Getting ready

This requires that you run web2py from source, and you have mercurial installed. You can install mercurial using the following command:

`easy_install mercurial`

This plugin will only work on Python distributions that have mercurial installed. You could package mercurial into the web2py application itself, but we do not recommend it. It makes very little sense to use this plugin if you are not a regular mercurial user.

## How to do it...

All you need to do to create the plugin is create a new controller, "plugin_mercurial.py":

```
""" plugin_mercurial.py
   Author:   Hans Christian v. Stockhausen <hc at vst.io>
   Date:     2010-12-09
"""

from mercurial import hgweb

def index():
  """ Controller to wrap hgweb

     You can access this endpoint either from a browser in which case
        the hgweb interface is displayed or from the mercurial client.

     hg clone http://localhost:8000/app/plugin_mercurial/index app
  """

  # HACK - hgweb expects the wsgi version to be reported in a tuple
  wsgi_version = request.wsgi.environ['wsgi.version']
  request.wsgi.environ['wsgi.version'] = (wsgi_version, 0)

  # map this controller's URL to the repository location and
  #instantiate app
  config = {URL():'applications/'+request.application}
  wsgi_app = hgweb.hgwebdir(config)

  # invoke wsgi app and return results via web2py API
  # http://web2py.com/book/default/chapter/04#WSGI
  items = wsgi_app(request.wsgi.environ, request.wsgi.start_response)
  for item in items:
    response.write(item, escape=False)
  return response.body.getvalue()
```

## Other Tips and Tricks

Here is a view of a sample report from the shell:

```
hcvst@ubuntu:~/temp$ hg clone http://localhost:8000/mercat/plugin_mercurial/index mercat-clone
requesting all changes
adding changesets
adding manifests
adding file changes
added 4 changesets with 49 changes to 48 files (+1 heads)
updating working directory
47 files updated, 0 files merged, 0 files removed, 0 files unresolved
hcvst@ubuntu:~/temp$
hcvst@ubuntu:~/temp$ ls -l mercat-clone/
total 36
-rw-r--r-- 1 hcvst hcvst   54 2010-12-09 14:25 ABOUT
drwxr-xr-x 2 hcvst hcvst 4096 2010-12-09 14:25 controllers
drwxr-xr-x 2 hcvst hcvst 4096 2010-12-09 14:25 cron
-rw-r--r-- 1 hcvst hcvst    0 2010-12-09 14:25 __init__.py
drwxr-xr-x 2 hcvst hcvst 4096 2010-12-09 14:25 languages
-rw-r--r-- 1 hcvst hcvst  135 2010-12-09 14:25 LICENSE
drwxr-xr-x 2 hcvst hcvst 4096 2010-12-09 14:25 models
drwxr-xr-x 2 hcvst hcvst 4096 2010-12-09 14:25 modules
drwxr-xr-x 3 hcvst hcvst 4096 2010-12-09 14:25 static
drwxr-xr-x 3 hcvst hcvst 4096 2010-12-09 14:25 views
hcvst@ubuntu:~/temp$
```

Here is a view from the `plugin_above`:

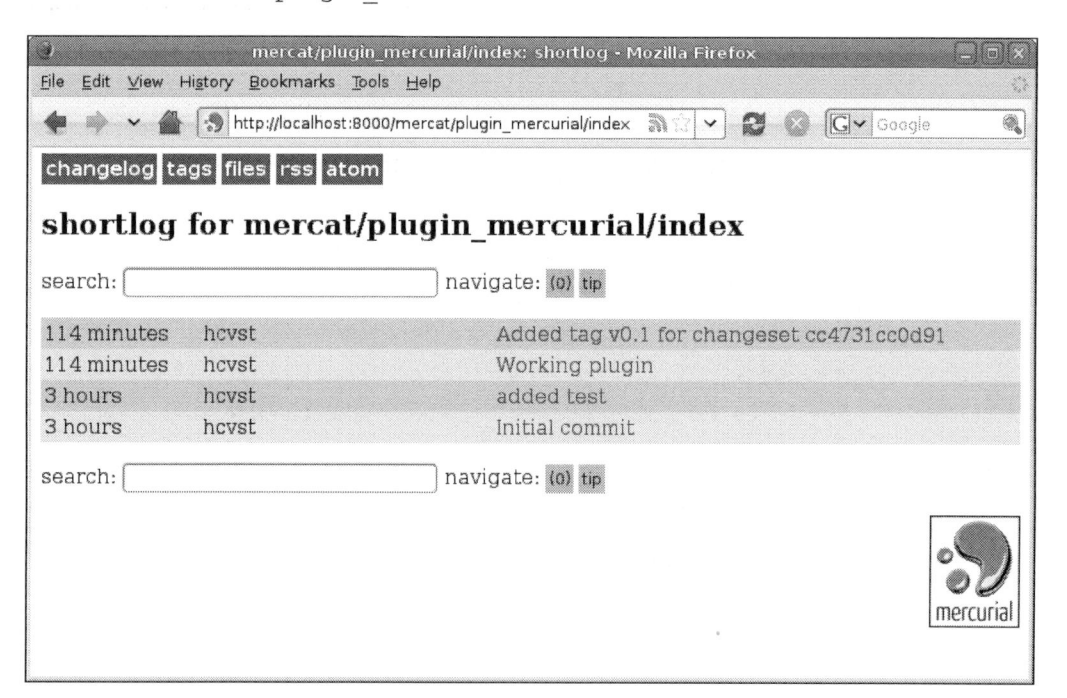

**shortlog for mercat/plugin_mercurial/index**

| 114 minutes | hcvst | Added tag v0.1 for changeset cc4731cc0d91 |
|---|---|---|
| 114 minutes | hcvst | Working plugin |
| 3 hours | hcvst | added test |
| 3 hours | hcvst | Initial commit |

You can also push to the repository. To be able to push to the repository, you need to edit/create the file `application/<app>/.hg/hgrc`, and add the following entries for example:

```
[web]
allow_push = *
push_ssl = False
```

Clearly, this is recommended for a trusted environment only. Also, see the `hgrc` documentation at http://www.selenic.com/mercurial/hgrc.5.html#web.

The `hgwebdir` WSGI application can expose multiple repositories, although for a web2py application-specific plugin, this is probably not what you want. If you do, however, want just that, try tweaking the `config` variable that is passed to the `hgwebdir` constructor. For example, you could pass the name of the repository to access through `request.args[0]`. URLs are even longer then, so you might want to set up some rules in `routes.py`.

```
config = {
  'app/plugin_mercurial/index/repo1':'path/to/repo1',
  'app/plugin_mercurial/index/repo2':'path/to/repo2',
  'app/plugin_mercurial/index/repo3':'path/to/repo3'
}
```

# Building a pingback plugin

Pingbacks allow blog posts and other resources, such as photos, to automatically notify one another of backlinks. This plugin exposes a decorator to pingback-enable controller functions, and a pingback client to inform a **Wordpress** blog, for example, that we link to it.

**Pingback** is a standard protocol, and version 1.0 is described at the following URL:

http://www.hixie.ch/specs/pingback/pingback

`plugin_pingback` consists of one single module file.

## How to do it...

First of all, create a `module/plugin_pingback.py` file, with the following code:

```
#!/usr/bin/env python
# coding: utf8
#
# Author:   Hans Christian v. Stockhausen <hc at vst.io>
# Date:     2010-12-19
# License: MIT
#
```

```python
# TODO
# - Check entity expansion requirements (e.g. &lt;) as per Pingback
# spec page 7
# - make try-except-finally in PingbackClient.ping robust

import httplib
import logging
import urllib2
import xmlrpclib
from gluon.html import URL

__author__ = 'H.C. v. Stockhausen <hc at vst.io>'
__version__ = '0.1.1'

from gluon import *

# we2py specific constants
TABLE_PINGBACKS = 'plugin_pingback_pingbacks'

# Pingback protocol faults
FAULT_GENERIC = 0
FAULT_UNKNOWN_SOURCE = 16
FAULT_NO_BACKLINK = 17
FAULT_UNKNOWN_TARGET = 32
FAULT_INVALID_TARGET = 33
FAULT_ALREADY_REGISTERED = 48
FAULT_ACCESS_DENIED = 49
FAULT_UPSTREAM_ERROR = 50

def define_table_if_not_done(db):
    if not TABLE_PINGBACKS in db.tables:
        db.define_table(TABLE_PINGBACKS,
            Field('source', notnull=True),
            Field('target', notnull=True),
            Field('direction', notnull=True,
                requires=IS_IN_SET(('inbound', 'outbound'))),
            Field('status'), # only relevant for outbound pingbacks
            Field('datetime', 'datetime', default=current.request.now))

class PingbackServerError(Exception):
    pass

class PingbackClientError(Exception):
```

```python
    pass

class PingbackServer(object):
  " Handles incomming pingbacks from other sites. "

  def __init__(self, db, request, callback=None):
    self.db = db
    self.request = request
    self.callback = callback
    define_table_if_not_done(db)

  def __call__(self):
    """
      Invoked instead of the decorated function if the request is a
        pingback request from some external site.
    """

    try:
      self._process_request()
    except PingbackServerError, e:
      resp = str(e.message)
    else:
      resp = 'Pingback registered'
    return xmlrpclib.dumps((resp,))

  def _process_request(self):
     " Decode xmlrpc pingback request and process it "

     (self.source, self.target), method = xmlrpclib.loads(
       self.request.body.read())

     if method != 'pingback.ping':
       raise PingbackServerError(FAULT_GENERIC)
       self._check_duplicates()
       self._check_target()
       self._check_source()

     if self.callback:
       self.callback(self.source, self.target, self.html)
       self._store_pingback()

  def _check_duplicates(self):
    " Check db whether the pingback request was previously processed "
```

## Other Tips and Tricks

```
      db = self.db
      table = db[TABLE_PINGBACKS]
      query = (table.source==self.source) & (table.target==self.target)
      if db(query).select():
        raise PingbackServerError(FAULT_ALREADY_REGISTERED)

   def _check_target(self):
     " Check that the target URI exists and supports pingbacks "

     try:
       page = urllib2.urlopen(self.target)
     except:
       raise PingbackServerError(FAULT_UNKNOWN_TARGET)
     if not page.info().has_key('X-Pingback'):
       raise PingbackServerError(FAULT_INVALID_TARGET)

   def _check_source(self):
     " Check that the source URI exists and contains the target link "

     try:
       page = urllib2.urlopen(self.source)

     except:
       raise PingbackServerError(FAULT_UNKNOWN_SOURCE)
     html = self.html = page.read()
     target = self.target

     try:
       import BeautifulSoup2
       soup = BeautifulSoup.BeautifulSoup(html)
       exists = any([a.get('href')==target for a in soup.findAll('a')])

     except ImportError:
       import re
       logging.warn('plugin_pingback: Could not import BeautifulSoup,' \
          ' using re instead (higher risk of pingback spam).')
       pattern = r'<a.+href=[\'"]?%s[\'"]?.*>' % target
       exists = re.search(pattern, html) != None

     if not exists:
       raise PingbackServerError(FAULT_NO_BACKLINK)

   def _store_pingback(self):
```

```python
    " Companion method for _check_duplicates to suppress duplicates. "

    self.db[TABLE_PINGBACKS].insert(
      source=self.source,
      target=self.target,
      direction='inbound')

class PingbackClient(object):
  " Notifies other sites about backlinks. "

  def __init__(self, db, source, targets, commit):
    self.db = db
    self.source = source
    self.targets = targets
    self.commit = commit
    define_table_if_not_done(db)

  def ping(self):
    status = 'FIXME'
    db = self.db
    session = current.session
    response = current.response
    table = db[TABLE_PINGBACKS]
    targets = self.targets

    if isinstance(targets, str):
      targets = [targets]

    for target in targets:
      query = (table.source==self.source) & (table.target==target)

    if not db(query).select(): # check for duplicates
      id_ = table.insert(
        source=self.source,
        target=target,
        direction='outbound')

    if self.commit:
      db.commit()

      try:
        server_url = self._get_pingback_server(target)

      except PingbackClientError, e:
```

```
            status = e.message

      else:
        try:
          session.forget()
          session._unlock(response)
          server = xmlrpclib.ServerProxy(server_url)
          status = server.pingback.ping(self.source, target)

        except xmlrpclib.Fault, e:
          status = e

        finally:
          db(table.id==id_).update(status=status)

  def _get_pingback_server(self, target):
    " Try to find the target's pingback xmlrpc server address "

    # first try to find the pingback server in the HTTP header
    try:
      host, path = urllib2.splithost(urllib2.splittype(target)[1])
      conn = httplib.HTTPConnection(host)
      conn.request('HEAD', path)
      res = conn.getresponse()
      server = dict(res.getheaders()).get('x-pingback')

    except Exception, e:
      raise PingbackClientError(e.message)
      # next try the header with urllib in case of redirects

      if not server:
        page = urllib2.urlopen(target)
        server = page.info().get('X-Pingback')

      # next search page body for link element

      if not server:
        import re
        html = page.read()
        # pattern as per Pingback 1.0 specification, page 7
        pattern = r'<link rel="pingback" href=(P<url>[^"])" ?/?>'
        match = re.search(pattern, html)

        if match:
```

```python
            server = match.groupdict()['url']

        if not server:
            raise PingbackClientError('No pingback server found.')
        return server

def listen(db, callback=None):
    """
    Decorator for page controller functions that want to support
        pingbacks.
    The optional callback parameter is a function with the following
        signature.
        callback(source_uri, target_uri, source_html)
    """

    request = current.request
    response = current.response

    def pingback_request_decorator(_):
        return PingbackServer(db, request, callback)

    def standard_request_decorator(controller):
        def wrapper():
            " Add X-Pingback HTTP Header to decorated function's response "

            url_base = '%(wsgi_url_scheme)s://%(http_host)s' % request.env
            url_path = URL(args=['x-pingback'])
            response.headers['X-Pingback'] = url_base + url_path
            return controller()
        return wrapper

        if request.args(0) in ('x-pingback', 'x_pingback'):
            return pingback_request_decorator

        else:
            return standard_request_decorator

def ping(db, source, targets, commit=True):
    " Notify other sites of backlink "

    client = PingbackClient(db, source, targets, commit)
    client.ping()
```

And here is how to use it:

- Import the module
- Decorate actions that should receive pingbacks with `listen`
- Modify actions that should send pingbacks with `ping`

Here is a concrete example, where we assume a simple `blog` system:

```
import plugin_pingback as pingback

def on_pingback(source_url, target_url, source_html):
  import logging
  logging.info('Got a pingback')
  # ...

@pingback.listen(db,on_pingback)
def viewpost():
  " Show post and comments "
  # ...
  return locals()

def addpost():
  " Admin function to add new post "
  pingback.ping(globals(),
    source=new_post_url,
    targets=[linked_to_post_url_A, linked_to_post_url_B]
  )
  # ...
  return locals()
```

## How it works...

The `plugin_pingback.py` module provides the core functionality of the `plugin_pingback` plugin.

The class `PingbackServer` handles the incoming pingbacks. The class `PingbackClient` is used to notify external sites of the backlinks. In your code, you should not have to use these classes directly. Instead, use the module functions `listen` and `ping`.

`listen` is a decorator to be used with controller functions you want to pingback-enable. Under the hood, it uses the `PingbackServer`. This decorator accepts the `db` as its first parameter, and optionally a second `callback` parameter. The `callback` signature is the function name (`source`, `target`, or `html`), where `source` is the ping- back source URI, `target` is the target URI, and `html` is the source page content.

`ping` is used to notify external sites of backlinks using the `PingbackClient`.

The first parameter is, as for `listen`, the `db` object, the second is the source page URI, the third is either a string or a list of target URIs, and finally there is the `commit` parameter (defaults to `True`). A DB `commit` is likely to be required at this point, as the controller function containing the ping is probably generating the source page. If the source page is not committed, the pingback system of the target page will not be able to find it, and thus rejects the pingback request.

## Changing views for mobile browsers

If your web application is accessed from a mobile device, such as a phone, then most likely, the visitor is using a small screen and limited bandwidth to access your website. You may want to detect this, and serve a light version of your pages. What **light** means depends on the context, but here we assume that you simply want to change the default layout for these visitors.

web2py provides two APIs that allow you to do this.

- You can detect when a client is using a mobile device:

  `if request.user_agent().is_mobile: ...`

- You can ask web2py to replace the default view `*.html` with `*.mobile.html`, for any action using the `@mobilize` decorator.

  ```
  from gluon.contrib.user_agent_parser import mobilize
  @mobilize
  def index():
    return dict()
  ```

In this recipe, we will show you how to do this manually, using third-party libraries: `mobile.sniffer` and `mywurlf`, instead of using the built-in web2py APIs.

### Getting ready

This slice uses the libraries `mobile.sniffer` and `pywurfl` to parse the USER_AGENT header from the HTTP request. We will create a single function that returns `True`/`False`.

You can install both of them with the following commands:

**easy_install mobile.sniffer**

**easy_install pywurfl**

### How to do it...

We will create our function so that, for example, if we have this request, `http://example.com/app/controller/function`, the regular view will be in `views/controller/function.html`, while the mobile view will be in `views/controller/function.mobile.html`. And if it does not exist, it will revert to the regular one.

## Other Tips and Tricks

This can be achieved through the following function, which you can place in any model file, for example `models/plugin_detect_mobile.py`.

```
# coding: utf8
import os

def plugin_detect_mobile(switch_view=True):
  from mobile.sniffer.detect import detect_mobile_browser
  if detect_mobile_browser(request.env.http_user_agent):
    if switch_view:
      view = '%(controller)s/%(function)s.mobile.%(extension)s' % \
        request
      if os.path.exists(os.path.join(request.folder, 'views',view)):
        response.view = view
    return True
  return False
plugin_detect_mobile()
```

# Background processing with a database queue

Let's consider a very typical application that requires users to register. After a user submits the registration form, the application sends out a confirmation e-mail, asking the user to verify the sign-up process. The problem, however, is that the user does not get an immediate response to the next page, since they have to wait for the application to connect to the SMTP mail server, send the message, save some database results, and then finally, return the next view. Another pathological case could be argued; let's say this same application provides a dashboard that allows the user to download PDF reports, or data in an OpenOffice `Calc` format. For the sake of argument, this process usually takes five to ten minutes to generate the PDF or spreadsheet. Obviously, it does not make sense for a user to wait on the server to process this data, since they would not be able to perform any other actions.

Instead of actually performing these actions that may take a while to run, the application can just register a request in the database to perform the said action. A background process executed by `cron` could read these requests, and then proceed to process them.

For the user registration, just provide a database table called `emails_to_send`; this will cause a background process that would run every minute, and send all of the e-mails in a single session. The user doing the registration benefits from a speedier sign-up, and our application benefits by needing to only make a single SMTP connection for multiple e-mails.

For report generation, the user could submit a request for the file in question. They might visit a download page on the application, which shows processing for files that have been requested. Again, a background process could load all report requests, process them into output files, and then save the results to the database. The user would re-visit the download page, and be able to download the processed file. The user could continue performing other tasks, while waiting for the report to finish.

## How to do it...

For this example, we will use the user report requests. This will be a dentistry website, where clients information is stored. The office clerk would like to know the demographic breakdown of their clients by zip code, to help determine where would be the best place to send out their new advertising campaign. Lets just assume this is a very large dentist's office that has over 100,000 clients. This report could take a while.

For this, we will need the following tables:

```
db.define_table('clients',
  Field('name'),
  Field('zipcode'),
  Field('address'))

db.define_table('reports',
  Field('report_type'),
  Field('report_file_loc'),
  Field('status'),
  Field('submitted_on', 'datetime', default=request.now),
  Field('completed_on', 'datetime', default=None))
```

When a user navigates to the `reports` page, they are presented with options for possible reports that could be downloaded. The following is an example of a controller function for a report request:

```
def request_report():
  report_type = request.vars.report_type
  
  # make sure its a valid report
  if report_type not in ['zipcode_breakdown', 'name_breakdown']:
    raise HTTP(404)
  
  # add the request to the database to process
  report_id = db.reports.insert(report_type=report_type,
    status='pending')
  
  # return something to uniquely identify this report in case
  # this request was made from Ajax.
  return dict(report_id=report_id)
```

## Other Tips and Tricks

Now for the script that would process all report requests.

```
def process_reports():
  from collections import defaultdict
  reports_to_process = db(db.reports.status == 'pending').select()

  # set selected reports to processing so they do not get picked up
  # a second time if the cron process happens to execute again while
  # this one is still executing.
  for report in reports_to_process:
    report.update_record(status='processing')

  db.commit()

  for report in reports_to_process:
    if report.report_type == 'zipcode_breakdown':

      # get all zipcodes
      zipcodes = db(db.clients.zipcode != None).select()

      # if the key does not exist, create it with a value of 0
      zipcode_counts = defaultdict(int)

  for zip in zipcodes:
    zipcode_counts[zip] += 1

      # black box function left up to the developer to implement
      # just assume it returns the filename of the report it created.
      filename = make_pdf_report(zipcode_counts)

      report.update_record(status='done',
        completed_on=datetime.datetime.now(),
        report_file_loc=filename)

      # commit record so it reflects into the database immediately.
    db.commit()
process_reports()
```

Now that we have the code to generate reports, it needs a way to execute. Let's add the call to this function to the `web2py cron/crontab` file.

`* * * * * root *applications/dentist_app/cron/process_reports.py`

Now, when the user requests the page, they will either see that the report is processing, or a link to download the generated report.

## There's more...

In this recipe, we used a `Poor-Man's Queue` example of dispatching tasks to the background processes. This method will scale up to a certain amount of users, however, at some point, an external message queue could be used to speed things up even more.

Since version 1.99.1, web2py includes its own built-in scheduler and scheduling API. It is documented in the latest edition of the official web2py manual, but you can also read more of it at the following link:

`http://www.web2py.com/examples/static/epydoc/web2py.gluon.scheduler-module.html`

There is a plugin that integrated celery into web2py:

`http://code.google.com/p/web2py-celery/`

The former uses database access to distribute tasks, and the latter uses **RabbitMQ** through celery to implement enterprise message queue servers.

# How to effectively use template blocks

As you may already know, the web2py template system is very flexible, providing template inheritance, inclusions, and a recently new (and under-documented) feature called blocks.

A **block** is a way that child templates can override certain portions of their parent templates, and replace or extend the content with their own.

For example, a typical layout template includes several places that could be overridden, based on the current page a user is located on. Examples include the title bar, portions of the navigation, perhaps a page title, or keywords.

In this example, we will consider a typical enterprise application that contains custom JavaScript on each page to handle elements local to only that page; the method of solving this will generate a base pattern for block usage.

## How to do it...

First, let's handle the basic pattern of using blocks, since this also solves the issue in our example application of needing a place to put extra JavaScript blocks within the `<head>` element of the HTML page.

Consider the following `layout.html` file:

```
<!doctype html>

<head>
  <title>{{block title}}My Web2py App{{end}}</title>

  <script type="text/javascript" src={{=URL(c="static/js",
    f="jquery.js")}}></script>

  {{block head}}{{end}}
</head>

<body>
  <h1>{{block body_title}}My Web2py App{{end}}</h1>

  <div id="main_content">
    {{block main_content}}
      <p>Page has not been defined</p>
    {{end}}
  </div>
</body>
```

And the following `detail.html` file:

```
{{extend "layout.html"}}

{{block title}}Analysis Drilldown - {{super}}{{end}}

{{block head}}
  <script>
    $(document).ready(function() {
      $('#drill_table').sort();
    });
  </script>
{{end}}

{{block main_content}}
  <table id="drill_table">
    <tr>
      <td>ABC</td>
      <td>123</td>
    </tr>
    <tr>
      <td>EFG</td>
      <td>456</td>
    </tr>
  </table>
{{end}}
```

This will render the following output file:

```html
<!doctype html>

<head>
  <title>Analysis Drilldown - My Web2py App</title>

  <script type="text/javascript" src="/static/js/jquery.js"></script>

  <script>
    $(document).ready(function() {
      $('#drill_table').sort();
    });
  </script>
</head>

<body>
  <h1>My Web2py App</h1>

  <div id="main_content">
    <table id="drill_table">
      <tr>
        <td>ABC</td>
        <td>123</td>
      </tr>
      <tr>
        <td>EFG</td>
        <td>456</td>
      </tr>
    </table>
  </div>
</body>
```

## There's more...

Notice the use of `{{super}}` when overriding the title block. `{{super}}` will take the HTML output of the parent block that it is overriding, and insert it at that position. So, in this example, the page title can retain the global sites title, but insert this unique page name into the title.

Another thing to note is that when a block is not defined in a child template, it will still render. Since there was no definition for the `body_title` block, it still rendered My web2py App.

Also, blocks deprecate the need for the old web2py `{{include}}` helper, as the child template could just define a block that represents the location for the main content of the page. This is a design pattern used heavily in other popular template languages.

*Other Tips and Tricks*

# Making standalone applications with web2py and wxPython

web2py can be used to make desktop-visual applications that doesn't require a browser or a web server. This can be useful when standalone applications are needed (that is, no web server installation), and also, this approach allows to simplify user interface programming without advanced JavaScript or CSS requirements, giving direct access to a user's machine operating system and libraries.

This recipe shows you how to use **models** and **helpers** to create a sample form, to store basic person information into a database using the **wxPython** GUI toolkit, in fewer than 100 lines of code, following the best practices of web2py.

## Getting ready

First, you need a working Python and web2py installation, and then download and install wxPython from (http://www.wxpython.org/download.php).

Second, you need **gui2py**, a small library that manages forms, bridging web2py and wx (http://code.google.com/p/gui2py/downloads/list).

You can also pull the source code from the project repository using Mercurial:

```
hg clone https://codegoogle.com/p/gui2py/.
```

## How to do it...

In this basic recipe, we will cover the following steps:

1. Import wxPython, gui2py, and web2py.
2. Create a sample `Person` table, with several fields and validators.
3. Create wxPython GUI objects (application, main frame window, and html browser).
4. Create a web2py SQL form for the `Person` table.
5. Define the event handler to process the user input (validating and inserting the row).
6. Connect the event handler, show the window, and start to interact with the user.

The full example follows, with a self-explained source code. Type it in, and save as a usual Python script, for example, in your home directory as my_gui2py_app.py:

```python
#!/usr/bin/python
# -*- coding: latin-1 -*-

import sys

# import wxPython:
import wx

# import gui2py support -wxHTML FORM handling- (change the path!)
sys.path.append(r"/home/reingart/gui2py")
from gui2py.form import EVT_FORM_SUBMIT

# import web2py (change the path!)
sys.path.append(r"/home/reingart/web2py")
from gluon.dal import DAL, Field
from gluon.sqlhtml import SQLFORM
from gluon.html import INPUT, FORM, TABLE, TR, TD
from gluon.validators import IS_NOT_EMPTY, IS_EXPR, IS_NOT_IN_DB, IS_IN_SET
from gluon.storage import Storage

# create DAL connection (and create DB if not exists)
db=DAL('sqlite://guitest.sqlite',folder=None)

# define a table 'person' (create/aster as necessary)
person = db.define_table('person',
  Field('name','string', length=100),
  Field('sex','string', length=1),
  Field('active','boolean', comment="check!"),
  Field('bio','text', comment="resume (CV)"),
)

# set sample validator (do not allow empty nor duplicate names)
db.person.name.requires = [IS_NOT_EMPTY(),
  IS_NOT_IN_DB(db, 'person.name')]

db.person.sex.requires = IS_IN_SET({'M': 'Male', 'F': 'Female'})

# create the wxPython GUI application instance:
app = wx.App(False)

# create a testing frame (wx "window"):
f = wx.Frame(None, title="web2py/gui2py sample app")
```

## Other Tips and Tricks

```python
    # create the web2py FORM based on person table
    form = SQLFORM(db.person)

    # create the HTML "browser" window:
    html = wx.html.HtmlWindow(f, style= wx.html.HW_DEFAULT_STYLE |
      wx.TAB_TRAVERSAL)
    # convert the web2py FORM to XML and display it
    html.SetPage(form.xml())

    def on_form_submit(evt):
      "Handle submit button user action"
      global form
      print "Submitting to %s via %s with args %s"% (evt.form.action,
        evt.form.method, evt.args)
      if form.accepts(evt.args, formname=None, keepvalues=False,
        dbio=False):
        print "accepted!"
      # insert the record in the table (if dbio=True this is done by
        web2py):
      db.person.insert(name=form.vars.name,
        sex=form.vars.sex,
        active=form.vars.active,
        bio=form.vars.bio,
        )
      # don't forget to commit, we aren't inside a web2py controller!
      db.commit()
      elif form.errors:
        print "errors", form.errors
      # refresh the form (show web2py errors)
      html.SetPage(form.xml())

    # connect the FORM event with the HTML browser
    html.Bind(EVT_FORM_SUBMIT, on_form_submit)

    # show the main window
    f.Show()
    # start the wx main-loop to interact with the user
    app.MainLoop()
```

Remember to change /home/reingart/web2py /home/reingart/gui2py to your web2py and gui2py installation paths.

Once you have saved the file, run it:

**python my_gui2py_app.py**

You should see the application window ready to receive data, and test it! It should work as a usual web2py application:

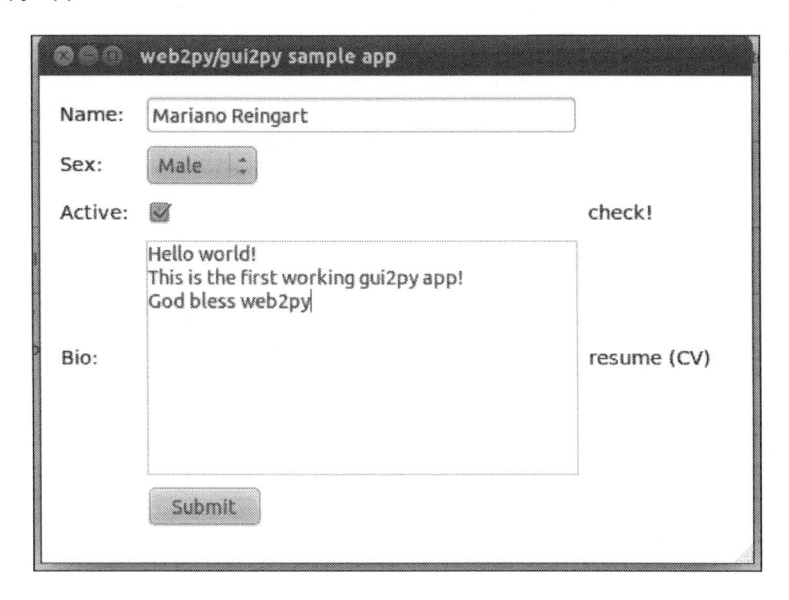

## How it works...

This recipe uses basic wxPython objects, in this case, the `wx.HTML` control (you can see the original `form_example.zip` that is the base to gui2py):

http://wiki.wxpython.org/wxHTML

`wx.HTML` is basically the **wxPython** browser, and it can display simple HTML markup (mainly intended to show help pages, reports, and do simple printing). It can be extended to render custom HTML tags (`FORM`, `INPUT`, `TEXTAREA`, and so on), emulating a normal browser.

First, the program should import the required libraries, define the models, and create a `wx` application and a basic window (a `Frame` in the `wx` world). Once the `wx.HTML` control is created inside the main window, the event handler should be connected to tell `wx` how to respond to user actions. The event handler receives the form data already parsed, it does the standard form validation and inserts the row data using DAL (in a similar way to web2py controllers). Finally, this is a GUI application, so it must call the `MainLoop`. It runs forever, waiting for the user events, and calling the appropriate event handlers.

The main advantage is that `wx.HTML` removes the need of a JavaScript engine, so the events can be programmed directly in Python, and it also assures the same results in different platforms where `wxPython` runs, without the troubles of HTML compatibility issues.

*Other Tips and Tricks*

As the code is a standard Python program, you can access advanced features directly in the user machine, such as opening files or socket connections, or using libraries to interact with webcams, USB devices or legacy hardware.

Also, this approach allows to reuse your web2py knowledge (DAL, models, helpers, built-in validation, and so on), speeding up the development of standalone visual GUI applications, following the best practices of web development.

## There's more...

This recipe could be further extended with more advanced wxPython controls, such as `wx.ListCtrl` or `wx.Grid`, enabling to make responsive fully-featured applications with spreadsheets capabilities, custom cell editors, virtual rows to browse huge quantities of records, and so on.

Also, `wx.AUI` (**Advanced User Interface**) allows to build modern looking applications with docking toolbars and panels, visual styles, and so on.

You can see more than 200 `wx` examples in the **wxPython Docs&Demo** package, available at: http://www.wxpython.org.

# Index

## Symbols

$app 270
.egg package 220
@service.amfrpc3(...) decorator 221
@service.json 210
@service.json, GET variable 210
! statement, Pdb command 297

## A

Add button 163
Advanced User Interface. *See* WX.AUI
Amazon Web Services. *See* AWS
amf3 RPC calls
   making from Flex, pyamf used 220-222
Apache httpd 16-20, 23
API 99
app 106
appadmin URLs 270
application
   associating, with domains 272, 273
   controllers, removing from URLs 274
   name, omitting 273
   name, removing from URLs 274
Applications Programming Interface. *See* API
asynchronous calls 214
AUI 334
Auth
   auth.settings.extra_fields 254
   auth_user 254
   customizing 254
   db.auth_user table 254
auth.settings.extra_fields 254
auth.settings.login_url 216
auth_user 254

auth_user table 51
autocompletion plugin
   using 169-171
auto tooltips
   adding, in forms 148-150
avatars
   getting for user profile page,
       pyGravatar used 256-261
AWS
   e-mails, sending with Boto 245

## B

badges
   creating 284-292
BasicJSONRPCData.py controller 213
BasicJSONRPC.py controller 213, 216
BDB module 300
block 327
body_title block 329
Bogdan 204
Boto
   e-mails sending with, through Amazon
       Web Services (AWS) 245
break filename
   lineno, Pdb command 297
built-in ajax function 173
button_text: string 165

## C

cache.disk 310
Calc format 324
call action 209
callback parameter 322
callback signature 322

**cancel button**
  adding, to forms 126, 127
**CAPTCHA** 253, 255, 256
**category tree**
  hierarchical 114, 115
**CGI**
  used, for running web2py on shared hosts 34
**checkout button** 225
**Cherokee**
  URL, for downloading 30
  URL, for installing 30
  web2py, running 26-30
**code_xml** 221
**color picker widget** 150, 151
**concurrent updates**
  blocking 133, 134
  detecting 133, 134
**config variable** 315
**confirmation**
  adding, on form submit 127, 128
**consumers** 263
**contacts application**
  building 53-60
**contacts_logs** 56
**continue, Pdb command** 297
**controller: string** 165
**cookies**
  used, for setting language 92-94
**corners, rounding**
  about 308
  background color, changing 309
  Gecko (Firefox), supported browser 308
  Opera (with a major hack), supported browser 308, 309
  WebKit (Safari, Chrome), supported browser 308
**crud.archive**
  about 76
  record history, storing 77
  stored record, timestamping 77
  using 76
**csv file**
  model, creating from 102-104
**Curriculum Vitae (CV)** 130
**custom logo**
  adding 84-86

## D

**DAL** 9, 99
**data**
  batch upload 104, 105
  de-normalizing temporarily 136-138
  moving, from one database to another 106, 107
  searching, dynamically 128
**database**
  accessing, from multiple applications 112-114
**Database Abstraction Layer.** *See* **DAL**
**database queue**
  used, for processing background 324-326
**DataController object** 214
**data object variable** 219
**data tables**
  improving, with WebGrid 180-183
**date** 121
**datetime** 121
**db.auth_user table** 254
**db.bottle table** 156
**db.commit()** 104
**DB commit** 323
**db object** 323
**db.vote entry** 64
**define_table method** 100, 102
**dialog_width: string** 165
**domains**
  applications, associating 272, 273
**downloads**
  speeding, up 96-98
**drop-down date selector**
  creating 171-173
**dynamic_search** 129

## E

**Eclipse** 302
**Eclipse IDE**
  URL 302
**EDIT button** 83
**e-mails**
  sending, with Boto through Amazon Web Services (AWS) 245

emails_to_send 324
exclusive_domain 273
express checkout 223

# F

**Facebook**
   authenticating, OAuth 2.0 used 263-266
**Facebook clone**
   building 68-75
**FastCGI** 23
**fast_download** 97
**favicons.ico**
   mapping 275, 276
**feedparser** 195
**feeds**
   aggregating 195-197
**files**
   uploading, LOADed component used 142-144
**fileuploader.js**
   using 139-141
**flatpages**
   creating 79-83
   defining 80
   examples 79
**Flex**
   amf3 RPC calls making, pyamf used 220-222
**flex mxml/AS3 code** 221
**Flickr photos**
   APIKEY, generating 243
   function, calling from controller 244
   function, calling from view 244
   function, creating in model files 243
   getting 243
**format field** 84
**form labels**
   removing 138
**forms**
   auto tooltips, adding 148-150
   cancel button, adding 126, 127
**formstyle attribute** 138
**form submit**
   configuration, adding 127, 128
**form_title: string** 165
**form wizard**
   creating 134, 135

**full_url() method** 238
**function: string** 165

# G

**GAE** 117
**get_configured_logger** 193
**get_days** 208
**GIS amps**
   making, mapscript used 246, 247
**Globally Recognized Avatars.** *See* **Gravatars**
**gluon.debug.set_trace()** 300
**gluon.debug.stop_trace()** 298, 300
**Google App Engine.** *See* **GAE**
**Google code feeds reader** 248
**Google groups feeds reader** 248
**Google Refine** 103
**Gravatars** 253, 267
**gui2py**
   URL 330
**GWT**
   URL 212

# H

**helpers** 330
**help, Pdb command** 297
**hgwebdir constructor** 315
**hgwebdir wsgi application** 312
**hgwebdir WSGI application** 315
**HTTP Accept-Language header** 92
**httpd.conf** 17
**hyphens**
   used, for replacing underscores, in URLs 275

# I

**icons**
   menus, customizing 88, 89
**IIS**
   web2py, running as proxy 39-44
**IIS 6.0 Management Compatability** 45
**image thumbnails**
   creating, from uploaded images 144
**Instant Payment Notification.** *See* **IPN**
**invoices**
   creating 284-292

**IPN** 223, 232
**is_active field** 77
**ISAPI**
  web2py, running 45-47
**isapi-wsgi** 45

## J

**Janrain**
  URL 52
**Java runtime**
  URL 302
**JavaScript**
  JSON-RPC from 211, 214-219
**joins** 119
**jqGrid**
  and web2py 175-179
**jQuery**
  web2py JSON service, consuming 208, 209
**jQuery.getJSON** 209
**jquery.multiselect.js**
  URL, for donwloading 162
  using 162, 163
**jquery.timers plugin** 187
**JSON-RPC**
  from JavaScript 211, 214-219
**jsonrpc library** 210
**JSON-RPC service**
  consuming 210, 211
**json-xml-rpc documentation**
  URL 215
**json-xml-rpc library** 214, 219
**jump lineno, Pdb command** 297

## L

**language**
  specifying, URLs used 276, 277
**language field** 276
**LaTeX** 279
**light** 323
**Lighttpd**
  about 23
  URL, for downloading 24
  URL, for installing 24
**LIKE** 121
**listen** 322

**list [first[, last]], Pdb command** 297
**LOAD command** 132
**LOADed component**
  used, for uploading files 142-144
**loggername** 193
**logging**
  about 191
  get_configured_logger 193
  issues 192
  loggername 193
**Logical OR** 119

## M

**M2Crypto module** 235
**make_taggable function** 137
**map_hyphen flag** 275
**mapscript**
  about 246
  used, for making GIS amps 246, 247
**MapServer** 246
**map_static flag** 273
**matplotlib**
  about 200
  plotting with 201, 202
  uses 200
**mColorPicker**
  URL, for downloading 150
**menus**
  creating 87, 88
  customizing, with icons 88, 89
**mercurial plugin**
  building 312-315
**mercurial version**
  URL 302
**mobile browsers**
  views, changing for 323
**model**
  creating 100, 102
  creating, from csv file 102-104
  creating, from existing MySQL
    database 107-110
  creating, from existing PostgreSQL
    database 107-110
**models** 330
**mod_proxy**
  web2py, running on shared hosts 35

**modular applications**
  designing 94-96
**Monit**
  used, for monitoring web2py process 311, 312
**multiple applications**
  database, accessing from 112-114
**multiple forms**
  embedding, in one page 130-133
**multi-table forms**
  creating, with references 154, 155
  creating 153, 154
**multi-table update form**
  creating 156, 157
**multi-user mode** 262, 263
**mx:method object** 221
**myplot function** 203

# N

**Name Value Pairs.** *See* **NVP**
**navigation bar**
  creating 89-91
**next: step next, Pdb command** 297
**Nginx**
  web2py, running 31-33
**number**
  representing, slider used 174
**NVP** 224

# O

**OAuth 2.0**
  about 253, 267
  used, for Facebook authentication 263-266
**onaccept function** 137
**onclick attribute** 128
**onclick function** 127
**onException handler** 217
**onvalidation function** 138
**operations**
  help page, sample 250, 251
  help, URL 250
  list page, sample 250
  lists, URL 250
  serving, SOAP used 249

**OR**
  with complex orderby 120
  with orderby 120
**os.getcwd()** 36

# P

**page**
  about 269
  multiple forms, embedding in 130-133
**page statistics plugin**
  about 307, 308
  plugin file 308
  plugin_stats 308
**parameter-based router** 268
**PATH_INFO prefix** 272
**path_prefix** 272
**pattern-based router** 268
**Payment Data Transfer.** *See* **PDT**
**PayPal**
  integration, Web2py 222-231
  web payments, standard 235-243
**PayPalEngine** 224
**PayPal integration, Web2py**
  about 222
  checkout confirmation/payment data transfer 227
  express checkout 223
  lst:confirmhtml 232
  standard integration 223
  technical documentation, URL 224
**paypal.py controller** 239
**PayPal web payments, standard**
  about 235, 237, 243
  full_url() method 238
  implementation 235
  M2Crypto module 235
  paypal.py controller 239
**PDB**
  about 296
  BDB module 300
  implementation 296
  Pdb command 297
  standard library 296
  technical documentation, URL 300

**Pdb command**
  break filename:lineno 297
  continue 297
  help 297
  jump lineno 297
  list [first[, last]] 297
  next: step next 297
  p expression 297
  quit 297
  return: step return 297
  ! statement 297
  step: step in 297
  where 297
**pdb.set_trace() 298**
**pdf label**
  creating 284-292
**PDF listings**
  creating 282
  example, URL 282
**pdf object 282**
**PDF reports**
  creating 279-282
  pdf object 282
  pyfpdf library 279
**PDF templates 293**
**PDT 223**
**p expression, Pdb command 297**
**PIL 13, 144**
**ping 322**
**pingback plugin**
  building 315, 321
  callback signature 322
  db object 323
  example 322
  listen 322
  ping 322
  PingbackServer class 322
  plugin_pingback.py module 322
  source 322
  using 322
**PingbackServer class 322**
**Planet Web2py 195**
**plugin_pingback plugin 322**
**plugin_pingback.py module 322**

**plugin_stats**
  hits 308
  total 308
  widget 308
**PluginWiki**
  about 203
  extending, RSS widget used 203-205
  URL, for downloading 203
**PostgreSQL 8**
**PP sandbox user guide 224**
**production deployment**
  setting up, on Ubuntu 12-14
**providers 263**
**psycopg2, installing 8**
**pyamf**
  URL, for installing 220
  used, for making amf3 RPC calls from Flex 220-222
**PyDev**
  about 302
  URL 302
**pyfpdf library 279**
**PyFPDF wiki documentation**
  URL 282, 293
**pyGravatar**
  URI, for downloading 256
  used, to get avatars for user profile page 256-261
**PyJamas**
  URL 212
**pyodbc, installing 9**
**pysimplesoap**
  about 252
  URL 252
**PySimpleSOAP library 249**
**Python**
  URL, for downloading 8
**python code 220**
**Python Debugger.** *See* **PDB**
**Python Imaging Library.** *See* **PIL**
**Python Paste**
  URL, for downloading 24
**pywin32**
  installing 8

## Q

**QGis**
  URL 247
**Queue.Queue 300**
**quit, Pdb command 297**
**quota 310**

## R

**RabbitMQ 327**
**RDBS 117**
**ReCaptcha 255, 256**
**record insert 118**
**records**
  creating, on demand 116, 117
**record update 119**
**Reddit clone**
  building 61-67
**references**
  multi-table form, creating 154, 155
**Relational Databases.** *See* **RDBS**
**RemoteObject. Endpoint, service URL 221**
**request.args(0) argument 56**
**request.lang 277**
**response.menu 87**
**return**
  return step return, Pdb command 297
**return function 298**
**robots.txt**
  mapping 275, 276
**root folder 275**
**router**
  simple router, creating 270, 271
**routes.py**
  cleaner URLS, creating 268-270
  request.args (a list) 268
  request.vars (a dictionary) 268
**rpc-client-JavaScript ZIP file 219**
**rss2 195**
**RSS widget**
  used, for extending PluginWiki 203-205

## S

**scaffolding application 50-52**
**SCGI**
  about 23
  URL, for downloading 24
  URL, for installing 24
**search functions**
  Ajaxing 183-186
**searching**
  by tag 110-112
**select_or_add widget**
  creating 163-169
**semi-static pages.** *See* **flatpages**
**service description (WSDL )**
  URL 250
**session.wizard variable 135**
**shared hosts**
  web2py running, CGI used 34
  web2py running, mod_proxy used 35
**shell script**
  used, for updating web2py 304-306
**Simple Object Access Protocol.** *See* **SOAP**
**slider**
  using, to represent number 174
**slow virtual fields**
  DB views, replacing 121, 122
**SOAP 248**
**source 322**
**sparklines**
  about 187
  creating, steps 188, 189
**SQLFORM.factory 135**
**SSL-secured web2py instance 262**
**standalone application**
  making, web2py used 330-333
  making, wxPython used 330-333
**standard integration 222, 223**
**star rating widget**
  URL, for downloading 158
**static folder 275**
**static site**
  converting, into web2py application 78, 79

step: step in, Pdb command  297
stop_trace  300
submenus
  creating  87, 88
systemListMethods function  215

## T

target  322
tasters%i field  156
teaching mode  262, 263
template blocks
  effective use  327-329
text fields
  shortening  151, 152
tweets
  displaying  197-199

## U

Ubuntu
  production deployment, setting up  12-14
  web2py, installing as service  39
underscores
  replacing, with hyphens in URLs  275
upgrade button  304
upload action  140
upload_callback action  140
uploaded images
  image thumbnails, creating from  144
upload progress
  monitoring  146-148
upload type field  98
URL() function  268
URL prefix
  adding  272
URLs
  cleaner URLs, creating with routes.py  268-270
  underscores, replacing with hyphens  275
  using, to specify language  276, 277
URL(vote)  67
user-defined folder
  web2py, running  36-38
user profile page
  avatars getting, pyGravatar used  256-261

uWSGI
  web2py, running  31-33

## V

views
  changing, for mobile browsers  323
virtual fields  122
VirtualHost configuration  18

## W

web2py
  and jqGrid  175-179
  existing static site, converting into  78, 79
  installing, as service in Ubuntu  39
  installing, in Ubuntu  10
  installing, on Windows  8
  PayPal, integration  222-231
  process monitoring, Monit used  311, 312
  RSS feeds, sample  197
  running, from user-defined folder  36-38
  running on shared hosts, CGI used  34
  running on shared hosts, mod_proxy used  35
  running, with Apache  16-23
  running, with Cherokee  26-30
  running, with IIS as proxy  39-44
  running, with ISAPI  45-47
  running, with Lighttpd  23-26
  running, with mod_proxy  16-23
  running, with mod_rewrite  16-23
  running, with Nginx  31-33
  running, with uWSGI  31-33
  setting up  302
  updating, shell script used  304, 306
  URL  8
  used, for making standalone applications  330-333
web2py debugger
  PDB  296
  Pipe class  300
  Queue.Queue  300
web2py, installing in Ubuntu
  about  10
  tk library, installing  10
  web2py, downloading  10

**web2py, installing on Windows**
  PostgreSQL 8
  psycopg2, installing 8
  pyodbc, installing 9
  Python, installing 8
  Python Win32 extensions 8
  pywin32, installing 8
  source package, downloading 9
**web2py JSON service**
  consuming, with jQuery 208, 209
**web2py, updating**
  generic views, updating 306
  shell script used 304
  static files, updating 306
  web2py_ajax, updating 306
**Web Feature Service client**
  URL 247
**WebGrid**
  data tables, improving with 180-183
**Web MapService client**
  URL 247

**Web Service Definition File.** *See* **WSDL**
**web URLs**
  URL 268
**where, Pdb command 297**
**Windows**
  web2py, installing 8
**wizard 134**
**wrapper function 219**
**WSDL**
  about 248
  used, for serving operations 249
**WX.AUI 334**
**WX.HTML.** *See* **wxPython**
**wxPython**
  about 333
  URL 330
  used, for making standalone
       applications 330-333
**wxPython Docs**
  URL 334

# Thank you for buying web2py Application Development Cookbook

## About Packt Publishing

Packt, pronounced 'packed', published its first book "*Mastering phpMyAdmin for Effective MySQL Management*" in April 2004 and subsequently continued to specialize in publishing highly focused books on specific technologies and solutions.

Our books and publications share the experiences of your fellow IT professionals in adapting and customizing today's systems, applications, and frameworks. Our solution based books give you the knowledge and power to customize the software and technologies you're using to get the job done. Packt books are more specific and less general than the IT books you have seen in the past. Our unique business model allows us to bring you more focused information, giving you more of what you need to know, and less of what you don't.

Packt is a modern, yet unique publishing company, which focuses on producing quality, cutting-edge books for communities of developers, administrators, and newbies alike. For more information, please visit our website: www.packtpub.com.

## About Packt Open Source

In 2010, Packt launched two new brands, Packt Open Source and Packt Enterprise, in order to continue its focus on specialization. This book is part of the Packt Open Source brand, home to books published on software built around Open Source licences, and offering information to anybody from advanced developers to budding web designers. The Open Source brand also runs Packt's Open Source Royalty Scheme, by which Packt gives a royalty to each Open Source project about whose software a book is sold.

## Writing for Packt

We welcome all inquiries from people who are interested in authoring. Book proposals should be sent to author@packtpub.com. If your book idea is still at an early stage and you would like to discuss it first before writing a formal book proposal, contact us; one of our commissioning editors will get in touch with you.

We're not just looking for published authors; if you have strong technical skills but no writing experience, our experienced editors can help you develop a writing career, or simply get some additional reward for your expertise.

## NumPy 1.5 Beginner's Guide

ISBN: 978-1-84951-530-6  Paperback: 234 pages

An action-packed guide for the easy-to-use, high performance, Python based free open source NumPy mathematical library using real-world examples

1. The first and only book that truly explores NumPy practically
2. Perform high performance calculations with clean and efficient NumPy code
3. Analyze large data sets with statistical functions
4. Execute complex linear algebra and mathematical computations

## Python 3 Object Oriented Programming

ISBN: 978-1-849511-26-1  Paperback: 404 pages

Harness the power of Python 3 objects

1. Learn how to do Object Oriented Programming in Python using this step-by-step tutorial
2. Design public interfaces using abstraction, encapsulation, and information hiding
3. Turn your designs into working software by studying the Python syntax
4. Raise, handle, define, and manipulate exceptions using special error objects

Please check www.PacktPub.com for information on our titles

# [PACKT] open source
community experience distilled

## Nginx 1 Web Server Implementation Cookbook

ISBN: 978-1-84951-496-5      Paperback: 236 pages

Over 100 recipes to master using the Nginx HTTP server and reverse proxy

1. Quick recipes and practical techniques to help you maximize your experience with Nginx
2. Interesting recipes that will help you optimize your web stack and get more out of your existing setup
3. Secure your website and prevent your setup from being compromised using SSL and rate-limiting techniques
4. Get more out of Nginx by using it as an important part of your web application using third-party modules

## Python Testing Cookbook

ISBN: 978-1-84951-466-8      Paperback: 364 pages

Over 70 simple but incredibly effective recipes for taking control of automated testing using powerful Python testing tools

1. Learn to write tests at every level using a variety of Python testing tools
2. The first book to include detailed screenshots and recipes for using Jenkins continuous integration server (formerly known as Hudson)
3. Explore innovative ways to introduce automated testing to legacy systems
4. Written by Greg L. Turnquist – senior software engineer and author of Spring Python 1.1

Please check **www.PacktPub.com** for information on our titles

Printed in Germany
by Amazon Distribution
GmbH, Leipzig